£20

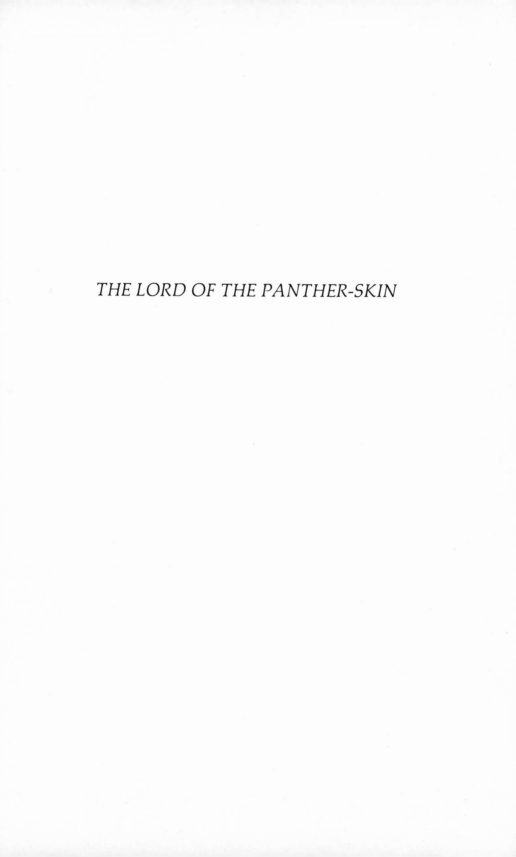

THE LORD OF THE PANTHER-SKIN

THE LORD OF THE PANTHER-SKIN

Shota Rustaveli

THE LORD OF THE PANTHER-SKIN
A GEORGIAN ROMANCE OF CHIVALRY

Translated by R.H. Stevenson

State University of New York Press
Albany 1977

UNESCO COLLECTION OF REPRESENTATIVE WORKS

SERIES OF TRANSLATIONS FROM THE LITERATURES OF
THE UNION OF SOVIET SOCIALIST REPUBLICS

This work from the Georgian has been accepted in
the series of translations sponsored by the United Nations
Educational, Scientific and Cultural Organization
in consultation with the Commission of the USSR for UNESCO
and the International Council for Philosophy and Humanistic Studies

The Lord of the Panther-skin

Published by State University of New York Press
99 Washington Avenue, Albany, New York 12246

Printed in the United States of America

Library of Congress Cataloging in Publication Data

Rustaveli, Shota, fl. 1190.

The lord of the panther-skin.

(UNESCO collection of representative works : Series of
translations from the literatures of the Union of Soviet
Socialist Republics)
Translated from the Georgian of the epic which was
probably based on a cycle of poems relating to the
legendary hero, Tariel. cf. J. Karst. Litt. géorg.
chrét. 1934, p. 130-133.
Includes bibliographical references.
I. Title. II. Series.
PK9169.R8E5   1976   899'.96   76-13225
ISBN 0-87395-320-7

CONTENTS

ABBREVIATIONS AND REFERENCES   xi

INTRODUCTION   xiii

THE LORD OF THE PANTHER-SKIN

Prologue   3

Of Rostevan, the king of the Arabs   6

How King Rostevan and Avtandil went hunting   11

How the king of the Arabs saw the lord of the
panther-skin   12

How Tinatin charged Avtandil with the quest for the
stranger lord   16

How Avtandil wrote out a charge to his vassals   21

How Avtandil went in search of the stranger lord   23

How Avtandil told Asmat his story at the cave   29

How Tariel and Avtandil met   34

How Tariel told Avtandil his tale   38

How Tariel fell in love   41

Nestan-Darejan's first letter to her lover   46

How Tariel wrote to his lady   46

How Tariel sent a letter to the Cathayans   47

How Nestan summoned Tariel   48

How the Cathayan king sent Tariel his reply   49

How Tariel and Nestan held converse together   49

How Tariel rode to Cathay and fought a great battle
there   51

How Tariel wrote to the king of the Indians, and how
he returned home in triumph   56

How Nestan-Darejan wrote to her lover   59

How Tariel wept and swooned   60

How Tariel wrote in answer to his lady   61

How they took counsel concerning the marriage of
Nestan-Darejan   61

How Tariel and Nestan-Darejan took counsel together and
made a plan   63

How the Khvarizm-shah's son came to India to be married,
and how Tariel killed him   66

How Tariel learned of the carrying-off of
Nestan-Darejan   69

How Tariel met Nuradin-Pridon   71

How Tariel gave help to Pridon   74

How Tariel received word of Nestan-Darejan from
Pridon   75

How Avtandil returned to Arabia   81

How Avtandil dispatched a request to King Rostevan,
and how the vizier gave utterance   87

How Avtandil talked with Shermadin   93

How Avtandil wrote a testament for the eyes of
King Rostevan   94

How Avtandil prayed   97

How King Rostevan learned of Avtandil's flight   97

How Avtandil set out to rejoin Tariel   99

How Avtandil found Tariel lying in a swoon   104

How Tariel told of the killing of the lion and
the panther   109

How Tariel and Avtandil returned to the cave and
found Asmat   110

How Avtandil set out for Pridon's city   114

How Avtandil journeyed to Pridon's city   116

How Avtandil departed from Pridon's realm to search for
Nestan-Darejan, and how he met with a caravan   123

How Avtandil arrived in Gulansharo   127

How Fatima conceived a passion for Avtandil   130

How Fatima wrote Avtandil a love-letter   130

How Avtandil replied to Fatima   131

How Fatima told of Nestan-Darejan   134

How Fatima told Avtandil of the Kajes' capture of
Nestan-Darejan   146

How Fatima wrote to Nestan-Darejan   153

How Nestan-Darejan wrote to Fatima   154

How Nestan-Darejan wrote to her lover   155

How Avtandil wrote to Pridon   158

How Avtandil departed from Gulansharo and returned
    to Tariel   159

How Tariel and Avtandil journeyed to Pridon's
    realm   165

How Nuradin-Pridon put forward a plan   167

How Avtandil put forward a plan   168

How Tariel put forward a plan   168

How Tariel went to meet the king of the Seas   172

How Pridon held a marriage festival for Tariel and
    Nestan-Darejan   176

How the three heroes went to Tariel's cave, and thence
    to Arabia   179

How the king of the Arabs held a marriage festival for
    Avtandil and Tinatin   186

How Tariel learned of the death of the king of the
    Indians   189

How Tariel arrived in India, and how the Cathayans
    made submission to him   192

How the marriage of Tariel and Nestan-Darejan was
    celebrated   196

Epilogue   200

APPENDIX A
    Personal beauty and planetary imagery   201

APPENDIX B
    "Generous" weeping and the demonstrative gesture   203

NOTES   205

THE LORD OF THE PANTHER-SKIN:
    A GEORGIAN PERSPECTIVE   221
        A.G. Baramidze
        Member of the Academy of Sciences of the Georgian S.S.R.

ABBREVIATIONS AND REFERENCES

Amiran-Darejaniani   *Amiran-Darejaniani: A Cycle of Medieval Georgian Tales Traditionally Ascribed to Mose Khoneli.* Translated by R.H. Stevenson (Oxford: Clarendon Press, 1958).

Antar   *Antar, a Bedoueen Romance.* Translated by Terrick Hamilton. 4 vols. (London, 1819-20).

Digenes   *Digenes Akrites.* Edited and translated by John Mavrogordato (Oxford: Clarendon Press, 1956).

Epic   *The Epic of the Kings: Shah-Nama: The National Epic of Persia, by Ferdowsi.* Translated by Reuben Levy (London: Routledge & Kegan Paul; Chicago: University of Chicago Press, 1967).

Layla and Majnun   *The Story of Layla and Majnun.* Translated by R. Gelpke (Cassirer [Distributed by Faber & Faber, London], 1966).

Visramiani   *Visramiani; The Story of the Loves of Vis and Ramin: A Romance of Ancient Persia.* Translated by Oliver Wardrop (London: Royal Asiatic Society, 1914; reprint, 1966).

INTRODUCTION

1

A Persian tale turned into Georgian; such, according to its Prologue, is *The Lord of the Panther-skin.*[1] It has been doubted whether the phrase is Rustaveli's own,[2] but the lack of evidence, either external or internal, to support the assertion is perhaps a matter of more significance. The narrative itself would hardly suggest an Iranian origin; Persians figure in one brief episode only, to be spoken of without kindness as foreigners suspected of a desire to domineer. It may be, however, that the Prologue's words should be understood as a rather mannered announcement of a story such as Persian writers tell; and taken in this sense they may be allowed a good deal of truth.

The enormous prestige of the work of the classical Persian poets in the Middle Ages and indeed down to comparatively modern times lies somewhat outside the awareness of the ordinary Western reader. Perhaps some suggestion of it is to be found in the story of the Sultan Mehmet II murmuring in the midst of the desolation of conquered Constantinople, "The spider weaves the curtains in the palace of the Caesars; the owl calls the watches in Afrasiab's towers." One of the apophthegms of Saadi of Shiraz rises to the lips of an Ottoman Turk on European soil.

A certain analogy to this Persian authority might perhaps be discerned in the influence of such Italians as Petrarch and Ariosto in the lands of the West, particularly in the England of Tudor and early Stuart times; but here the effects were altogether more limited and superficial. A few of the more scholarly men of letters, like Milton, might turn out casual pieces in Tuscan from time to time, but Italian verse was not written throughout Europe as was Persian from the Caucasus to India: the only Western comparison that could really be sustained in some manner, though of a scope very narrowly restricted beside the vast sweep of Persian predominance, would be the mastery of Greek poets over Latin.

There can be no doubt as to where within the framework of such an analogy we should look for our Iranian Homer. The position of the man known as Firdausi (c.940-c.1025), first, in both senses, of the great Persian poets, is indeed even more commanding than that of his Greek counterpart, inasmuch as he not only gave to literature a large part of a civilization's heritage of legend but also established a whole idiom of verse-writing that, secure in the protection of an approved style, story-tellers over half a continent writing in a whole catalogue of languages were to employ for centuries to come. No doubt Firdausi's imagery had its roots in the work of earlier writers, but with the *Shah-nama*, his splendid evocation of Iranian myth, folklore and chronicled history, the figurative stock-in-trade of what may for our purposes be called the Persian tradition—the narcissus eyes, the raven's-wing hair, the tree-like or cypress-like bodies, the rose cheeks, the ruby lips, the jet eyebrows, the lion-heroes, the "planetary" imagery— was freed once and for all from any provincial limitation to which it may earlier have been subject.

Nowhere was admiration for the works of Firdausi and his successors greater than among the Georgians: this admiration, however, did not lead them, as it often did Turks, Afghans and Indians, into slavish imitation; inheritors of an ancient indigenous civilization which subsumed the culture of Orthodox Christianity, they had much to sustain their identity. Nevertheless, in Rustaveli's time and for long afterwards they undoubtedly regarded the Persians as the masters of letters; he who drew a term from their vocabulary[3] or an allusion or an image from their verse could hardly go wrong. Only once, in a reference to Rustam, the greatest of its heroes, does Rustaveli look at the *Shah-nama* directly; but that it was from Firdausi that he learned much of the business of conducting kings, princesses and lion-like warriors through romantic adventures can scarcely be doubted. As for his debt in imagery, it must suffice to draw attention to the description in the Persian epic of Rudaba, the future mother of Rustam: "[She] is more radiant than the sun . . . for stature she is as a plane-tree . . . . Her eyes are like the narcissus in the garden and her lashes draw their blackness from the raven's wing . . . . If you seek a brilliant moon, it is her face. . . ."; to Rudaba's retort to those who try to discourage her passion for the hero's destined father by asserting that she will one day find a more splendid husband: "My heart is torn for a star; how then should I be happy with the moon?"; and to the solar image applied to the spendor of a monarch's aspect: ". . . the garden from end to end is lit up by him . . . he is like the flaming sun."[4] The world in which Rustaveli's characters live and move is one that received its creation from Firdausi of Tus.

A work which, although native to Georgia and indeed instinct with the Georgian spirit, is so much influenced by the *Shah-nama* that it may properly be associated here with the Firdausian legacy is *Amiran-Darejaniani* ('The Story of Amiran, son of Darejan'), a cycle of tales of adventure written in a vigorous, unadorned style and dating probably from the early or middle decades of the twelfth century. Certain passages in the national chronicles apart, it is the only original Georgian work with a chivalric content composed before Rustaveli's time that has come down to us. Widely read, there is evidence to suggest, from its earliest days, it could hardly have failed to exert a powerful influence on *The Lord of the Panther-skin*, an influence of which the line in the poem's Epilogue, "Amiran, son of Darejan, was praised by Mosé Khoneli," may hold some acknowledgement. And in fact many passages in Rustaveli's romance, some few of which receive comment in the notes, reflect happenings in this Caucasian appanage to Firdausi's territory.

In the case of the *Vis and Ramin* of the eleventh-century Persian poet Gurgani,[5] the question of indebtedness is somewhat more complicated. It has been maintained that Rustaveli had an acquaintance with the original, but, be that as it may, considerations of style make it impossible to suppose that the version to which he habitually had recourse was not the Georgian prose translation, *Visramiani* ('The Story of Vis and Ramin'), traditionally ascribed to Sargis Tmogveli, a feudal magnate of the Tamaran period. This rendering, which has always held a much higher place in Georgian literature than has the work of Gurgani's own pen in Persian, is carried out in the free medieval manner and has some claim to be regarded as a creation in its own right.

In addition to large quantities of the common stock of Persian romantic expression, *Visramiani* possesses a number of more distinctive figurative formulations—notably weepings, swoonings and leaping flames of grief and passion, all of a highly conventionalized kind—which seem to have served Rustaveli as models. The wanderings of Tariel, the Lord of the Panther-skin, over the world in quest of his lost Nestan look, too, like a reflection of the search Shah Moabad makes for his queen.[6]

Two passages from *Visramiani* may be taken to illustrate the affinities of its style with that of *The Lord of the Panther-skin*. The first, which tells how Ramin first saw Vis, probably lies behind Rustaveli's account of Tariel's corresponding experience (p. 42):

> The face of Vis appeared; it was as if lightning shone forth from a cloud, or suddenly the sun arose; and at her appearing the heart of Ramin was taken captive. It was as if a sorcerer had poisoned Ramin, for at one look his soul was reft from him.
>
> When Ramin saw Vis's face, it was as if an arrow of the length of a stadium had struck his heart; from his horse he dropped, light as a leaf, the fire of love enflamed his heart, burned his brain, and carried away his mind. In the twinkling of an eye passion took hold of him, love deprived him of heart and soul. From his love such a tree came forth, whose fruit was roaming in the field and madness. When he fell from his horse he fainted, and for a long time lay unconscious. His roselike face changed into saffron, and his red jacinth lips became blue as the sky. . . .[7]

The second describes Ramin's love-sickness:

> . . . he would ever seek a lonely spot and sit alone; he wept without ceasing, and at night he had no sleep, he laid not his head upon the pillow. He stared at

the stars, and besought God to change his fate. He
had no rest, neither by day nor night. He roamed
about like a madman; like a wild ass and a wild goat
he avoided men. Wherever he saw a cedar, it was to
him the likeness of the form of Vis, and he could not
tear away his eyes; wherever in a garden he found a
red rose, he kissed it for its likeness to her. . . .[8]

The most immediately striking, however, of the Persian in-
fluences on Rustaveli, direct or indirect, is perhaps that of
Layla and Majnun, a work composed in 1188-89 by the second
to appear of the great Persian poets, Nizami of Ganja. Like the
Shah-nama and *Vis and Ramin*, this telling of one of the most
famous love stories of the East may very possibly have been
available to him in his own tongue; a Georgian translation
seems to have been made almost immediately after the appear-
ance of the original. In addition to the suns, moons, cypresses
etc. of established tradition and the tears, swoonings and con-
suming fires of the story of Vis and Ramin,[9] it contains some
notable correspondences to *The Lord of the Panther-skin* in
both phrase and incident. A more particular bond is however
suggested by an observation in the Prologue to the latter: "In
the speech of the Arabs our *lover* means 'madman' . . . ." This
allusion to the derivation of the Georgian *mijnuri* from the
Arabic *majnun* seems to glance at the star-crossed love that
drives Nizami's Arab hero beyond the bounds of human rea-
son; in any case Rustaveli makes a direct comparison when he
tells us that not even Qays (Majnun) had woes such as Tariel's
to bear (p. 161). A distraught lover's roaming in desert places
is indeed in some sense the master theme of both the Persian
and the Georgian poem and, while Rustaveli has nothing of
the mystical spirit of his fellow-Transcaucasian, it can hardly
be doubted that he made a conscious transposition of the idea
from the Beduin setting of long-standing poetic convention to
the chivalrous world of his own imaginative vision.[10]

The *Shah-nama*, *Visramiani* and *Layla and Majnun* were all
storehouses of the images and phrases of Persian poetic idiom;
to each, furthermore, Rustaveli had a particular indebtedness.
His work is his own; the creative originality of a great poet

informs it: and yet, by his references to Rustam, Vis, Ramin and Qays, he himself seems to invite us to view him as a romancer writing in the tradition of the great Persian story-tellers.

A further Persian debt of sorts seems possible in respect of the once widely popular story of Vamiq and Azra, but here all is speculation.[11] The adventures of these lovers may possibly have furnished Rustaveli with one or two ideas—the most likely, perhaps, being that of three brothers in arms living by a code of all for one and one for all—but it would be difficult to point to anything in them that suggests he may have been beholden for anything very substantial.

As a pendant to this brief consideration of Persian influences, a few lines should be devoted to a tale of adventure which, although belonging to a literature in general resistant to the Persian dominance, shows distinct signs of indebtedness to Iranian models. The Arabic *Romance of Antar*, enormous in length[12] and equally enormous in popularity, is embodied in rhymed prose in which are set many passages of declamatory verse. It seems to have achieved its present form about the end of the thirteenth century, but by then it had been in the making for perhaps half a millenium. Antar himself is a hero of a mold somewhat different from that of Rustaveli's paladins; his feats, while titanic, are presented with less luxuriance of hyperbole and, though both poet and lover, he is not possessed of the same extreme sophistication. His story certainly contains passages that almost force upon one the conviction that it was known to Rustaveli in some form; and indeed, since there is evidence to suggest that its reputation was well established in the Arab world as early as the beginning of the twelfth century, there would be no difficulty in arguing that by his time it probably did have its readers in Georgia. It is introduced here, however, not primarily as a possible influence on the composition of *The Lord of the Panther-skin*, but on the ground of a kinship in ethos. As was remarked above, the world in which Rustaveli's characters live and move received its creation from Firdausi; yet, as befits its legendary and "heroic" subject-matter, the early part of the *Shah-nama* that concerns us has in its atmosphere a certain primeval quality. The Georgian poem, on the other hand, is quick with a spirit of chivalry very distinctively of the Middle Ages. It is *Antar's* possession of this same

spirit — ardent, generous, apt for every flight of verbal extra-
vagance — that, for all the differences between the two in form
and content, renders it, from one standpoint, perhaps *The
Lord of the Panther-skin's* closest analogue.

In studies intended for the general reader Rustaveli's Orien-
tal affinities have in general received too little attention: Geor-
gian critics, naturally enough, tend to take them as a matter
of course requiring no very extended consideration; a stronger
assertion is usually made of *The Lord of the Panther-skin's*
resemblances to Western tales of chivalry. Such resemblances,
reflections of the similarities of feudal societies, certainly exist;
and striking many of them are. But some knowledge of the in-
fluences from the world of Islam that permeated the minds of
Rustaveli and his audience is needed if the reader brought up
on the European romances is not to be disconcerted by modes
of expression and attitudes of mind far removed from those
associated with the deeds of Gawain or Amadis of Gaul.

In the West, the claims of lord[13] and comrade,[14] set so high
in the heroic literature of the early Middle Ages, came, in the
course of the generations that followed the composition of
The Song of Roland, to count for relatively little.[15] From about
the middle of the twelfth century friendship between man and
man seems to exist mainly for its demands to provide dramatic
tension by running counter to those of love; a familiar example
from a later period is supplied by Chaucer's *Knight's Tale*.
Loyalty to lord or king may receive some passing lip-service,
but the springs of action lie elsewhere: the prevailing ethos
is that of courtly love, the political reality is usually the power
of great all-but-independent fiefs. A monarch is more likely to
be portrayed as a cuckold, like the Arthur of Chrétien de
Troyes or Mark in the Tristan story, than as a figure of ma-
jesty commanding the devotion of his lieges.

In the world of Rustaveli all is very different: the son of a
people which, geographically exposed to some of the more
acute hazards of history, had risen to greatness under the leader-
ship of a strong monarchy, he cannot regard lightly any of the
bonds that hold men and women together in the life of the
community. On the contrary, he reinterprets the traditional

loyalties of the heroic world in terms appropriate to the more sophisticated society of his own day, adds the newer concept of *Frauendienst* ('service of ladies'),[16] examines the criss-cross of tensions that may arise between the three, and brings them at the last into a harmony within his unifying vision of an ideal chivalrous society. Put into Western terms, it is rather as though, in addition to transforming Oliver's sister from the briefly-glimpsed figure of *The Song of Roland* into a heroine of courtly romance, Bertrand de Bar-sur-Aube, the author of the thirteenth-century *Roman de Girart de Viane*, had had the will and found a way to celebrate the old warrior virtues of the *Song* in a contemporary idiom.

In setting out in quest of the mysterious Lord of the Panther-skin, Avtandil is honoring two distinct obediences; the queen who lays the command upon him speaks to her vassal as well as her lover: the task has "a two-fold fitness." Conscious of his responsibilities as a great feudatory and officer of state, he takes thought for the security of the realm during his absence and likewise makes provision for the government of his own march-land principality: "Lead the men-at-arms and the barons in battle," he enjoins his lieutenant; "take all things in your governance; send messengers to court and ascertain all that is done there; write letters in my name . . . ." It is difficult to picture Launcelot preparing to leave Arthur's Britain on a quest with his mind full of the problems relating to the conduct of military activity and civil administration that would arise during his absence.

The object of his search found, Avtandil swears brotherhood with him and then returns to Arabia in order to reconcile this new commitment with his lady's service; confronted with a conflict between the former and his faith to his queen's father, he obeys the call of friendship; and then when all is done he comes back once more to throw himself on the mercy of his old liege lord. He has given proof of his devotion to his lady, to his comrade, and to the throne.

Such an exacting triad of loyalties does not leave much room for casual deeds of knight-errantry: Avtandil has no time for chivalrous shows of courtesy towards people met with on his travels;[17] nor do we find him turning aside to champion the cause of the oppressed. When pirates attack he proves himself a very effective protector of the merchants in whose company he is sailing, but it was to further his own purposes that he joined them, and his interests are for the moment identical with theirs. He makes a handsome-looking gesture, certainly, in waiving all claims on the treasure captured after the fight—but then, as he himself says candidly enough, it would be of small use to one as wealthy as he; and he is prompt to turn the traders' gratitude to account. Utterly single-minded in the pursuit of his aims, he does not balk at assassination any more than at a trying erotic encounter.

As well as serving as a pattern of loyalty, Avtandil's character, with its business-like approach to the problems of life, is of great assistance in keeping the story free of such merely episodic matter as the disposition of a knight-errant must inevitably attract: the remarkable absence of such matter from *The Lord of the Panther-skin* is however to be attributed primarily to Rustaveli's possession of that rarest of qualities in a medieval narrative writer, a sense of form. On a first reading the poem's construction may seem rather bewildering, but further study will soon make apparent the relevance of each scene to the general plan. Avtandil's two expeditions, the first in the service of the throne and his lady, the second in that of his friend, form balancing elements of architecture, while Rustaveli's skill in the use of the difficult story-within-a-story technique enables him to move at will through time and space without loss of cohesion. Such a mastery in the handling of convolutions of plot and such a sure sense of proportion are, it may be suggested, seldom to be met with in any literature.

Structural comparisons with contemporary Western works are interesting. In *Cligés* a third of the tale has gone by before Chrétien can reach even the birth of his hero; it is yet further on in Gottfried von Strassburg's admittedly not quite complete story that Tristan meets Isolde; in Wolfram von Eschenbach's *Parzival* there is no apparent relationship between incident and totality. It may be doubted indeed whether any other medieval romance, Eastern or Western, is possessed of such unity in such complexity of design.

Another gift of Rustaveli's, and one no commoner among writers of his kind, is the power to suggest place and to evoke milieu. In most tales of chivalry the outline of each castle or forest seems to come into view enshrouded in the same mist of conventional generality as covered the last. No reader of *The Lord of the Panther-skin*, however — as made his way to and fro between the court of Arabia, with its vivid splendors, generous and perceptive personal relationships, and quick responses to joy and sorrow; the great rocks in the wilderness that afford the distraught Tariel a refuge; the Indian capital, with its erratic policies, intrigues and unease; the bachelor world, all fresh air and exercise, of the hard-riding Pridon, and the sensuous, pleasure-loving entrepôt of Mulghazanzar — can ever have been oppressed by a sense of sameness or of lack of immediacy. The transitions and contrasts, furthermore, are put to most effective use. Scenes of comedy at Mulghazanzar, for example, both afford valuable light relief and serve as an introduction to a new phase, in which the story's movement quickens and anguish yields place to hope and constructive action.

This is not the place for an assessment of Rustaveli according to the canons of formal Western literary criticism; his work must become much more widely known before there can be any valid appeal to general opinion. All that has been attempted here is some slight and partial clearing of the approaches to one easy of access to perhaps fewer readers than is any other among the master-poets of the world.

2

The remoteness of its structure, idiom and thought-patterns from those of English renders Rustaveli's language all but impossible to translate. "She split her almonds," he will write, in the confident expectation that his readers will understand that the lady opened her eyes wide with astonishment (cf. p. 154). A literal treatment of three lines may illustrate some of the problems posed by the frequent coagulations of imagery (cf. p. 137): "When I went inside, before her there stood pools of tears. Inside the abyss of ink lay lances of jet. From the lakes of ink into the bowls full of jet there was a stream. Between the coral and the cornelian shone twin pearls." Even in passages less recondite than this, an unyieldingly literal approach can lead to quite grotesque results: it would have the khan of Cathay, for example, write to Tariel (cf. p. 51): "Put us on our oath, and you will have bound our neck with a twig."[18] Complete capitulation to the "what we would say in English" argument, on the other hand, will often lose the whole essence: the assertion that a lady's lashes were killing a young man cannot be turned into the language of yesterday's newspaper without suffering a certain loss of identity. The endeavor has been to evolve a manner that can reflect something of both the poem's fast-moving, terse vitality and its highly formalized expression. Wardour Street English has no friends today, but Rustaveli's quatrains would cry out against any attempt to render them into specifically twentieth-century idiom. Balances must be struck.[19]

No early manuscripts of the poem have survived, and in the centuries that elapsed before its first printing in 1712 it suffered much at the hands of copyists and also, probably, of interpolators. Edition differs from edition greatly in word and phrase, and many quatrains have suffered rejection at the hands of this critic or that: the text on which this translation is based, that published by the Georgian Academy of Sciences in 1957, contains 1,669 quatrains, and may be regarded as comprehensive.[20] Very many lines are still subject to differences in interpretation, differences due sometimes to figurative ambiguities, sometimes to elliptical brevity of expression. Difficulties may also arise from word-play such as that which has certain quatrains (e.g., 137, 172, 304, 494, 708, 1532) end with the same three, four or five syllables in each line and with two or more identical verbal forms. Often enough, it may fairly be said, even when there is no textual uncertainty it seems to be a case of *quot homines, tot sententiae*. It would indeed hardly be possible in even the most monumental study to take notice of every reasonable interpretation that has been put forward for every obscurity.

The rhyme-scheme of Rustaveli's sixteen-syllable lines is *aaaa*, the rhyme for the quatrain being either double or triple; the accentuation is light and variable, but has something of a dactylic and trochaic character. The following is a rough-and-ready transliteration[21] of the quatrain with which the story opens (a is pronounced somewhat as in English "hat," e as in "met," i as in "hit," or the vowel sound in "mien," o as in "not" or "note," u as in "put;" s is always unvoiced): scansion Western rather than Georgian:[22]

ĭkŏ/ ˉarăbĕts/ rōstĕvăn,/ mēpĕ/ ghmrtīsăgăn/ svĭănĭ,
māghălĭ,/ ūkhvĭ,/ mdābălĭ,/ lāshkăr-/mrāvălĭ,
   kmĭănĭ,
mōsă/mārtlĕ dă/ mōtskălĕ,/ mōrjmŭlĭ,/ gāngĕ/bĭănĭ,
tvīt mĕ/ōmărĭ/ ūĕbrŏ,/ kvlā mŏ/ūbărĭ/ tsklĭăni.

It will be evident that the successful handling of the verse-form in a long work requires a mastery of rhythmic movement, as well as an accomplishment in rhyming as high as that demanded by the qasidas and ghazals of other Near Eastern literatures.

Prose translations have generally preserved the identity of each quatrain with a separate numbered paragraph, and departure from this practice may be thought to call for some apology. It is undoubtedly true that in the mind of anyone acquainted with the original, *The Lord of the Panther-skin* lives in its quatrains as does *The Rape of the Lock* in its couplets; but it is also true that flow and speed are of the essence, and it may be argued that a translator should not feel bound to subject the natural continuities of prose to visual interruption. It is hoped that the running numbers will facilitate reference to the quatrains of the original.

Some inconsistency in the treatment of proper names of Arabic and Persian derivation must be admitted to. To present familiar, evocative Husam, Husain and Fatima in the guise of the Usam, Usen and Patman of the text would, however, be to fail to respond to the bazaar-and-caravanserai orientalism of the part of the poem in which they appear — while insistence on the Arabic origin of Asmat or the Persian base of Pridon (a form well established in Georgian), names whose bearers belong to the world of chivalrous idealization with which that orientalism is contrasted, would introduce a certain distortion of vision.

3

A bibliography of Rustaveli published in 1957 contains no less than 2,481 items, and much has appeared since. Although *The Lord of the Panther-skin* has been rendered into all the principal European languages, as well as into many tongues less widely known, it has on the whole received strangely little critical attention outside the land of its origin. In 1910 the best that the eleventh edition of the *Encyclopaedia Britannica* could do for it lay in the aloof adjective "curious." Since then, however, the record of the English-speaking world has improved somewhat, the basis of all subsequent study therein being Marjory Scott Wardrop's prose translation, *The Man in the Panther's Skin: a Romantic Epic by Shot'ha Rust'haveli* (London: Royal Asiatic Society, 1912; reprint, 1967). *The Knight in the Tiger's Skin*, a modified and enlarged version issued in Moscow in 1938 (reprint, New York: International Publishers, n.d.), has a useful introduction by Pavlé Ingorokva, but is shorn of the copious notes of the 1912 publication. Miss Wardrop's work is still invaluable to the student, although account must naturally be taken of subsequent advances in the study of the text. Venera Urushadze's rendering in unrhymed quatrains, *The Knight in the Panther's Skin* (Tbilisi: Sabchota Sakartvelo, 1968), affords a most interesting insight into the response of a native. A chapter is devoted to the poem in C.M. Bowra's *Inspiration and Poetry* (London: Macmillan; New York: St. Martin's Press, 1955).

A most useful short study of medieval Georgian literature is to be found in W.E.D. Allen's *A History of the Georgian People* (1932; reprint New York: Barnes & Noble, 1971), chapter 28; the material on society and government in chapters 19-23, furthermore, is very relevant to the study of Rustaveli, inasmuch as his Arabia and India reflect Georgian conditions. A general consideration of the literature is also offered in David Marshall Lang's *The Georgians* (London: Thames and Hudson; New York: Praeger, 1966), pp. 152-78; the same writer's *Popular and Courtly Elements in the Georgian Epic* (Rome: Accademia Nazionale dei Lincei, 1969), may also be mentioned. C. Toumanoff's chapter (14) in *The Cambridge Medieval History* (2d ed., 1966, 4:1) contains a masterly sketch of the history and culture of the medieval kingdom.

Notes

1. Many heroes have followed Paris (*Iliad* 3. 17) and Heracles in wearing the skin of one of the Cats; the leopard-skin cloak round Rustam's shoulders (*Epic*, pp. 72, 75, etc.) is an instance that can hardly have been absent from Rustaveli's mind. There would be biblical warrant for rendering the animal element in his poem's title, *vep'khi*, as 'leopard'; its modern meaning is 'tiger'; the sense he intended is uncertain. The consistent use of 'tiger' would entail what for an English translator would be the embarrassment of having a romantic heroine looking 'like a tigress' (p. 63). *Vep'khistqaosani*, the title of the poem, is literally, 'The One clad in the Skin of a Vep'khi'.

The panther, furnished with attributes deriving ultimately from Aristotle (*Historia Animalium* 9. 6) figures in the bestiaries as a symbol of Christ. Richard de Fournival's *Li Bestiaires d'Amours* (ed. Cesare Segre [Milan, Naples: R. Ricciardi, 1957], in which it serves the purposes of profane love (pp. 45, 117-18) was probably the immediate source of the central image in Nicole de Margival's *La Panthere d'Amors* (ed. Henry A. Todd [Paris, 1883; editor's title]) in which the god of Love tells the poet (p. 18, lines 463-69):

> Amis, la beste qui est bele
> Et noble senefie cele
> Dont si desirrez a savoir
> Se s'amour peüsses avoir.
> Et je te dirai la mistere;
> Car tout aussi com la panthere
> Est d'estre bele renommee. . . .

If Rustaveli's *vep'khi* is indeed a panther, Aristotle may, perhaps through the Georgian version of the *Physiologus*, be the ultimate source of his image no less than of Nicole's. At any rate it is clear that the skin is associated in the poet's mind with both the passion which envelops the wearer's being and her who inspires it.

2. It has indeed been questioned whether he wrote any part of either Prologue or Epilogue.

3. It could well be argued that the words noticed as Arabic in the following pages should rather be given a Persian label: without exception they established themselves in Persian and, terms relating to Islam apart, their presence in classical Georgian is to be ascribed mainly if not entirely to Iranian influences.

4. *Epic*, pp. 39-40, 41, 397.

5. English translation by George Morrison (New York and London: Columbia University Press, 1972).

6. *Visramiani*, pp. 137-39. While, as remarked below, Rustaveli's

conception of the roaming, distracted lover derives largely from Nizami's *Layla and Majnun*, it also owes much to the story of Vis and Ramin, in which the idea emerges several times.

7. Ibid., p. 47.

8. Ibid., p. 62.

9. The tears and swoonings in *The Lord of the Panther-skin* and *Visramiani* have in common a certain formalized quality that distinguishes them from those in Nizami's poem. The fires are admittedly a medieval commonplace; we need look no further than the figure of Chaucer's Troilus for 'the hote fir of love' (*Troilus and Criseyde* 1, line 490). Rustaveli could have found such flames in the lines of the master, Firdausi: nevertheless *Visramiani*, *Layla and Majnun* and *The Lord of the Panther-skin* form a trio in which their frequency is quite striking.

10. It is unnecessary to labor the difference between the distraction of lovers such as Qays and Rustaveli's hero Tariel and the straight-forward insanity which attacks some paladins: Chrétien de Troyes' Yvain, for example, under the stress of unkind words from his lady, tears his flesh, strips off his clothes and flees to the forest, there to conduct himself "like a madman or a savage" *(Le Chevalier au Lion*, ed. Mario Roques [Paris: H. Champion, 1960], p. 86, lines 2806-30). Malory's Trystram and Launcelot act in somewhat similar fashion *(Le Morte d'Arthur* 9.18, 11.8): attention may however be drawn to Launcelot's embarrassment upon recovery — "A, Jesu, mercy! . . . Yf this be sothe, how many be there that knowyth of my woodnes?" (12.5). It is difficult to think of any reaction that would be more wholly alien to either Nizami's or Rustaveli's hero. Qays's distraction for the most part takes a form close to religious ecstasy; Tariel's is a form of service to love much like that described in the French twelfth-century romance *Eneas* (ed. J.-J. Salverda de Grave [Paris: 1929], 2: 92, lines 8930-34):

> Amors l'ot mis an grant trepoil,
> Amors lo faisoit trespanser,
> Amors lo faisoit tressüer
> et refreidir et espaumir
> et sospirer et tressaillir.

Lovers of this type may flee the world of men; they may be in some sense "possessed": they are not, take them for all in all, out of their wits.

11. None of the apparently once numerous Persian versions of this romance is extant in its entirety, but that of the eleventh-century writer Unsuri is thought to have served as a basis for a work by one Lamiy, a Turkish poet of the early sixteenth century, which has survived. The tale would appear to have been known in Georgia in the

latter part of the twelfth century; in one of his odes the panegyrist Shavteli couples the name of its hero, Vamiq, with that of Vis, the heroine of the *Vis and Ramin* story, in a way that suggests that he expects the two names to be more or less equally familiar to his readers. Unsuri's is the version most likely to have been in circulation.

Lamiy sends a prince of China with his foster-brother in search of a princess with whose portrait he has fallen in love: in the alliance formed later with a third hero, the fidelity shown by a waiting-woman, the assumption by certain of the characters of a merchant's disguise and a bereft lover's anguished wandering, resemblances might be seen to the sworn brotherhood of the three paladins of *The Lord of the Panther-skin*, Asmat's devotion, Avtandil's masquerade and Tariel's distraction; some argument could perhaps also be built on the various imprisonments and rescues that occur. On the other hand it may fairly be maintained that such themes as these form the small change of romance everywhere, and that we are not entitled to assume that every passage in Lamiy's work necessarily had the backing of a Persian original.

12. The English translation (see "Abbreviations and References") is heavily abridged.

13. Pur sun seignur deit hom susfrir granz mals

E endurer e forz freiz e granz chalz,

Si·n deit hom perdre del sanc e de la char.

(*La Chanson de Roland*, ed. Cesare Segre [Milan, Naples: R. Ricciardi, 1971], p. 207, lines 1117-19.)

14. Mult dulcement a regreter le prist:

— Sire cumpaign, tant mar fustes hardiz!

Ensemble avum estét e anz e dis;

Ne·m fesis mal ne jo ne·l te forsfis.

Quant tu es mor<z>, dulur est que jo vif. —

(Ibid., pp. 385-86, lines 2026-30.)

15. Exceptions such as those to be found in the presentation of the old warrior virtues in the *Nibelungenlied* and of the friendship theme in the widely popular story of Amis and Amiloun hardly affect the validity of this generalization.

16. A well-known theory brings this idea into Western Europe from the Muslim world by way of Moorish Spain: a similar percolation would be equally possible on Christendom's Transcaucasian marches.

17. We are told that on his quest he treated travelers with courtesy; but this was as a preliminary to interrogation.

18. The "twig" must be taken as representing halters of plaited withies.

19. On every page considerations of intelligibility and usage require the turning of "his rose" into "the rose on his cheek," or some similar expansion: "the sun" is regularly rendered as "the sun-fair

hero/maiden"; "the moon" and "the star" receive the same treatment.

20. The critical edition published by A. Shanidze and A. Baramidze (Tbilisi: Metsniereba, 1966) and, still more, that edited by Pavlé Ingorokva (Tbilisi: Merani, 1970) are more rigorist as regards the number of quatrains accepted.

21. The technical paraphernalia of transcription has been confined to points of etymology in the notes.

22. For the Georgian prosody, see p. 237.

THE LORD OF THE PANTHER-SKIN

Prologue

The Power that gave the earth and the skies their creation, whose breath, wafted from heaven, endued all creatures with life, has granted us mortals this world, with its endless diversity:[1] its likeness is imprinted upon all who hold sway as monarchs.

O One, O God, thou hast conferred their form on all creatures! Defend me, give me strength to trample upon Satan, give me the love of a lover longing unto death, lighten the burden of sin I must bear with me beyond the grave!

How can I hymn the praises of that hero whose lance, shield, and sword bring him glory, or of Queen Tamar[2] — Tamar, whose radiance is like the sun's, whose cheek is ruby, whose hair is jet; Tamar, who fills all beholders with rapture unutterable?

Tears of blood flow from my eyes as I sing of Tamar; I, not unworthy, have composed her eulogy: her eyes' jet pools have served for ink, my wasted form, reed-thin, for pen:[3] compassion's lance must pierce my hearers' hearts.

I was commanded to fashion sweet verses in her honor, to tell of her eyebrows, lashes, tresses, lips and teeth — of the crystal and ruby set within her cheek. . . . An anvil's soft lead breaks the hardest stone!

Now have I need of tongue, heart and skill for song: give me strength; with your aid all will be achieved! Thus will the fame of Tariel endure, nobly enshrined in verse — aye, the fame of all the three star-fair heroes wont to bear aid one to another. Come, let us sit and shed unceasing tears for Tariel; never, truly, has another such as he been created! My heart pierced as by a lance, I, Rustaveli, set myself to write a poem: before this there was only a tale passing among the people — behold now a rope of pearls![4]

I, the lord of Rustavi,[5] have composed this work; for the sake of her who has at her command hosts of warriors,[6] I have lost my wits, come near to death. I am wasting away — nowhere is there a cure for lovers! Let her give me healing, or the earth a grave.

A Persian tale, this, turned into Georgian; a thing like a rare pearl passed from hand to hand I found, and put into verse. A work deserving of praise; may it find favor with the lady proud and beautiful for whose sake I run distraught.

Her beauty has blinded my eyes; they long once more to behold her: my heart, alas, is mad for love — it must roam, it must wander. Who will pray for me? Enough that the body should burn in love's fires, let the soul know some comfort! . . . My verse has to tell of the deeds of three heroes.

A man should accept without repining the lot that fate sends him; it is for the laborer to toil, the warrior to fight bravely. Even so must the lover surrender himself to love, learn well how to know it. Let him cast no blame upon others, that he himself may escape reproach.

Poetry, before all else, is a branch of philosophy: divine, fit for heaven, it delights those who hear it. Even here below it gives pleasure to noble souls: to say much in a few words — therein lies its excellence.

As with the racehorse tried over a distance, as with the player proving his skill in the maidan,[7] so is it with the poet who has put his hand to a long work when utterance grows hard and the lines are slow to form. Behold the man at his craft now! When the Georgian flows no more and the verse falters, he will not let his words fall short nor yet suffer cheapening; rather will he take courage and strike again deftly.

A couple of verses scribbled somewhere do not make a man a poet; let none on the strength of such trifles think himself the peer of the masters; as crass as a mule is the fellow ready to brag of a few odd, ragged lines.

There are, too, those poems that are no more than snatches: one cannot look in such things for words that will pierce the heart; they are like the wretched little bows that boys have for hunting — good enough to bring down small game, but of no use against larger beasts. Then there are those of yet a third sort, songs that go with drinking and gaiety, the game of love and the laughter of friends: they may win our applause when all is done with accomplishment. . . . But only the man whose design is a large one can be called a true poet.

The poet must not squander the powers that are in him: one lady alone should command his devotion; he should call forth the whole of his art for her praise; he should have but one longing; he should give her glory in song.

Now let it be known to all that the lady I laud here is she of whom I have sung in the past, and none other. Great will my renown be, no task of dishonor this! Cruel as a leopard, she is yet life itself to me: in this tale she is pictured under a name not her own.[8]

I would speak of a love first whose nature is heavenly; hard is it to discourse on, to treat of in words: a thing not of this world, it draws the soul to heights beyond: he who attains to it will receive strength against grief. But far is it beyond the understanding of even the wisest men; it makes the tongue weary and brings fatigue to the ear of the listener. My theme is rather the earthly passion that visits us mortals — which has yet some likeness to the mystic when there is nothing wanton in it, only silence and longing.

In the speech of the Arabs our *lover* means 'madman';[9] lovers are robbed of their wits by a cruel denial. . . . Some seek nearness to God but are wearied by soaring; others grosser of nature will run after women.

A lover should be even as fair as the sun itself, deep of mind, possessed of riches, generous of heart, in the flower of youth, and with time at command. He should have eloquence of tongue, a good understanding, endurance, and the strength that brings victory over mighty antagonists. He who falls short of this is not to be reckoned a lover.

Love is a thing rare and fine, hard to comprehend;[10] it can in no way be likened to the desire of the flesh. Love is one thing, desire another; and deep indeed is the chasm that stretches between them. Let them not be confounded — give ear to my words!

The lover must be constant and free from all stain and adultery; when parted from his lady he should for ever be sighing; his heart must yearn for one and one only, though she be cruel and unkind.[11] Love-making with no heart to it I find utterly hateful.

This one today, that other tomorrow; parting without a pang — this is not worthy of the name of love! It resembles nothing so much as the idle games boys play together: the true lover is he who can endure the woes that Fate sends him.

The lover's first duty is concealment of sorrow; he should cherish his passion in secret, should always seek solitude. Pining, yearning and burning in the furnace of grief — all these from afar.[12]. . . He must bear his lady's displeasure, hold her in fear and in reverence. Let him betray his secret to none,[13] let him not bring shame on his beloved with clownish lamentation; let him reveal his passion in no way, nowhere make it known. For her sake he must look on sorrow as joy, for her sake he must be consumed in love's fires.

How can any man in his right mind put trust in the babbler who noises his love abroad — what good can come of that? The lover will only do harm to his lady, and to himself also. How can he endue her with fame when with his tongue he dishonors her, why should her heart have to suffer such wounds?

Strange that men should be without care to keep their love hidden! How can they bring shame upon those who are wasting away in their longing? If they care nothing, so be it — but why offer a wrong thus? Yet, in truth, to an evil man an evil word is dearer than his heart or his soul!

If a lover weeps for his lady, he does as is fitting: let him roam alone through desert places[14] as one who has renounced the world: his mind should be filled with the thought of her wholly.[15] But let his love stay concealed when he moves among men.

Of Rostevan, the king of the Arabs

In Arabia there once ruled a king, Rostevan, who was blessed by God with good fortune. Of great majesty was he, liberal of gifts, gentle, lord over many warriors and vassals; just, gracious, mighty, far-seeing, peerless in battle and eloquent of speech.[16]

(25-41)

Only one child had he, a daughter who illumined the world like the sun. All who looked on her were bereft of heart, wits and soul: it would take a man profound of mind to praise her, and a tongue like a myriad. Tinatin[17] was her name — let it be known now on every hand! The sun itself was dimmed when she grew beyond childhood.

One day the king had all his viziers assemble before him. Serene in his majesty, he disposed them about him and addressed them thus graciously: "I would have your counsel, therefor are we met together. — When a rose withers and fades it must soon fall, and another will flower in the beauty of the garden: now my sun has set, and I am looking out on the dark of a moonless night.

"For indeed my time is past; old age, the sorest of all ills, has fastened upon me. Death will come — if not today, then tomorrow; such is the rule of the world. What manner of light is that on which darkness attends? Now let us bestow the crown on my daughter,[18] whom the sun does not equal in beauty."

The viziers replied: "O King, why speak thus of your years? Even when the rose has withered we must hold it in regard, for in scent and hue it is still the loveliest of flowers. Does a star dare to vie with the waning moon? No, do not speak thus, O King; yours is no withered rose, and your worst counsel is worth more than the best of another. — Yet your heart must have its desire; make queen the lady whose beauty is brighter than the rays of the sun. For all that she is a woman, she has been destined by God to rule and knows well how to govern — no idle flattery this; we have often said as much when we were not in your presence. Her acts, like her beauty, shine forth as the sun. . . . And, male or female, the lion's whelps are all equal."

Avtandil[19] was the captain of the host and the son of its marshal. Still beardless, he was more splendid in his form than the cypress; he was like the sun and the moon; he resembled rare crystal.[20] Tinatin's lashes had wreaked havoc in his heart with their lustre, but he kept his love concealed closely within him. When he was denied sight of her the rose on his cheek would fade, but when he saw her once more the fires would leap up anew, and the pain of his wound become yet more bitter. Wretched indeed is the lot of the man who suffers from love; it strikes through to the heart.[21]

Avtandil rejoiced over the king's resolve to give the crown to his daughter; the torment of his passion was eased. "Often now," he thought, "shall I look upon that face fair as crystal; perhaps my wan cheek will be cured of its pallor!"

The mighty monarch of the Arabs had this proclaimed throughout his realm: "I, her father, am going to install Tinatin as your sovereign, that she may shed light over all, even as the radiant sun. Come, therefore, all of you to look upon her and offer her praise!"

All the Arabs came; the great men thronged thickly. There was Avtandil the sun-fair, captain over great hosts; and there too was Sograt[22] the vizier, who of all men at court stood nearest the king.

A throne was set in place that all declared to be priceless. Tinatin, radiant in her beauty, was led up by her father and seated herself upon it. With his own hands he laid the crown upon her head, then he surrendered the scepter and put about her the royal robes: like the sun, the maiden looked out over all, her gaze filled with understanding.

The king and his warriors fell back, made obeisance, called down blessings upon her and acclaimed her as queen. On all sides her praises were sung; horns were blown, joyously sounded the cymbals. But the maiden closed her eyes and wept; tear followed tear through lashes dark as the raven's wing: for she deemed herself unworthy to sit on her father's throne. The king addressed her thus: "Every father at the last gives place to his child: before this was done I had no peace within me." And he went on: "Do not weep, daughter, but give ear to my words. This day you have become the queen of Arabia, called by me to the lordship of the realm; and henceforward its welfare lies in your charge. Let wisdom inform your every act; be mild and prudent in your rule. Even as the sun shines alike on roses and dunghills, let your favor fall unwearyingly on both the great and the humble. He who is generous of hand binds the free man to him and keeps the devotion of the already bound: therefore be lavish in giving, even as is the ocean in sending forth again the inflowing waters.[23]

(41-58)

"Royal bounty has splendor; it is like a cypress in Eden. All, even the false of heart, will obey the munificent. To eat and drink is indeed good, but to what end do we store up riches? What you bestow in gifts remains yours, the retained is lost utterly!"

The maiden listened wisely to this advice from her father: she heeded his words, did not fret under instruction. Glad in heart, the king drank and gave himself up to diversion. . . . The sun strove in vain to match Tinatin's radiance.

Presently Tinatin summoned her faithful steward, well tried in loyalty: "Bring here my treasure, sealed by your own hand," she said; "bring my whole inheritance." It was brought; and without measure, without reckoning, without ever tiring, did she give it away then. With everything come to her since childhood did she part in that one day, enriching small folk and great. "I will take my father's guidance," such was her declaration: "let none seek to keep any of my treasures concealed."

She said, "Go and carry forth all that there is to be carried! — Master of the Horse, let your beasts be driven here in their herds." Her command was obeyed; and countless were the horses she gave away; unfaltering still was she in her liberality. Her warriors laid hands on her treasure like brigands; they seized it like booty taken from Turks; her sleek, well-tended Arab steeds were one and all borne away. Her largesse was like a snow-storm showering down from the heavens; not a man, not a woman, went away without wealth.[24]

The whole of that day was given over to feasting; the warriors gathered and sat down to the banquet. But the king's head was bowed and his demeanor had gloom in it; men began to ask one another what could be the cause of his grief.

At the table's head sat Avtandil, the sun-fair, the glorious, delight of beholders, the host's leader, the peer of the lion and panther; and old Sograt the vizier sat at his side. What, they wondered, could be the cause of the king's pallor and melancholy? Since the feast had been marred by no untoward happening, some thought filled with sadness must surely have come to him. At length Avtandil said, "Sograt, let us ask him why we have fallen from favor: come, we must try to amuse him — why should he treat us thus?"

Sograt and Avtandil the graceful arose, filled their goblets and went up quietly to the king; smiling they knelt before him. The vizier spoke then with ready words, lightly: "O King, you are fallen into melancholy; your countenance is not now illumined by laughter. And indeed you have cause for grief, for now your daughter has squandered your rich, priceless treasure, has given it all away in prodigal largesse. — Do not make her queen at all, why should you bring down such sorrow upon your head?"

The king looked up with a smile at this, wondering to hear such audacity. But he gave gracious thanks, saying, "That was well spoken!" Then he went on: "Call me tight-fisted, and you lie in your teeth with your chatter! No, the cause of my sorrow is not to be found there: my grief lies in this — the days of my youth are gone, old age is coming upon me, yet in all my dominions there is none I could ever turn into a true man of arms. And then, although I have a daughter, brought up in all tenderness, God has not granted me a son — hard is the lot that is mine in this world! None is there like me with the bow or at ball-play. . . . It is true that Avtandil, whom I trained as my pupil, has got within him some small trace of my quality."

Avtandil the proud listened quietly to the words of the king: head bent, he gave a smile that illumined his countenance; his white teeth shone forth like the rays of the sun. "Why do you smile," the king asked him, "what are you holding back?" And again: "What makes you smile thus, why are you deriding me?" Avtandil replied, "If I may speak freely I will tell you; but do not let my words move you to anger; do not let my presumption bring me to ruin!"

The king said, "How could I take amiss any words of yours!" And he invoked the name of Tinatin, fairer than the sun, in an oath of assurance. Then Avtandil went on: "Now I will speak boldly: you should not brag so much of your skill as an archer — it is good to be modest in speech. Now I, Avtandil, earth under your feet, who stand here before you, am likewise a bowman. Let us lay a wager; for judges we can turn to your retinue. You ask who there is to compare with you. . . . Of what use boast and counter-boast? In sport it is the ball and the ground that decide."

"No more! Come, we will shoot together — do not think to escape this! We will take trustworthy men to deliver a judgement, and we will see on the ground which of us earns the acclaim."

Avtandil acquiesced in this, and the matter was settled: laughing like carefree boys, they showed their affection: it was determined between them that he who was vanquished should go three days bareheaded.[25] The king said to Avtandil, "We will take twelve attendants, to keep me furnished with arrows and to serve me as squires. Your Shermadin[26] is in himself worth the sum of these — let him and them keep a faithful and unerring count of the arrows loosed, and of the hits also." Then he gave out his orders for those who served him when hunting: "Go out and scour the plain, drive beasts in crowds for us — see to this!" Warriors were told to make ready, to come and assemble: and so ended the banquet on this day of rejoicing.

How King Rostevan and Avtandil went hunting

Early in the morning Avtandil rode out on a white horse: as fair as a lily was he to look upon; he was clad in crimson; his face shone in its beauty like rubies and crystal. His turban was golden; splendid was he to behold in the gear of an archer. His coming announced, Rostevan made ready and mounted. Off they went to the hunt; those who would drive the game formed a ring round the chace; there was much joyous noise; everywhere there were warriors. For their wager the king and Avtandil were to shoot and slaughter in rivalry.

The king gave his commands: "Twelve attendants are to ride with us, to have our swift-shafted bows always ready and to ply us with arrows, to weigh hit against hit and to keep count of the shots." Game came thronging from all sides, beasts in countless droves — deer, goats, wild asses and light-footed antelopes. Lord and vassal pursued them — what sight could be fairer? Behold now bows and arrows, arms strong and untiring! The dust from their horses' hooves darkened the sun; their shooting and slaughtering covered the plain over with blood. When their arrows were gone the attendants supplied more; and never a beast was struck but it fell in its tracks.

Driving the herds before them, they coursed over the ground; the death that they dealt out roused the wrath of the heavens; the ground was dyed red with the blood of the creatures. — All who beheld Avtandil declared that he was as fair as a cypress in Eden.

They rode over the whole chace, a thing done by no others: then on the far side, where a stream flowed between rocks, their quarry leaped into thickets where a horse could not follow. The king and Avtandil were both weary now, great as their spirit was. Laughing, each declared that he had won in the contest: two joking friends, they were gay then together. The attendants who had been following came up in a little; and the king said, "Now tell us the truth without flattery!"

They replied, "We will speak in all honesty, we will not deceive you: O King, you are not the peer of Avtandil! Kill us all here out of hand if you will; you are not his equal, and nothing can make you so! Every creature his arrow struck fell straight to the ground. You have slaughtered between you beasts to a hundred score, but Avtandil has slain twenty for one you have killed. Not one shaft that he shot failed to strike on its mark, but we have cleaned the earth off from many of yours."

For all that the king cared, it might have been a game of backgammon: he rejoiced to hear what the young lord he had trained had achieved, for he held him as dear as the nightingale does the rose.[27] He smiled and was happy; grief was gone from his heart.

They got out of their saddles now under the shade of the trees. The warriors came up and stood round about them, as thick as chaff on the ground; the twelve attendants, the bravest of the brave, stayed close by the king. And thus they took their ease, with the stream and the edge of the woodland before them.

How the king of the Arabs saw the lord of the panther-skin

By the edge of the stream they saw a stranger lord, sitting weeping. He held a black horse by the rein. . . . He looked like a lion, a hero. Arms, saddle and bridle were all thickly encrusted with pearls. On the rose of his cheek tears from his heart's fires lay frozen.

He wore as a garment the skin of a panther; on his head he had a cap likewise made of the beast's skin; in his hand he held an enchased whip thicker than the arm of a man.[28] — They gazed on this unknown with delight; they admired him.

One of the attendants went forward to speak to the grief-stricken lord; piteous indeed to behold was he as he wept there with head bent; through the jet of his lashes drops of crystal came raining down. — The man approached, but could not bring himself to utter a word. Not daring to speak, overawed, he gazed in amazement: at length, calling up all the courage within him, he said, "The king summons you to him!" and went closer quietly. But the young lord in his weeping did not hear what he said, did not know he was there, even. Not a word did he hear, nor yet the noise that was made by the warriors. Strange sobs burst out from a heart that was burning; tears mixed with blood flowed forth as from flood-gates. His thoughts were gone from his bowed head, flown to far-distant places.

The attendant then uttered the king's command for a second time: as the lord did not cease from weeping, pay heed or part his rose-red lips in speech, he went back without an answer thereafter. "He will have no truck with you," he reported to Rostevan; "my eyes were dazzled as by the sun, and my heart was sorely dismayed. For all my trying, I could not get him to listen to me."

The king was surprised; his heart was moved now to anger; he had all twelve of his attendants go forward. "Take your arms," he said, "and bring before me that lord sitting over there!"

The attendants advanced: the stranger was aroused from his bitter weeping now by the clank of their war-gear. He looked round about; and when he saw the great assemblage of warriors a single cry broke from him: "Woe is me!"

He drew his hand across his eyes, wiping away the hot tears, put right sword and quiver and summoned the strength of his arms. Then he mounted his horse — why should he give any heed to such minions! — and rode off unregarding.

The attendants sought to lay hands on him — but what he did to them then might have drawn pity from enemies! Some he dashed together and slaughtered unmercifully; others he cleft down to the breast with his whip.

Filled with fury and rage, the king loosed his warriors: he recked nothing of them until they got up to him — but as many as did so were quickly dead men! One on another, they were hurled to the ground;[29] and greatly did Rostevan grieve at the sight.

The king and Avtandil mounted to make after the stranger. Proud and haughty, he rode off; his body swayed gracefully; he was as fair as the sun; his horse was the peer of Merani.[30] When he perceived he was being pursued by the king he struck his steed with his whip and disappeared in an instant: it was as though the earth had swallowed him or he had been snatched up into the heavens. In vain did they search for tracks, they could find never a trace of him: greatly amazed were they! Thus, like a Div,[31] did he vanish away.

The warriors mourned for their dead and hastened to bind up wounds. The king said, "What I have seen here has put a weight on my spirit." And he went on, "The happiness that was mine until this day has grown wearisome to God: he has turned it to bitter grief, he has dealt me a mortal wound beyond any man's curing. But let his will be done!"

When he had said this he turned about and rode off, his brow darkened. The horn would sound for the hunt no more, the slaughter of beasts was stayed. Some said, "This is rightly done!" — but there was too some murmuring.

Sombre and melancholy, the king retired to his chamber: only Avtandil, who was as a son to him, followed. The household dispersed then; all joy was fled away; the sweet-sounding harp and the lute were no more heard.[32]

When Tinatin learned of her father's deep sorrow, she, the sun's rival, rose and repaired to the door of his chamber. "Is he asleep or awake?" she asked of the chamberlain. The chamberlain replied, "He is sitting brooding; pale is his cheek and wan: he has only one companion, Avtandil, who is seated before him. The sight of a certain stranger lord has caused this distemper."

(94-111)

Tinatin said, "I will withdraw; it is not the time now to enter. But if he asks for me, tell him that only a moment before I was here."

After a little the king asked, "What of my daughter — my joy, jewel, life's spring?" "Pale of cheek," the chamberlain answered, "she came here not long since: but she withdrew as soon as she had learned of your melancholy."

The king said, "Go and summon her: I cannot endure to be longer without her. Give her this message: 'Light of your father's life, why did you turn away? Come, dispel my grief, heal my heart's wounds; and I will tell you why all my joy has now gone from me.' "

Tinatin rose and came in answer to her father's command; like the waxing moon was her face in its loveliness. He had her sit at his side, and then, kissing her tenderly, he said, "Why did you not come before, why did you wait to be called here?" The maiden replied, "Who, O King, even among the boldest, would dare enter your presence, knowing your spirit to be troubled? Your dark humor might bring down the stars from the heavens! . . . But men should grapple with difficulty, not vainly repine."

"My child," the king said, "great as is my grief, to see you, to have you with me, is enough to bring joy back. My melancholy is banished now, as by some elixir: but when you have heard the story you will say, I think, that my sorrow had reason. — I came upon a certain stranger lord, wondrous to look upon; his beauty filled the heavens and the earth too with light. He was weeping, but what grieved him or for whose sake he wept I could not discover. When he would not come to me I was angered and tried to make him my captive. Wiping the tears from his eyes, he mounted as soon as he saw me: I shouted to my men to lay hands upon him, but great was the slaughter he wrought then among them! He disappeared like a demon, gave no greeting after the manner of humankind; and still I do not know whether he was a true man or a phantom.

"Grievous is my perplexity: what was this thing that I saw? — He slaughtered my warriors, made blood flow in torrents. . . . Can he have been a mortal, since he vanished in such a way? Until this time I have known nothing but happiness, but now assuredly am I hated of God! His gracious favors have at last turned to bitterness, the days of my joys are departed. Let every man pity me — none can bring comfort: whatever my length of days, I can know no content of mind."

The maiden said, "I will speak boldly: O King, why reproach either God or Fate? Can you accuse him who sees and cherishes all creatures of cruelty? Can evil have been wrought by the creator of good?

"This is my counsel: you are a king, and lord over many rulers; wide are the dominions through which your writ runs. Send men to all quarters to gather intelligence; you will soon know whether or not he whom you saw was a mortal."[33]

Emissaries were summoned, and dispatched to the four corners of the earth with this charge: "Go forth, spare your-selves no labor, search for that lord — be zealous in the task: let letters be written when you cannot gain access."

They set out, and for the whole of a year they all journeyed, looking for the stranger lord, making inquiry again and again. But never a mortal man could they find who had seen him; and at length, wearied to no purpose and sick at heart, they returned and said, "O King, we have traveled over the earth, but the joy of finding that lord was denied us; nor did we meet with any who had ever set eyes on him. We have failed to achieve anything; you must think of some other plan."

"My child spoke truth," said the king: "what I saw was the deceit of some fiend come down from the sky for my un-doing. — I have done now with melancholy, no longer will I grieve."

And then, joyful of heart, he gave the word for diversions: every minstrel and tumbler to be found in any quarter was called on: there was largesse of gifts, all were summoned to the palace — when did God create another as generous-handed as he!

How Tinatin charged Avtandil
with the quest for the stranger lord

Attired for his ease, Avtandil was sitting alone in his cham-ber, singing gaily to a harp, when Tinatin's negro slave came

before him and said, "The cypress-like, the moon-fair, calls
you to her presence."

These were the words Avtandil had longed for! He rose and
put on the finest of his tunics, the richest. He rejoiced that he
was now to see that lady who was as fair as a rose: never had
he and she been alone together. . . . Sweet indeed is it to look
on beauty, to be near to the loved one!

Proud and bold of mien — he feared no man's eye — he
answered the summons. And now he beheld her he had wept
for so often. The peerless lady sat pensive; her beauty, dazzling
as lightning, made the moon's face seem darkness; she wore
unlined ermine, with a loose veil of a price beyond reckoning.
Her black lashes were lovely; about her white throat her long
tresses lay thickly; thus she sat, thoughtful, behind her crimson-
hued veil. Quietly and gently she bade Avtandil be seated: a
slave placed a stool, and he took it with deference: he was
filled with great joy; now he could see her before him.

The maiden said, "It is hard to speak; I wished to stay silent,
but this pain is not to be longer endured! . . . Do you know why
I have summoned you, why I am oppressed by sadness, bereft
of understanding?"

"What words of mine," Avtandil replied, "can give ease to
your sorrow? When the moon meets the sun[34] it fades, wastes
away. I can no longer think, I am filled with disquiet: tell me
what grieves you, and where the cure lies."

In words of great beauty the maiden said to him: "I have
until now kept some distance between us: what you scarcely
dared hope for has come to pass suddenly, and you are amazed
at this. . . . But first I must tell you of the pain that afflicts me.

"Do you remember how, when you and Rostevan were hunt-
ing out on the plain, you saw that stranger lord who wiped
away tears? Ever since that day the thought of him has weighed
heavily on me: seek for him, I beg you, in every corner between
earth and sky.

"Never before this day have we had converse together, but I
divined that you loved from afar. I know that tears have hailed
down from your eyes without ceasing, that love has made
you a prisoner, taken your heart for its captive.

"Listen well: you can do me service doubly befitting: first, as a paladin you have no peer among mortals; and then I am loved by you — this is truth, not imagining! Be he near, be he far, go and search for that young lord: deliver me from the power of this demon of sorrow — thus will your love for me be made even stronger. Plant the violets of hope in my heart, let strewn roses adorn it. Then return here, my lion; I will go to meet you like the sun;[35] come to me.

"Allow your search three years. If you find him, come back in triumph, give the news joyfully. If you do not, I shall be assured that he was but a phantom; you will find me, your rose, unwithered, in bud still.

"This do I swear: if I take any other for a husband — even were the sun itself to take a man's form for my sake — may I be shut out from Paradise, may I be swallowed up in Hell, may my love for you pierce my heart with a dagger and kill me!"

"Sun-fair lady of the jet-black lashes!" Avtandil replied: "there is but one answer, one thought in my mind: I looked only for death; you have now restored life to me. I will go forth assuredly as your true man to serve you." He said again, "Sun-fair one, created by God as a very sun, obeyed by all of the stars in the heavens, gracious indeed are the words I have heard! My rose cannot wither, with your rays shining upon it."

Oaths were exchanged once more, they confirmed their troth. Long did they talk, their white teeth flashing like lightning; the pain that they had both of them known was now eased. They conversed, talked of a hundred things as they sat there together; their cheeks were crystal and ruby, their lashes were jet. Avtandil said, "All who look on you are bereft of their reason; the flame of your loveliness has turned my heart into ashes."

He took his leave at last: ill able to endure parting, he looked back with an eye bemused. Down hailed his tears; his cheek's rose was frozen; tremors ran through the frame that was compact of gracefulness; he had received pledge for pledge, his part it was to love. "Sun-fair lady," he said, "thus early does parting show on the rose! The crystal and ruby have fled from my countenance, now am I yellower than ever was amber.

Woe unto me, if we must endure a long severance! But a man should readily die for his lady; I will hold to this law."

He lay down on his bed and shed tears without ceasing; like an aspen in the path of the wind, he shivered and trembled. When slumber came he dreamed that his lady was near him, and with a start he cried out aloud: twentyfold grew his sufferings. The parting of that day had filled him with longing; tears like pearls softly fell on his cheek's rose.

In the morning he garbed himself — fair was he to look upon! — got into the saddle and rode to the palace. Then he sent this message in by the mouth of the chamberlain: "O King, I desire to tell you of the design I have formed. Your sword has brought the whole earth under your sway, and this should be made known now to all of our neighbors. I will go forth and ride round the marches, and fight on them; I will stamp Tinatin's rule on the hearts of your enemies. I will bring joy to all true men, the unruly I will cause to weep; I will send back gift after gift with my duty and greetings."

The king in his reply showed himself very grateful: "Never, O my lion, have you faltered in battle; this project is worthy indeed of your valor. You may depart — but what shall I do if you are long gone from me?"

Avtandil went in, made obeisance and spoke words of thanks then: "O King, I wonder that you should deign thus to praise me! — Perhaps God will give it to me once more to behold you, will lighten my darkness, will grant me the joy of seeing your face illumined by gladness."

The king embraced and kissed him like a son — never have such as they been known, such a lord, such a liegeman! Avtandil rose then and went forth; such was their parting. And Rostevan, the wise and gentle-hearted, wept for him.

Avtandil, the valiant lord, set out, riding proudly; he journeyed for twenty days, and many a night and day did he join on the road. The delight of the world was he, in very truth! His thoughts were always of Tinatin, and for her sake flames burned in his breast.

When he reached his own domain he was received with rejoicing: the barons came out to meet him and welcomed him with lavish gifts. The sun-fair hero showed himself on that

journey no lingerer: his attendants came forward to the glad
sound of the drum.

He was lord of a stronghold, girt by rock, that kept the
march-lands in awe; here, after spending three days pleasantly
in hunting, he summoned his vassal Shermadin to confer with
him. This was the Shermadin already named as his follower;[36]
he had grown up with Avtandil and was wholly devoted to
him; but as yet he knew nothing of the fires in his lord's breast.
Avtandil now told him of the hope his sun-fair lady had given
him:

"Shermadin, I feel ashamed; I confide to you all things that
concern me, yet you have known nothing until this day of the
tears I have shed! But now my woe's source has bestowed joy
upon me. I have been brought near to death by love and long-
ing for Tinatin; hot tears have poured from my eye's narcissus
down over the frosted rose on my cheek. Until this time I have
kept my sorrow close hidden, but now she has uttered words
that have heartened me, and you see me filled with gladness
before you.

"She said to me, 'Find out who that lord was who vanished
before you; then return, and I will grant you the desire of your
heart. I want no husband but you, not though he were as fair
as a tree growing in Eden.' With her words she brought heal-
ing to a heart that had long burned.

"First, I am a vassal, eager to go forth in my sovereign's ser-
vice. Devotion is due to rulers, we lieges owe loyalty. Then
she has quenched the fires aflame in my breast; my heart is
burning no longer within me to cinders. . . . A man should not
flinch before sorrow, but meet it with fortitude.

"No lord and vassal anywhere hold each other as dear as do
we; for this give good heed, I beg, to what I now say to you. I
am going to put you in my place, to rule and to command all my
warriors; this is a charge I could give to no other. Lead the men-
at-arms and the barons in battle; take all things in your govern-
ance; send messengers to court and ascertain all that is done
there; write letters in my name; send forth costly gifts; act, in
brief, so that none may perceive I am gone. Whether fighting or
hunting, bear yourself as do I.

"Wait for me up to three years; keep my secret close. It may be that I shall return — that the cypress will not fall into the sere. If I do not . . . mourn for me, weep for me; then break to the king the heavy news of my death — let grief take you like wine, tell him I have suffered the fate that none may escape. Give away my treasure to the poor; gold, silver and copper. Thus can you aid me best, prove your zeal in my service. Do not forget me soon, think of me often; let your care follow me, pray for my soul. Let your mind turn to my boyhood, hold me in memory tenderly."

When Shermadin heard this he was astonished and troubled: hot tears like pearls started forth from his eyes as he said, "What manner of joy can my heart have without you? . . . I know you will go, that I have no power to stop you — but how can you say you will leave me here in your place? How could I hold sway and govern in the way you are wont to? Better to sleep in my grave than to see you ride forth alone! Let us set out together — let me come, I will go with you!"

"Listen," Avtandil replied, "and I will tell you the truth of the matter: when a lover departs on a quest he must go all alone. Pearls are not won without bargain and purchase! . . . For treacherous falsehood a lance-thrust is fitting.

"What other man could I entrust with my secret? None save you is worthy of receiving my confidence. In what other hands could I place my authority? Who, tell me, would bear himself as well as you will? — Strengthen the march-lands' defences against the incursions of enemies. . . . If God does not forsake me utterly I shall maybe return.

"Be it a hundred or be it one, Fate can slay just as easily. . . . Though I go alone, I shall not come to harm if the heavenly powers give protection. If I am not back within three years, put on mourning and make lamentation. — You shall have a commission charging all my vassals to give you obedience."

How Avtandil wrote out a charge to his vassals

He wrote thus: "My vassals, old and young alike; followers well-tried, heedful as very shadows to my will, trusty and loyal —give ear to what is here proclaimed when you are assembled together.

"Listen to what I have written to you — I, Avtandil, your loving lord; the penning of this has been the work of my own hand. I am going to leave for a time the life of song and of feasting and go on a quest; for meat I shall trust to my hand and my bow. I have a task that will take me to a land very far distant, and for a whole year I shall travel alone.[37] This would I beg of you: let me return to a realm still unravaged by enemies.

"I have chosen Shermadin to hold sway in my place: until he knows whether I have lived through all or have died he will be to you like a kindly sun that cherishes the rose with its rays; but all evil-doers will he have melt like wax. You know that he has always been like a brother or son to me; render him such obedience as you would give me myself. Let the trumpet sound at his bidding, in all things let him act in my name. If I do not return within the term set, put away joy and mourn for me."

When he had written this charge out — rare master of words was he! — Avtandil tied gold round his waist and made ready for the quest he was about to set forth on. "I will ride out on to the plain now," he said; his warriors were mustered in ranks. No time did he lose then; straightaway he departed. "Go, all of you now," he commanded; "I do not wish to have any companion." His attendants dismissed, he was left all alone. He made about and then galloped off through a reed-bed. . . . The thought of his lady, Tinatin, was never out of his mind.

He made off over the plain, away from the warriors. He was gone from the sight of all. there was none who could follow him; no sword could give him hurt, his arm would protect him. . . . But heavy was the weight of grief that he bore for his lady's sake.

The warriors looked and searched for their lord, but nowhere could they find him, the sun-fair one. Their faces turned ashen, joy was changed into sorrow. Those who were best mounted sought everywhere for him: "O lion," the cry rose, "what man could God choose to put in your place?" This way and that they galloped, from all sides men were brought in for questioning. But in vain; Avtandil had vanished from ken, and his followers shed scalding tears in their wretchedness.

(166-82)

Shermadin called together the lords and the great men, showed them Avtandil's charge, and then read it aloud. Stricken to the heart were they all when they heard it; there was not an eye without a tear, every man smote his breast. Then they said, one and all, "Grievous indeed is our loss, but to whose hands save yours could he have committed the governance? We will all obey you, assuredly, in whatever you may command." Thus they recognized that Shermadin was possessed of authority; each man made him obeisance.

How Avtandil went in search of the stranger lord

Let the wise Denys[38] here give his testimony: Pitiful indeed is a frost-covered rose to behold, or one who has lost his ruby hue, whose frame is worn reed-thin.

Riding fast over the plain, Avtandil passed beyond the Arabs' borders and then through other lands. Yet parting from his sun-fair lady had cleft his heart in twain: "Were I but with her now," he said, "these hot tears would not be falling!"

The drops took his cheek as the snow's chill a rose: many a time did he put his hand to his dagger, filled with the longing to plunge it into his heart. He said, "Fate has made my woes ninety — a hundred times more bitter: sundered am I from all joy, from the music of harp, lyre and flute!"

Like a rose denied the sun his cheek became ever more faded; yet he did not despair utterly, he told himself to endure. He passed through places on his quest that were strange indeed; he treated travelers with courtesy and put questions to them. Thus did he pursue his search, his tears flowing always to swell the waters of the ocean. For bed he had the ground, his arm served him for pillow.[39] "Beloved," he said, "although we are parted my heart remains with you: joy would it indeed be to die for your sake!"

He journeyed over the whole earth; no place he had not passed through remained under the sky. But never a man did he meet who had heard of the stranger lord; and so, save for three months, three years passed away.

He came to a region very wild and desolate then; for a month he did not see a soul, not a single son of Adam. Truly, neither Vis nor Ramin[40] knew such sorrows as his! . . . His thoughts were with his lady always, by day and by night.

At length he stopped to rest on a high mountain-summit; a wide plain stretched out before him, seven days' journey across. At the foot of the slope below flowed a river that could be easily forded; both banks were covered with trees right down to the water's edge. There on the crest he took some ease and made a reckoning of time: no more than two months, so he counted, was left to him. "Alas," he said with a sigh, "would that the truth might yet be revealed to me!" Once more his heart desponded: "No man can turn evil into good, none can be born again!"

He began now to reflect and to ponder: "If I turn for home, all this time of my search will have gone for nought. — What shall I tell my star-fair lady, what shall I have to say for the long days if I cannot bring with me even a rumor of the lord I have been looking for? Yet, if I do not return, if I spend more time on my quest to no purpose, the term will be reached that was given to Shermadin. His cheeks stained with tears, he will go to the king to make due report and, even as I asked him to do, he will tell him that I am beyond any doubt dead. There will be lamentation, weeping and bitter grief — and then if I return, a living man, from my wanderings. . .?" Such were his thoughts; and, disturbed in spirit, he wept. "O God," he said then, "why are you so unjust to me? Why have you had me travel on a fool's errand such distances? Why have you rooted out joy from my heart and planted in its stead sorrow? . . . Never will I cease from weeping in all the days that are left to me!"

But then he said, "Patience!" and went on thus in thought: "Let me not die before my hour, let my heart not be dismayed. Without God I can do nothing, in vain do my tears flow. None can change his fate; that which is not ordained to be, will not be." Yet again he reflected: "Better death than a shameful life! If you go back you will see Tinatin the sun-fair; she will question you about the stranger lord most assuredly — and what, miserable wretch, will you have then to say?" Meditating thus, he made off towards the reeds and the river that flowed through the woodland.

"I have now seen all the creatures that live under the heavens, but nowhere have I learned anything at all of the stranger lord. Truly, those who declared him a Kaj[41] had the right of it. . . . But weeping avails nothing; why shed idle tears?"

When he had reached the foot of the mountain Avtandil crossed over the river and rode on through the trees: fretted by their rustlings, he spurred his horse towards the plain. His strength and his pride alike were now weakened. . . . A moustache black as jet adorned his crystal-fair countenance.

Sighing and groaning, he had resolved to turn homeward; and now, making forward, he picked out his road. Never a living soul did he see for a month then: he met with terrible beasts, but they did not dismay him.

Although all his groaning and sighing had crazed him, he needed to eat, as is the way with the children of Adam: he shot a beast — he had an arm that was stronger than Rustam's[42] — then dismounted by a reed-bed and with flint and steel lit a fire. Turning his horse loose to graze, he roasted the flesh.

Presently he saw six horsemen approaching him: "These must be brigands!" was the thought in his mind. "What could bring honest men here, where no mortal has trodden before me?" — But with a friendly demeanor he went forward to meet them, bow and arrow in hand. Now he could discern a swooning, smooth-cheeked youth with a wound in his head and blood on his breast, supported by two men with beards fully grown. The two were weeping and lamenting; the youth had come to the point of death.

"Who are you, brothers?" Avtandil called. "I took you for brigands!" They replied, "Have no fear, but come and give us your aid: or, if you can do nothing, add your sorrow to ours at least. Join us in our grief, weep with us in our wretchedness, let your cheeks too be rent."

Avtandil rode up then and spoke to those stricken souls. Still weeping, they told him their story: "Three brothers are we — as brothers we shed these tears — lords of a strong city in the land of Cathay.[43] We heard tell of good hunting and set out with a great following: at length we arrived on the banks of a river and, well pleased with the sport, stayed for a month in the region. Great was our slaughter of beasts on hill and on dale.

"After we three had put to shame all the bowmen we had brought with us we began to dispute among ourselves for the first place. Each was ready to boast now that he was the mightiest hunter and we fell to quarrelling, unable to agree where the truth of the matter lay. Today we sent off our following, loaded with deer hides; for we had agreed that in order to determine whose arm had the greatest skill we should go by ourselves and shoot, with none to look on. Fearing no danger and keeping only three squires with us, we dismissed our whole company and set out over the plain; and so we passed through many woods and ravines, slaughtering beasts and every bird that started up.

"Suddenly we saw before us a young lord with a face full of sorrow: he was mounted upon a black steed like Merani,[44] and he wore panther's skin on his head and his back alike. Never has the eye of man looked on such beauty! Dazzled by his radiance, we said as we gazed on him, 'The sun has surely come down on to earth from the heavens!' We were filled with the desire there and then to make him our captive, and in our foolhardiness we endeavored to do so: therein lies the cause of our sighs, groans and tears.

"I, the eldest, begged my brothers to let the stranger be my prize; the second had his eyes on his horse: the third was eager to vanquish him single-handed, and we let him have his way with a nod. Then we advanced upon the young lord, who was riding on, calm in his beauty.

"Fair were the roses on his cheeks; crystal mingled with ruby. . . . But now his gentle thoughts were turned into raging. No heed did he pay us, he would not hold converse — but he gave us a cure with his whip for our boldness!

"We drew back and left the stranger then to our brother: our brother said, 'Stay!' and sought to lay hands on him. As he did not put his hand to his sword we held off, but then he brought his whip down on our brother's head, and we saw the blood spurt: the blow cracked the skull and our brother fell senseless, like a corpse, to the earth. Thus was our presumption humbled, brought down to the ground! Proud, stern and haughty, the stranger rode off now: with never a glance back, quietly, without haste, he departed. — Look, there he goes, he who is as fair as the sun and the moon!" And, weeping still, the unhappy wretches pointed out the sun-fair lord far in the distance: there he was, mounted upon the same black steed.

And now no more would Avtandil's tears fall like snow on his cheeks; not in vain had he quested in foreign lands for so long: when a man gets his desire, when he finds what he has been seeking, then indeed can the memory of past woes be put from him! — "Brothers," the hero said, "seeking that young lord I left the land where I was bred, to journey from place to place without a single companion. Now from you I have gained something I have been denied hitherto. — May God give you no more cause to grieve after this; even as he has granted me the fulfilment of my heart's desire, may he show your brother his mercy!" Then he directed their gaze to the place where he had himself halted: "Move over there gently," he said; "put him down in the shade, and give rest to your weariness."

As soon as he had said this he put spurs to his horse — and was off, flying like a falcon unloosed, fair as the moon when it meets the sun, bright in its cloth of gold. Now were the fires in his breast all extinguished.

As he drew closer he began to ask himself how he could best manage the meeting: "Unwise words may drive a madman to yet greater distraction! The man of sense approaches a difficult matter with care and a level head. — Since this lord is so deranged that he will not allow any man to speak to or even to look at him, an encounter could lead only to blows passing between us: he would kill me or I should slay him; and either way his story would remain shrouded in mystery."

Then he said again, "Is all to go for nothing, all the hardship I have endured? — Be he what he may, he must have somewhere some refuge: I will follow him wherever he goes, though he should seek the shelter of walls, till he reaches it; and then look about for some means of achieving my purpose."

And so for two days and two nights they went onward; the one following the other; without rest day or night; with no food to sustain them. Never did they make a halt, not for so much as an instant: tears flowed from their eyes without ceasing and watered the plain.[45]

They made on through the third day; and then at dusk some great rocks, pitted with caves, rose up before them. Below ran a stream, thickly bordered with rushes; there were many huge trees, their tops beyond mortal sight. Across the stream and through the rocks towards one of the caves rode the stranger lord: Avtandil dismounted, tied his horse to the foot of one of the great trees and climbed up into its branches.

When the stranger lord — who had still not ceased to weep — came out from the trees, a maiden clad in a black mantle appeared at the mouth of the cave; wailing aloud, she shed tears that swelled the ocean. The lord dismounted and embraced her: then he said, "Asmat,[46] my sister, our bridges have fallen into the sea: never shall we find in time her for whose sake these fires burn within us!" As he said this he beat his breast, and his tears rained down in a torrent. The maiden would have fallen to the ground in a swoon, had she not had him to hold her. . . . Then each wiped away the tears from the face of the other. So fiercely did they tear their hair that the forest was darkened: wailing and lamenting, they clung together: the rocks threw back their voices.[47] Avtandil looked in wonder on them and on what they did.

When the maiden had composed her spirit she led the horse into the cave and took off its saddle and bridle; she undid the lord's belt after that and unarmed him. Then the two withdrew into the cave, and the day had its ending.

Sorely perplexed was Avtandil! "How can I get light on this matter?" he wondered. When morning had brought its light the maiden, still garbed in black, came out. Cleaning the bridle with a corner of her veil, she put it on the black steed; then the saddle: and after that, deftly, without clatter, she brought out the armor.

It looked as though the young lord were accustomed to come and go in this fleeting way: the maiden wept, beat her breast and tore her thick tresses. After they had embraced the lord kissed her and got into the saddle. Asmat, the unhappy one, was plunged into yet greater sorrow. — Avtantil now once again saw the lord's face from close at hand: his chin was still beardless, his lip's hair was hardly grown. "Surely he is the heavens' sun itself!" was the thought in the Arab's mind. The scent of the aloe filled the air and his nostrils. . . . Truly, for the stranger, slaughtering a lion would have been as the killing of a goat for the brute itself!

The young lord rode back along the way he had come in the evening, passed through the reeds and out on to the plain. "God has been kind, he could not have done better, in truth, for me," said Avtandil, hidden behind a tree and watching in wonder. "I will seize the maiden and make her tell me his story. In return, I will tell her mine, and so all will be made plain. No need for sword-blows between him and me!"

How Avtandil told Asmat his story at the cave

Avtandil climbed down from the tree and loosed his horse, which he had tied to it; then he mounted and rode up to the cave's open entrance. Deep in grief, bathed in tears, the unhappy maiden came running out, for she thought that the young lord, fair as the rose, fair as crystal, was back again.

But no, it was another face, a face that she did not know! With a shriek she turned to fly to the rocks and trees for a refuge. Leaping to the ground, Avtandil seized hold of her: now was she like a partridge caught in a net; and the rocks resounded with her cries. She would not submit to the hateful stranger, would not even look upon him: like a partridge in the talons of an eagle she trembled.[48] She kept calling for aid to one "Tariel," but there was no one to help her. Presently Avtandil knelt before her and, raising the fingers of his hands in entreaty,[49] said, "Peace! You have nothing to fear from me: I am but a mortal man. — I have seen the rose and the violet grow pale here: tell me, who is this lord with the form of a cypress and such beauty of countenance? I will not harm you, you have no cause for dread — put an end to this wailing!"

Like one trying to appeal to cool reason the maiden replied, weeping, "If you are not out of your mind, let me go: if you are indeed crazed, return to your senses! You ask glibly for a story that would come passing hard in the uttering: do not waste your breath, you have no hope of drawing anything out of me."

Again she said, "Little do you know what it is that you ask of me! Even the pen could not put down such a tale as this. For once that you bid me tell it I will say No a hundred times. . . . Laughter is better than tears, but to my soul sorrow is sweeter than song."

"You do not know, lady, where I hail from, or what I have suffered. I have spent long years on this quest, and found never a man who could help me. Now that I have found you — harsh words, these — I cannot release you: tell me the story; you have no cause to distrust me."

"What am I to you, or you to me," said the maiden, "that our paths should have crossed thus? Well did you know he was gone, and so, like the frost when the sun is set, you have dared to show me this insolence! I will tell you shortly, and with no waste of words, that nothing will make me speak, whatever you do with me."

Kneeling before her, Avtandil now begged with great urgency: but nothing could he draw from her; and at length, patience gone, anger darkened his countenance, rage reddened his eyes. Seizing her by the hair, he put his dagger to her throat and said, "This is not to be borne! Would you condemn me to shed tears in vain? You have but to speak and I will set you free on the instant: but if you will not, may God kill my enemy as I will slay you!"

The maiden replied, "Poor means these to gain your end! If you do not take my life I shall be well and whole: why then should I tell you anything, since I shall be suffering nothing? But if you do take me off, I shall have no head left to talk with." And she went on, "What, sir, do you think me? Who are you I am speaking with? — Never while I live will you win from me this secret. Kill me and welcome, tear me to pieces like a letter of no account! Do not think that to die would be at all grievous to me: you would release me from weeping; death dries up the ford of tears. For me the whole world is like straw — that is the value I put on it. I do not know who you are: why should I put any trust in you?"

"This is not the way," Avtandil thought, "to get anything out of her; I must try something else." Letting her go free, he went and sat down at a distance; then he began to weep. "I have angered you," he said, "and now all hope is gone from me." Still she did not soften, but sat with a clouded brow. Avtandil spoke no more, but his sobbing continued; in the rose-garden of his cheek a pool grew from his tears. . . . Moved to compassion at last, the maiden wept likewise; pity for the weeping lord caused the hot tears to flow. But still she did not speak to him; no word passed across her lips. "Her thoughts have grown more kindly!" Avtandil said to himself now. His face covered with tears, he went and knelt before her to make supplication. "I know," he said, "that I do not deserve any kindness: I have angered you, and therefor am I as wretched as the outcast, as the orphan. But all hope is not gone yet: sin shall be forgiven, it is said, seven times.[50] Although I have not thus far found any favor with you, a lover — understand this — should receive pity always. I have no other resource; there is no one to aid me; I will give my soul for your kindness — what can I do more?"

The maiden moaned when she heard that he was a lover; a hundred times as fast fell her tears; once more did she wail aloud. God granted Avtandil his desire, his heart now had comfort. "Her color changed at those words," he thought; "it must be love that calls forth the scalding tears." Then he spoke to her again: "A lover is pitied, sister, even by enemies! You know that he will not strive to avoid death; he will look for it, rather. Such a one am I, a madman whose sorrows can have no more enduring. I was sent forth in search of this lord by my lady, the sun-fair, and to places the very clouds could not reach have I won through. And now I have found you here, his heart yours, yours his!

"I have set my lady's face in my heart like a picture: mad for her sake, I have foregone all manner of joy, taken myself into exile. Now do one of two things: make me a captive or set me free: grant me life — or kill me and pile woe upon woe."

The maiden replied to him with words that were gentler: "Now have you found speech of a better turn. You were sowing hatred's seeds in my heart but a moment since; a friend truer than a sister will you find in me now. I will do all I can to aid you, since you plead in the name of love; if I do not, grief will assuredly drive you distracted. I am ready to die for your sake — and what more can I do?

"If you take my guidance, without a doubt you will find what you are seeking: but if you will not, you can never attain your desire, however many your tears. You will curse Fate, and die at the last a death that is shameful."

"This," Avtandil replied, "puts me in mind of a story. — Two men were journeying along a road when the one that came behind saw the first fall into a well. He hastened up to it, called down, and then, when he had wept and made lamentation, said, 'Stay there, my dear friend, and wait for me; I am going to fetch a rope to haul you out with.' Greatly astonished at this, the man at the bottom laughed and shouted up, 'What else can I do but wait; where could I make off to?'

"Sister, there is a rope round my neck, and you hold the end in your hands: if you do not give me your help I have no power to do anything. You know what is best for me, you can bring the mad back to reason — it is the head of the sick man that needs to be bound up."

The maiden said, "Sweetly have your words fallen, sir, on my ear: I cannot doubt that you are an honorable lord, deserving of the praise of the wise. Since you have endured this much, listen well to what I tell you, and you will yet attain your desire. — This story can be told you by one and one only; you must have it from his own lips to give it belief. Wait here until he returns, however long the time, and let your mind be at rest; do not let the snow of tears freeze the rose on your cheek.

"I will tell you our names, if you wish to know them: that distracted lord is Tariel; I am Asmat the unhappy, whose breast is consumed by hot flames, whose sighs never cease. That is all I can say. He roams over the plain, the fair one, the mighty one; I eat alone, alas, of the game that he brings here. He may be back any moment, he may not return here for many days: I do not know. But I beg you to wait, do not take your departure. When he comes I will plead with him and do all that I can to win him over; I will make you known to each other so that he may receive you as a friend and tell you his story. Thus may you take back joy to your lady."

Avtandil listened to what the maiden said and accepted her guidance. At that moment they heard a splashing in the ravine and, looking round, they saw that Tariel, fair as the bright moon, had ridden across the stream. And on this they made haste to withdraw out of sight. — "Sir," said the maiden, "God has granted your desire; but now you must hide yourself here inside this cave, for the man does not live who can meet his anger with safety. I will try to persuade him that you are not an enemy." And then she concealed him with all speed in the cave.

Tariel — splendid to look upon, with his sword and his quiver — dismounted: their tears flowing to swell the ocean, he and the maiden wept loudly — Avtandil, unseen, seeing all through an aperture. For a long time did they shed tears, the young lord and the maiden in the mantle of black; the flood turned their faces' bright crystal to amber. Asmat at last took off Tariel's hauberk and brought it in; she led in the horse after that. By now they were calm; their lashes, jet knives, had cut off the tears' flow. (Avtandil watched through his opening still — a prisoner, save for the irons.) The young lord, sighing yet more woefully, sat down upon a panther-skin spread out by the maiden; tears of blood welled up to his jet-colored lashes.

Hoping that he might eat some roast meat, the maiden took flint and steel to a small fire and lighted it. . . . He tore off a piece of the meat that she gave him; but then, too weary to use his jaws, spat it out. After that he lay down and slept — but not for long; starting, he shrieked aloud and leaped up like one possessed. Still crying out, he beat his breast with a stone and his head with a stick, blow after blow.[51] A little way off the maiden sat and tore her cheeks as she looked at him.

"Why have you returned?" she asked after a time. "Tell me what has happened." He replied, "I came upon a king who was out hunting with a great train and a wealth of gear; before him, on the plain, many beaters were scattered. The sight of men hurt my spirit; the fires in my breast burned more fiercely. . . . I did not go forward to meet the king — that did I spare myself — but fled ashen-cheeked from them and hid in a wood. 'If I can keep clear,' I said to myself, 'I will make away tomorrow at dawn.' "

The maiden's tears flowed a hundred, ten thousand times faster. "You roam alone through the forests with the brute

beasts," she said, "with no friend to converse with you or af-
ford you distraction. You cannot thus help your lady, why do
you waste your days? You have journeyed over all the earth —
could you not have found somewhere a companion who might
have brought comfort; who would not have irked you, at least,
if he could not lighten your load of grief? If both you and your
lady die, what good will come of it?"

"These words, sister," Tariel replied, "are worthy of your
heart's tender compassion: but there is not upon the earth any
salve for this wound. How is the man to be found who has not
been born? — Death, the sundering of body and soul, is my only
joy! Could it be the will of God that another should share my
fate, even if I wished for the talk, the companionship? Who
has borne, who has tried to bear, such sorrows as mine are?
Save for you, sister, I have no friend anywhere."

"I entreat you not to be angry," said the maiden: "since God
has made me your counsellor I cannot conceal from you how I
judge of the matter. — To exceed measure is bad, and you have
passed beyond bounds."

"I do not understand what you want; make it plain," an-
swered the young lord. "How can I, on my own, without God,
create a man to sustain me? God has willed wretchedness for
me — what can I do to escape it? . . . I know well I am like a
wild beast; to such a pass have I come."

"I have wearied you with much admonishing," said the
maiden again; "but if I bring before you a man come of his
own free will to be your companion, one whose friendship
would gladden you, will you give me your oath that you will
not kill him or do him harm?"

"If you can bring me such a one,"responded the young lord,
"greatly indeed will I rejoice to behold him. By my love for
her for whose sake I roam over the plain in distraction, I swear
that I will not use him ill or show him any discourtesy, but will
do all that I can to please him and give him the love of a friend."

How Tariel and Avtandil met

The maiden then rose and went to bring out Avtandil. Say-
ing "He is not angry!" to give reassurance, she took him by the

hand and led him forth into view. As fair was he to look on as the moon at the full; when Tariel saw him he thought he was like the sun in his splendor.

Tariel came forward. . . . Like the sun were those two, or like the moon when from a cloudless sky it sheds its beams on the plain beneath. The cypress could not compare with them; in their glory they resembled the seven planets — what can I say more?

They cared nothing for being strangers, but kissed each other in greeting: their lips, red as the rose, parted; and their white teeth shone forth. Embracing, they wept together; their jacinth cheeks lost their ruby hue, turning to amber.

Tariel took Avtandil by the hand, and they sat down together; then for a long time the two wept scalding tears. Asmat soothed their spirits with words of rare beauty: "Do not bring yourselves to destruction; do not let your grieving darken the sun!"

The rose on Tariel's cheek had been no more than touched by frost: "I am impatient; tell me your story," he said to Avtandil: "who are you, where do you come from — where do you have your home? As for me, I am one forgotten of death; even that has abandoned me."

"Most courteous Tariel, lion and hero," replied Avtandil with eloquence, "I am an Arab, and in Arabia I am the lord of great palaces. I am burned up by love, consumed in unquenchable fires. She who has been acclaimed queen by warriors strong of arm, my sovereign's daughter, is the lady of my devotion. I am not known to you, but you have seen me, if you can recall the time. Do you remember the day when you dealt out slaughter among our stout men-at-arms?

"We saw you upon the plain and thrust ourselves forward; my lord's anger rose, and we found ourselves sadly at odds with you. We first sent a summons; when you would not come, we unloosed our warriors — and then did you dye the plain red with their blood! With your whip alone, without use of sword, you took off the heads of all! The king mounted to pursue you, but you vanished without a trace; to the terror of our men, you disappeared like a Kaj.[52] This bewildered us yet more; we were utterly amazed then. The king's humor darkened —

monarchs, you will well know, do not like to be thwarted. They looked for you everywhere and dispatched letters of inquiry; but none could they find, young or old, who had seen you. Then my lady, lovelier than the sun or the airs of the heavens, sent me forth with this word: 'Bring me intelligence of that lord who vanished, and I will grant you the desire of your heart.' She told me that I must be ready to endure three years of tears, separation — do you not marvel that, banished from her smile, I have lived?

"Until the other day I could find never a man who had seen you: then I met with certain Turks[53] who had shown you insolence; you had dealt one a mortal blow with your whip, but his brothers told me about you."

The fight came back now into Tariel's memory. "I recall that day," he said, "although it was long ago. You and your lord were hunting: I was weeping, thinking — alas — of her for whose sake I am fated to suffer.

"What did you want of me, what were you seeking, what was there to link us? You were taking your pleasure, you were happy — I was bathing my cheek in tears! You sent, in your temerity, men forward to take me; yet in the event it was not I that you bore away, but their corpses!

"I saw that your lord was drawing close when I glanced back; so I vanished without parley — I would not strike a blow at a king. It is as though my horse could render itself invisible, truly: I can escape quicker than a man can blink from those who displease me. As for those Turks, I do not think that I wronged them: their insolence did not deserve anything better.

"But welcome indeed are you, sun-fair hero of the cypress-form! I rejoice to look on you. Much have you striven, well are you known to sorrow — for hard is that man to find whom God himself has abandoned!"

"Why," Avtandil replied, "should you thus sing my praises, you who deserve to be lauded by sages' tongues? Am I worthy of this? — But *you* are the peer of the sun, the radiant light of the heavens above; the pain, the many tears, have left no mark upon you. This day has banished from my mind the thought of her who put my heart into darkness; I renounce her service; all must be now as you wish. Jacinth is more pre-

cious than enamel, a thousand times! I ask no more than to be
your comrade until the day of my death."

"What warmth has now filled your heart! Great is my won-
der," said Tariel. "What have I done for you that you should
make me such a return as this? — But it is ever thus; lover must
pity lover. What could recompense you for being parted from
your lady? You went forth to seek me in your sovereign's ser-
vice; you have striven like a man, and by God's grace you have
found me. . . . But how can I tell you my story — why I roam
in this fashion? If I endeavored to do this, I should be con-
sumed as in flame."

"What can tears do with such a fire as this, O lion?" said
Asmat. "I cannot urge you to unfold the tale; to speak so is
not for me. But here, in this noble lord, in this slave to love,
I see one who is ready to hazard his life for you. If he knew
the cause of your wounds, he would do all that in him lay to
give aid. He begged me to tell him your tale, but why should I
speak if God will give you yourself the strength to recount it?
If he hears it I think you may find you gain comfort; let all
things be done even as heaven would have them."

Tariel was silent for a space, burning in the flame of his an-
guish. Then he said to Asmat, "You have been with me from the
beginning; do you not know that there can be no cure for my
wound? The sight of this lord of long sorrow now adds to my
grief. How can a man find that which God has never created?
My heart suffers as in a furnace; my road is cut; I am caught
in a net. The world's joys are gone; straw and cloak are all
that remain to me.

"Yet two blessings have been granted to me this day by the
merciful God, by him of whom the sun is a semblance: two
lovers, first, through me will find union; and then, these hot
fires will wholly consume me."

"When a man has sworn brotherhood," he said to Avtandil,
"he must not flinch from death or grief, even for the sake of a
brother or sister. How can God save one without destroying
another? — Give ear and I will tell my story, let what will be-
fall me."

To Asmat he said again, "Come and sit by me; bring water
to pour on my breast if I swoon. . . . If I die, weep for me,

sigh without ceasing; dig a grave, let the earth cradle me here."

He undid his shirt at the throat and sat down to tell his tale: for a space he sat like the sun hidden by clouds, unable to part his tightly-clenched lips to give utterance. Then at length, hot tears bursting from his eyes, he groaned and cried out aloud. "O my beloved," he sobbed, "O my own, lost to me! My hope and life, my thought, heart and soul! Who cut you down, O tree planted in Eden? — O heart burned a hundred times, are you not now in ashes?"

How Tariel told Avtandil his tale

Give ear to this story — to deeds and words my tongue scarcely can put in speech! . . . From her who has brought me to madness and melancholy, for whom I have shed tears of blood, I can look for no joy.

You will know — who does not — that there are in India seven realms. Over six of these the lord was King Parsadan. Generous, wealthy, valiant, suzerain over vassal-kings, he had the frame of a hero and a face as fair as the sun: he was mighty in battle, a leader of armies.

On the seventh throne sat my father, the terror of enemies, one who destroyed all his foes without treachery. Saridan was his name: none was there who dared work against him, in secret or in light of day. Free from care, he spent his time in hunting and other diversions.

But loneliness began to weigh on him, cares to crowd into his heart: and at length he said, "I have conquered my enemies' march-lands and driven out all who oppose me; here do I reign in splendor and might. . . . Now I will go to King Parsadan and offer him my allegiance." And he resolved to send an envoy to the king with this message: "You are lord of all India; I would show myself before you in loyalty; I would fain be remembered as a vassal who kept his faith."

Parsadan rejoiced when he received this, and he sent back the reply: "I, the world's ruler, offer up thanks to God, since you who sit, even as do I, on an Indian throne, have decided thus. Come to me, and I will receive you like a son or a brother."

(307-324)

Parsadan bestowed on my father a domain and the office of amirbar.[54] (In India the amirbar is the host's marshal also.) My father ruled with a sure hand; lord over others, he lacked only the power of a sovereign.

The king treated my father as his peer: "I will wager," he would say, "that no other monarch has such an amirbar!" — My father hunted, made war, forced enemies to sue for peace; I am no more his equal than is any man mine.

No child had been born to the king and his sun-fair queen: much did this grieve them, and in time the warriors of the host too began to grow troubled. Ah, cursed be the day when my mother bore me! — "I will bring him up as my own son," the king said; "he will have rank in my kindred."

So the royal pair took me as their child and bred me to be lord of the realm and their armies: they had sages instruct me in the acts and conduct befitting a king. And I grew to be as fair as the sun, to have the frame of a hero.

Asmat, tell me of anything that is false in my story! — At five I was like a rose newly opened; slaying a lion was like killing a sparrow.[55] Parsadan no longer grieved over the lack of a son. — Asmat, you can tell of my cheeks, and the color gone from them! The sun was to me as the dusk is to daybreak. All who beheld me declared that I was like a tree growing in Eden: I am but a shadow now of what I was then.

When I was five the queen conceived a child. [*When he had said this the young lord sighed, and then uttered through tears: "She bore a daughter." He nearly swooned away, but Asmat poured water on his breast; and he went on.*[56]] Even from the first days, the peer of the sun was she for whose sake I burn in flame!

Letter followed letter forth to announce the birth, messenger went after messenger. All India received the news, the sun and moon rejoiced, the heavens sparkled with gladness. All men were happy and made celebration.

To sing the praises of the princess is beyond the power of this tongue of mine! With splendor of rejoicing Parsadan held festival; kings came from all parts, bearing gifts of many kinds; treasure was given away, and the warriors were laden with largesse.

When all was over they began to attend to our upbringing.
. . . Even then the princess was three times as fair as the sun. . . .
The king and queen loved us equally. — And now I will tell
you the name of her my heart burns for.

[*But when he tried to utter her name the young lord swooned
right away. Avtandil wept also, his heart charred to ash in
fire. Asmat poured water on Tariel's breast to restore him,
and soon he continued.*]

Give ear, though this will surely be my last day upon earth!
Nestan-Darejan was the name that she bore. She was a wise
and gentle child, like the moon, fairer than the sun, when she
was seven. — What heart, were it of tempered steel or of ada-
mant, could endure to be parted from her?

She grew up, while I became old enough to go to the wars.
Seeing in his daughter now one who could reign as queen, the
king gave me back into the care of my father. At that time I
played at ball and hunted, killing lions like cats.[57]

The king built a bower for the princess to dwell in; made of
bezoar it was, not fashioned from stone. Inside there was a
canopied throne of jacinths and rubies, and in front of the
door a little garden, with a pool of rose-water to bathe in.
And there she for whom I burn as in flame abode.

Day and night the scent of aloes was wafted from censers.
Sometimes the princess sat inside the tower, sometimes she
went down into the shade of the garden. The king made it the
duty of his sister Davar — a widow who, when married, had
lived in Kajeti[58]—to teach her. The bower was furnished richly
with silk stuffs and with gold brocades; to none was it given
to look upon the maiden, upon the crystal and rose of her
beauty. She had Asmat and two slaves to wait on her; they
played together at dice. And here she grew up, lovely as a tree
planted in Gibeon.[59]

I reached the age of fifteen. . . . The king was like a father to
me: he had me with him each day; I might not even sleep at
home. I was as strong as a lion, as fair as the sun, as splendid
to behold as a tree growing in Eden. My prowess with the bow
and in sports won me praise; wild beasts and game were brought
down by my arrow. I would come back from the plain to play
at ball in the maidan, then go home for feasting — there was

always diversion. But now the fate of my lady, fair as crystal and ruby, has cut me off from the world!

The day came when my father died: all feasting and gaiety ended at Parsadan's court then. Those who had walked in terror of Saridan rejoiced; the loyal made lamentation and enemies' hearts knew great gladness. Grief-stricken, groaning day and night, I sat in darkness a full year; from no man would I take any comfort. Then certain lords came to fetch me, charged by the king with this message: "Tariel, my son, put off your mourning garb; we are even more grieved than you by the loss of him we looked on as our equal." Sending a hundred gifts and enjoining an end to my sorrowing, he conferred upon me all the authority that my father had exercised. — "You are now my amirbar; take the duties that belong to the place."

Though flames burned remorselessly in my breast for my father's sake, those lords led me out now from my shadows. The king and queen of India made celebration for my coming forth; they came forward to meet me and kissed me fondly, like parents. — Honoring me like a son, they had me sit by their thrones; then they both spoke to me gently of what it was now my part to do. Filled with horror at the thought of taking my father's place, I was loath indeed to accept the office; but they would brook no refusal. I had to submit, and took my oath as amirbar.

Long years have passed since then — I can remember no more than this. . . . Yet, for all that it will be hard, I will tell you my story. This world is for ever working evil, false is it and treacherous! Long have I been burned by the sparks of its striking!

How Tariel fell in love

[*When he had wept for a space he went on with his tale.*] One day after hunting the king took me by the hand: "Let us go now and see my daughter," he said to me. — Do you not marvel that I can think of that time and yet live?

He bade me take some partridges to give to the princess. I put my hand on them and we went on — I to be plunged into flame. Then did I begin to pay the debt owed to Destiny. . . . A heart of rock can be pierced by a lance of adamant only!

I beheld her garden; the fairest of all fair places of delight was it. The song of birds sounded there more sweetly than sirens' voices: many were the pools of rose-water for bathing in: over the door hung a curtain of velvet.

When the king passed through the entrance-curtain I halted before it: I knew that it was his wish to keep the sun-fair princess from the eyes of all. I could see nothing, only hear the sound of voices in converse; and then the king told Asmat to take the partridges from me.

Asmat drew the curtain aside, while I still remained standing. Then I beheld the princess — and mind and heart were pierced by a sudden lance! Asmat came and asked me for the birds. I was now on fire. . . . Alas, I have burned in those flames ever since that day! The light that was brighter far than the sun is extinct now! [*Tariel could not continue, but swooned with a heavy groan. Avtandil and Asmat wept aloud, their voices returning in echo. "Alas," they said in sorrow, "powerless are those arms now that threatened mighty heroes once!" Asmat sprinkled water upon the young lord, and he came to himself soon; but for long he could not speak, so oppressed was his heart by grief: his tears watered the ground as he sat moaning bitterly. Then he went on.*]

Alas, the sorrow that lies in her memory! — Those who trust in Fortune can thrive on her gifts and be happy; but in the end they will surely not be spared her base treachery. I praise the understanding of wise men who contemn her. . . . But listen to my story, if life remains in me.

I surrendered the partridges, but not one step could I take then; all strength went out of me and I fell in a swoon. — When at length I came to my senses I heard weeping and lamentation; like travelers about to go on board ship, the royal household stood clustered round me.

I found myself lying in a magnificent bed in a very large chamber. The king and queen were shedding tears in floods over me, they were rending their faces, their cheeks were all torn. Muezzins had been summoned; and they declared my illness to be the work of Beelzebub.

(342-58)

When the king saw my eyes open he embraced me: "My son, my son, are you still alive?" he said through his tears. "Speak to me!" I could give no answer, but started like one mad; and then swooned once more, as blood rushed to my heart.

The muezzins and mullahs stood round me, the Koran in their hands; and each of them read from it. They thought me possessed by the Enemy — there was no end to their nonsense! ... Burned by a raging fire, for three days I lay lifeless.

The physicians too were perplexed. "What illness can this be?" they wondered. "It is nothing our skill can cure; some distemper has fastened upon him." Sometimes, babbling demented words, I would leap up like a madman. — The tears shed by the queen would have formed a great ocean.

I lay between life and death for three days in that chamber; then I came to myself and remembered everything clearly. "How wretched," I said, "is my present condition!" Then I prayed to the Creator for strength: "O God, hearken to this, my beseeching, and do not abandon me. Give me the power to endure; let me rise up and be gone. My secret must surely be betrayed if I stay here — do but let me get home!" My prayer was heard, and I began to mend; my wounded heart turned to iron.

I was able by and by to sit up; and the king's messengers carried the news to him. The queen ran to me, the king followed — in his haste came bare-headed. His joy was such that he scarcely knew what he did. . . . While the rest remained silent, he gave praise to God.

The royal pair sat down on either side, and then had me take some broth. Presently I said, "Sire, I am now restored, and am eager to ride out to see the streams and the open plain." A horse was brought and I mounted, with the king for companion. We rode over the maidan and along the river bank; and then I went home, taking leave of the king at the gate. Thereafter my affliction began to grow greater; one sorrow came crowding in hard on another. "Let death come now," I said; "what hope of anything better?" Tears changed my hue from bright crystal to saffron; the blades of ten thousand knives cut through my heart.

The guard of my chamber came and called out my treasurer; I wondered what could be passing between them. Then my treasurer told me that a slave of Asmat's was outside; and I bade him ask the man what news he brought with him. After that the slave entered. . . . He gave me a love-letter: I read it and was amazed — could I have caused burning then in the heart of another? All unlooked-for was this! Distress lay heavy on me, like the weight of a tree.

I felt bewildered: "How can she[60] love me — how dare she declare her love? But I cannot disdain her; she would hold silence against me, she would despair and reproach me!" And so I wrote an answer such as love demands to that letter.

Some days passed; and my heart's flames burned ever more fiercely. No longer did I watch the warriors on the plain at their exercises, nor did I go to court. Many were the physicians that came at this time to see me. Then was it that I began to pay for the joys and sorrows Fate sends. The physicians could do nothing for me; my heart lay in twilight. No one discovered the fires that were burning me. It must, they thought, be my blood; and the king gave the command for my arm to be bled: I let this be done, to hide the true cause of suffering.

After the bleeding when, melancholy of mood, I was lying alone in my chamber, my attendant came in to me. I looked up at him in inquiry, and he told me Asmat's slave had come. Saying to myself, "What am I to her, and what can she be to me?" I bade him bring the man in.

The slave gave me a letter which I read through in no great haste. Could we soon have a meeting? I wrote in answer: "It is indeed time — you may well wonder at me. I will come if you summon me: do not think that I shall be slow."

I asked my heart, "Why are you thus struck by the lances of melancholy? . . ." Then, "I am the amirbar," I said, "obeyed like the king by all India. — Should suspicion be aroused they will probe this matter not once but a thousand times. And if my secret is discovered I shall be driven from this land into exile!"

A messenger in quest of news arrived next from the king. I had him brought in: the monarch desired to know whether I had now had my bleeding. I sent back the reply: "The blood has been drawn from my arm and my state is now better: I am about to attend at court, and for this I rejoice."

I went to the palace. Saying, "May this be the end of the matter!" the king had me mount, though without quiver or other gear. Then he took horse himself and let loose his falcons: the partridges cowered now! He gave the bowmen their tasks and they all uttered glad cries. — We coursed over the plain, and sat down to feast afterwards; the minstrels and singing-girls raised their voices in song. Many a jewel of great price did the king give away then; none of the day's companions was left unrewarded.

In vain did I strive to put away wretchedness; the thought of the princess made flames burn in my heart yet more fiercely. When all was over and done I took my comrades back home with me; they declared with one voice that I resembled a cypress. With feasting and wine I sought to conceal bitter suffering.

My treasurer came presently to me and whispered, "A woman is asking if she can see the amirbar. Her face, though it is under a veil, deserves the praise of the wise." "Take her to my chamber," I replied; "she has come on my summons."

My friends moved to break up the feast on my rising. "Do not stir," I said; "it is nothing. Before long I shall once more be with you." With that I repaired to my chamber, which had one of my slaves as a guard at the door. I steeled my heart now to encounter dishonor.

The woman advanced on my entry and made me a reverence. "Joy indeed is it to stand thus before you!" she said. Astounded — who ever humbled herself so to a lover? — I thought, "She can know nothing of love and its conduct, or she would sit still and quiet, without making a move."

I sat down on the couch, but she did not sit beside me; she dared come no closer than the edge of the carpet. "Why do you hold back," I asked, "if it is love that has brought you here?" She gave no answer to this; utterance seemed to be hard for her.

At last she said, "Shame is burning my heart; you have mistaken my purpose. But I hope that this may remain a close secret: I cannot say God's grace is denied me if you grant me this favor."

She rose and went on, "I feel confused, sorely troubled, before you. Do not hold me to blame for what is said only at the command of my mistress; it is from her heart that this boldness comes, and not mine. — This letter will tell you what I have not put into words."

Nestan-Darejan's first letter to her lover

I looked at the letter; it was from her for whose sake my heart burns in flame. "O lion," the sun-fair lady wrote, "keep your wound closely hidden! Do not despair — I am yours, and I find vain agonies hateful! Asmat will tell you of all I have said to her.

"Vapors, swoonings, expirings — is this how you would play the lover? Deeds of prowess were a far better offering to make to your lady! — The people of Cathay[61] are all pledged to pay tribute; and the injuries that they do to us can no longer be borne.

"I have long wanted to marry you, but there has never been a fit time until now to speak. . . . A few days since, sitting under my canopy, I saw you, robbed of your reason; and later I ascertained what had befallen you.

"I will speak to you straightly; listen to what I say: go and fight the Cathayans; give me cause to think well of you. Have done with vain weeping, with those tears on your cheek's rose! I have turned your darkness to dawn; what more could the sun do?"

Asmat spoke boldly, without fear. Ah, how can I find words for the turmoil within me, for the joy that was mine? My heart throbbed and trembled — and then all but failed me. My face became like crystal once again; the color of my cheek returned.

How Tariel wrote to his lady

I pressed her letter against my eyes, and then wrote back in answer: "O moon, you are as fair as the sun in the heavens! May God keep me from all that would not be worthy of you! This must be a dream. . . . I cannot believe I am still alive."

(375-89)

I said to Asmat, "There is nothing more I can send now as my reply. Say: 'O sun, you have risen to bring forth your light to me, you have brought me back to the world of living. All swooning is done with — I will not flinch, I swear, from the service, be it what it may, you require of me.' "

Asmat said, "She spoke thus to me: 'This is the best plan to follow: no one who sees you will have any thought of messages passing between me and him; and when he comes to see me it will look like a passage of love with you.' And then she exhorted me, 'Tell the amirbar to keep this a secret!' "

Greatly did this wise counsel from her whom even the sun did not dare look on rejoice me: now it had been granted to me to hear the rare words of her who made the light of day seem like darkness. — I would have given Asmat a golden bowl full of costly jewels, but she said, "I do not want them; I have enough and to spare of such things." One ring, of a dram's weight, was all she accepted. — "This for a token; I have no lack of bracelets." And with these words she arose and was gone.

My heart was now pierced through no longer by lances; joy lightened my darkness; the fires were quenched which had burned me. I went back to my comrades at their wine and then, in my rapture, made a bestowal of gifts: delight filled the hearts of all.

How Tariel sent a letter to the Cathayans

I sent an envoy after this to Cathay with a letter: "The power of the king of the Indians is like unto God's: every man loyal to him is fed if he hungers, but he who withholds obedience will assuredly curse himself.

"Lord and brother, we have no mind to brook insult! Set out for this city without delay on this summons. If you will not come to us, we shall go to you, in war's panoply: better to obey than to settle the score with your blood."

I gave up my heart to joy when I had sent off the messenger, went to court and was gay, and no longer suffered in the furnace of torture. Fate granted lavishly all I desired then — it has brought me since to such madness that the very brutes shun me!

The time came when I was gripped by the desire to go roam-
ing. Reason calmed my mind, my comrades came and feasted
with me, but joy was denied me by the depths of my longing.
I was seized sometimes by melancholy, and then I would curse
my fate.

How Nestan summoned Tariel

One day, on returning from the palace, I went to my chamber
and sat there. Slumber did not close my eyes, my thoughts
were full of my lady — my heart was rejoicing over that letter
of hope.[62] Presently the guard at my door called out my at-
tendant and in a low whisper said a few words to him. "Asmat's
slave has come!" I was told; and I had him brought in before
me. Asmat wrote that *she* summoned me, she who had pierced
my heart through with a dagger. Joy lightened my darkness
and my fetters were loosened.

I said nothing to the slave, but had him accompany me.
There was no one to receive me in the garden, but Asmat ap-
peared, gay and laughing. "I have drawn the thorn from your
heart," she said; "come and look on your new-sprung rose."
With that she raised a heavy curtain, and under a canopy en-
crusted with rubies I saw my lady; her face was as fair as the
sun. Her eyes ink-dark pools, she turned on me a tender gaze.

There I stood, but, although I had come on her summons,
never a word did she say; she only gave me a gentle look, such
as dear friends might have bestowed on them. — She called
Asmat to her presently, and a few words passed between them:
then Asmat came and whispered in my ear, "Go now; she can-
not speak to you." And once again I burned, as in flame.

Asmat led me out and I passed under the curtain. "O Fate,
you gave me hope, you gave my heart healing," I said; "why
have you thus put an end to my gladness?" The pain of parting
brought my heart now to yet greater sorrow. — As we walked
through the garden Asmat promised me joy. "Do not grieve
because of this," she said; "close the terrace of sorrow, open the
portals of happiness. Modesty demanded reserve, and forbade
her to speak to you." "Sister," I replied, "for my heart's com-
fort I look to you. Do not cut me off from my soul, I beseech

you, but extinguish the fires in my breast with intelligence. Send messages constantly, let letter follow hard upon letter — hold nothing back from me."

I mounted and rode away, shedding tears in a steady stream. . . . I went to rest, but my distraction kept sleep at a distance. My cheeks lost their crystal and ruby and turned to a deathly hue; yet I dreaded most sorely the coming of day.

How the Cathayan king sent Tariel his reply

In due time the envoys returned from Cathay; this was the arrogant and insolent reply they brought with them: "No cowards are we, nor do we lack strongholds. — Who is this king of yours? When did he become lord over us?"

And further to this their ruler had written: "King Ramaz to Tariel: Greatly did the burden of your letter amaze me. — You summon *me*, who hold sway as their lord over many peoples! I will never receive aught again from your hand."

I gave orders now for the host to be mustered and dispatched lieutenants to marshal the armies of India, more numerous than the stars. From near and far they came hastening; plains, rocks and ravines were filled then with warriors. None lingered at home, they made speed on the road. I had them assembled before me, and their gear, well-ordered ranks, bold demeanor and dexterity pleased me; likewise their swift horses and their Khvarizmian[63] armor.

I raised the royal banner of red and black up on high and gave orders for the countless host to set out in the morning. Then I wept, and lamented my cruel lot sorely: "If I do not see my sun-fair lady," I said, "how can I steel myself to depart?"

I went home, and greater yet grew my heart's melancholy; from my eyes the hot tears poured forth as from flood-gates. "My fate," I said, "is still all in darkness; why did my hand reach for a rose that was not for its culling?"

How Tariel and Nestan held converse together

Great was my surprise when a slave made his entry! To me, sitting there in the depths of my grief, he gave a message from

Asmat. "Your sun-fair lady calls you to her," it said; "come, and have done with tears and moaning at Fate and its ways!"

My joy in that hour does not need any telling. . . . I repaired at dusk to the garden and went in at the gate. Asmat was standing at the spot where she had met me before: "Come, O lion, the moon awaits you!" she said with a smile. She led me then into that fair tower of many storeys — and there was my lady, lovely as the moon at the full. Splendid and rare, wondrous of face and form, she was sitting beyond the curtain, attired in a robe that was green in hue.

I stepped forward and stood at the edge of the carpet: the fires in my breast ceased to rage; my heart's darkness was lightened; up to a great height shot joy, like a pinnacle. Reclining on a cushion — fairer far was she than the sun's rays! — the princess kept her face covered, with only a glance at me. "Asmat," she said, "ask the amirbar to seat himself." Asmat placed a cushion before the sun-fair one, and, giving up to joy that heart Fate had so long abused, I sat down. . . . Can I repeat the words she uttered and live still!

"The other day," she said, "you were grieved when I dismissed you without a word: I withered you as the sun withers the flower in the field then; tears flowed from those eyes that are like two narcissus-pools. But it was my part to show restraint and reserve towards the amirbar.

"Yet, although a woman should have much care for modesty, the worst of all things is a sorrow that is silent and hidden. If my lips have worn a smile, inward grief has been known to me: and so I sent Asmat with a message of truth to you. What we have both known in our hearts I now give to words in a promise — I am yours; I assure you of this with my solemn oath. If I deceive you, may God bring me to the dust, may I never sit in the ninth heaven![64]

"Go and fight the Cathayans, cross the border, give battle; may God grant you victory, may you come back in triumph! — But what shall I do until you return here? . . . Give me your whole heart, and take mine in exchange."

"For your sake I will burn as in flame," I said: "you have not slain me — no, you have granted me life itself. You are to my eyes no less fair than the sun. Now I will go and prove myself in war with the Cathayans a very lion of valor.

(406-23)

"What you have given me is more than any man could be worthy of. Grace unlooked-for — yet it is not strange, come from God! The light of your loveliness has flooded my dark heart; I am yours until the day the earth covers me."

I took my oath upon a sacred book, and she hers. Thus did she then give her love declaration: "If any other man wins the favor of my heart, may God slay me! — In all the days to come I will live with this utterance."

I stayed with her for some time; sweet were the words that were spoken then; we ate, as we talked, fruit that was very delicious. At length, shedding tears, I stood up to take my leave: my heart was illumined by her dazzling beauty.

Pain indeed was it to turn from her countenance, from the crystal and ruby; yet the world was made new and a great joy possessed me. Mine now was that radiance that shone like the sun! I marvel that parting from her did not bring death to me — truly, my heart is rock!

How Tariel rode to Cathay and fought a great battle there

In the morning I mounted and had the clarions and trumpets sound: eager indeed was the whole army to take the field! None could call me a coward — I set out for Cathay like a lion. With no care for the winding track, my host marched by the shortest way.

I passed the border of India; and then, after I had for some time gone forward, an envoy arrived from Ramaz, the Cathayan khan, bringing a fair-worded message: "Indians, your goats could assuredly eat our wolves!" He first presented rich treasures as a gift from his master, then said, "These are the terms of the entreaty he makes to you: 'Do not bring slaughter — that were unworthy — but take from us a solemn oath that will put our necks within halters. Without raising a hand we will surrender ourselves and our children and all our possessions. Forgive the wrongs we have done you, for we sorely repent of them; show us mercy like God's, bring your host no further forward. Do not lay our land waste, do not loose heaven's wrath upon us! We will hand over strongholds and cities — but do not come with the whole of your army.' "

I called together my viziers, and at our council they said to me: "Because of your youth we, your advisers, venture to speak thus. — These Cathayans are very treacherous; we have seen that once already. They may be planning to kill you foully, to bring grief upon us. This is our counsel: go forward with some few picked men, but have the rest of the host follow, not far behind you; and communicate constantly, keep sending messengers. If the Cathayans show good faith, give them trust and make them swear oaths by God and by heaven: if you find them false-hearted, your wrath can break over them."

I judged this advice good, and this was the reply that I sent back: "King Ramaz, I have been told of the terms you put forward. Life is indeed better than death, and stone walls could not shelter you! — I will come with a small company and leave the rest in the rear."

I went on with three hundred picked men, leaving behind the rest of the host with this charge: "Follow close in my track and be ready to give aid; I will call on you to come to me if need should arise."

After we had journeyed for three days another courier from the khan arrived; he presented me in his turn with many rich robes and then delivered this message: "Valiant and mighty hero, eager am I to look upon you; other such gifts shall be yours when we meet." And then: "This is truth: I myself am coming in all haste to see you." I sent this reply: "I will obey your command and we will meet lovingly, like father and son."

I went on, and then made a halt presently on the edge of a forest. More messengers now came up and gave salutation; with them they brought some fine steeds as a gift. "Well might kings," they said, "desire to behold you!" And they went on, "The king sends this message: 'I am on my way; I have left my palace and shall be with you early tomorrow.' " I lodged them in a fine pavilion and treated them graciously: they lay down for the night together like guests after a wedding.

No kindness done in this world can pass away utterly! One of those messengers, unbeknown to any, came back and said to me: "I owe a debt that would take much repaying: in youth I was for a time in the care of your father, and no part at all can I have in betraying you. — I have hastened to tell you of treachery

I heard being plotted; it were pity indeed to see one with your form, with your rose-cheek, a dead man! I will tell you all; keep your wits now and attend.

"Do not be deceived; they are playing you false: in one place a hundred thousand, in another thirty thousand warriors are lying in wait. That is why they have shown themselves so urgent in calling you. You must be alert or you will surely be lost.

"The king will come a little way to meet you, whom all men admire as the summit of excellence. To speak to you with fair words is their plan — but they will have their armor on, hidden! Their host will close in from all sides when a puff of smoke rises; and, a thousand against one, they must overwhelm you."

I spoke to the man graciously and gave him my thanks. "If I live I will reward you with the desire of your heart," I said. "Go back now to your comrades, lest suspicion be roused in them. If I forget you, may I go down the road to perdition." — To none did I speak of the matter; I kept it close like so much idle talk: what will be, will be — words can be spared well! But, long though the way was, I sent a courier back to the host with this message: "Make haste, ride hard over the hills and the mountains!"

In the morning I gave a friendly reply to the messengers: "Tell Ramaz to come forward; I too will press on to the meeting." I journeyed on, untroubled by danger, for half a day after that. There is a Providence; if I am to be killed today, of what use to try to hide?

From the top of a hill I saw dust rising on the plain. "Here comes King Ramaz," I said; "he has spread a net, but soon will their flesh know my sharp blade, my straight lance." Then I spoke of great deeds to my escort: "Brothers," I said to them, "those men plan to attack us with treachery, but why should this take the strength of your arms away? Die for your king, and your soul goes to heaven! Now let us fall on the Cathayans and use our swords to good purpose!"

Proudly, with stern words, I gave the order for arming; and we all put our mail on for battle. I marshalled my warriors then and rode forward with great speed: that day my brand was to shatter my enemies!

As we drew near, the Cathayans perceived we were wearing our armor, and a man came from their king to us, bearing a message: "We have no thought of treachery, and it is with displeasure that we see you thus in your war-gear!" I sent back this reply: "I know what you have planned for me, but matters will not fall out in the way you have schemed for. Now come and give battle as honor requires of you! I have put my hand to my sword-hilt to work your destruction."

When once they had received this, there was an end to their messages; they sent up their signal-smoke and laid bare their secret. The warriors rose from their hiding-places and bore down, rank upon rank, from both sides, upon us. . . . But, by heaven, they could do nothing against me!

I took my lance in my hand and put on my helmet: great was my eagerness to destroy them in battle! Then I put my men into line and began to make forward. Marshalled in countless ranks the Cathayans waited, well-ordered and calm.

I drew near: "He is out of his wits!" they said when they saw me. I, the strong in arm, charged where the foe stood thickest, struck a man with my lance, overturned his horse and killed both beast and rider. My lance broke and I drew my sword — to him who had the whetting of you, O blade, be all praise!

I swooped down like a hawk on a covey of partridges,[65] dashed one man down on another and heaped up horses and men in a pile like a mountain. The men that I struck spun round and round just like dragonflies; I made slaughter of all those in the two leading bands.

They pressed in from all sides, and round me the battle raged fiercely. None could stand against my blows; I made blood flow in torrents: those I had cleft hung splayed from their horses like saddle-bags. . . . Wherever I went, they fled before me in terror.

As dusk was beginning to gather a sentinel called down from a hill-top, "Make haste and fly; heaven has once more turned upon us a face of wrath! A fearful dust is approaching that portends a disaster — the countless host that is coming must most surely destroy us!"

As soon as they had received my message the warriors left behind had set out; and hard had their riding been, by day and

(442-59)

by night. The plain could not hold their numbers, they streamed over the mountains; and now they came in sight, sounding their drums and their trumpets.

The Cathayans at once turned to fly, and with shouts we pursued them: I unhorsed King Ramaz; he and I then fought with swords. We showed mercy and took captive the whole of his army. Those who, vanquished and terrified, had made away were overtaken by our rearguard, seized and dashed down to the ground. Well were my men rewarded for the loss of their night's sleep! Even the unwounded prisoners gave out groans like the sick.

We dismounted to take our rest there on the battlefield: I had been deprived by a sword-cut of the use of an arm. My men came to look on me and to sing my praises — but they could not find words for that: the acclaim I received was enough for one man! Some blessed me from afar, others sought to embrace me; those lords who had watched over my youth wept for joy. All were amazed at the work of my sword.

I sent off my warriors this way and that to lay hands upon booty; heavily laden were they when they came back again. Well pleased indeed was I with my achievement, for the ground was dyed red with the blood of my enemies: the gates of all the cities were opened to me without further fighting.

I said to Ramaz, "I know the tale of your treachery! Now you are a captive, strive to redeem yourself. Let there be no defending of strongholds, bid them all to submit to me. Else, why should I pardon the wrong you have done?"

Ramaz replied, "No resource now remains to me: let me have one of my barons to carry out my commands, and I will have him go to the governors of all of my fortresses. Everything will be surrendered into your hands and possession." — I gave him one of his barons, with men for an escort, to act for him, and had all the governors brought into my presence: they all made submission and surrendered their castles. Thus did I give the Cathayans cause to repent that they had ever taken up arms against us.

How can I describe to you the wealth of their treasure! I made a march through Cathay and saw the whole of the land. The handing-over of treasure-chamber keys was done so that

all could see. I quieted the country: "Be easy in your minds,"
I said; "the sun[66] will not burn you, of that you can be assured."

I examined all the treasures one by one, first to last: weary
should I be were I to tell you of all of the wonders! I found a
veil of a fabric most rare and most strange — had you seen it
you would have been eager to learn what its name was. I could
not find out what the stuff was, or what the work done upon
it: all those that I showed it to spoke of a miracle, marvelling.
The fabric did not seem to be woven after the fashion of bro-
cades or of carpets. . . . It was like steel finely tempered, even
so was it strong.

This veil I put aside for her whose beauty illumined me; then
I selected the choicest treasures to send to King Parsadan; a
thousand strong-legged camels and mules were to carry them:
and at the same time I dispatched the good news.

How Tariel wrote to the king of the Indians, and how he returned home in triumph

I wrote this letter: "O King, good fortune is yours! The
Cathayans — ill did it fall out for them — tried to work
treachery; that is why I am late in sending intelligence. I have
made their king captive and am now on my way to you with
booty and prisoners."

When I had put everything in order I set out from Cathay;
the treasures of the plundered kingdom all went along with
me. I could not find enough camels, so loaded up bullocks.
Great was my joy, for my desires were attained now. And the
king of Cathay went with me, a prisoner.

My lord came forth with a loving welcome when I arrived
back in India. It would not befit me to tell you how he then
sang my praises! He undid my arm's bandage and put on a
softer. — Fine pavilions had been erected in the maidan for him
to receive me in. A banquet was held; and so the king spent the
day. He had me sit close by him, he gazed at me and treated me
lovingly; and the whole of the night that followed we spent in
gay, joyous feasting.

(459-76)

In the morning we went into the city, and then came the king's command: "Let the warriors assemble; bring the Cathayan before me; lead in the prisoners."

When I brought in the captive King Ramaz, Parsadan looked on him kindly, as though on a son. I spoke of the false traitor so as to make him seem a man to be trusted: in such a fashion as this does a brave man best crown his achievements. — Parsadan received the Cathayan graciously and talked, as king to king, with him for a space of time. When dawn came he summoned me, and his words carried clemency: "Shall I give pardon to the Cathayan, my enemy?" "To the sinner," I replied, "God himself extends his forgiveness; it befits you to show mercy to those who are humbled." Then he said to Ramaz, "I send you away with a pardon; but do not come before us again in dishonor." A tribute of ten thousand dinars and much coin of Cathay, together with satins and brocades, was imposed by him: and then, after bestowing rich raiment upon Ramaz and his nobles, he gave him a gracious dismissal. Such was the price of his anger.

The Cathayan gave thanks and said, bending in humble obeisance, "God has brought me to repent of my treacherous deeds; put me to death if I ever again do you injury!" And then he departed, his train following after.

Next day this message from the king reached me with the light of the morning: "All the time you were away, for three months, I ate of no game that had been brought down by an arrow. In truth you have earned rest. . . . But come out, if you are not too weary."

I made ready forthwith and rode off to the palace: there I found a pack of hunting-leopards, while falcons were everywhere. As splendid as the sun in his majesty, the king sat in readiness: well pleased was he to see me in my radiance! — Softly, so that I should not hear, he said to the queen: "Tariel has returned from the wars truly glorious to look upon: he brings light to the heart, be it never so dark, of every man who beholds him. Now do without delay the things I enjoin on you. — I have formed a plan without telling you, and the time has now come for it to be unfolded: since we have named our daughter heir to our throne, let all look today on the maiden who is like a cypress in Eden. Set her at your side and await my return in the palace; I shall have joy in my heart when I come."

We set out with great numbers of hounds, hawks and falcons, and went hunting over hillside and plain; but we returned home early, without having gone far. Nor did we spend long in ball-play; we played two games only before making an end.

The people crowded the city's streets and the house-tops to see me, the victor in war: I wore a tunic with tassels. Like a rose pale of hue and bathed in tears was I then! All who beheld me swooned — that is truth. I had round my head the fabric I had found in the Cathayans' chief city; well did it become me. . . . The crowd was ravished with yet greater delight.

The king dismounted and we entered the palace: when I beheld my lady I started back, for her cheek's beauty dazzled me. She was clad in an orange-colored robe; groups of ladies-in-waiting were standing behind her; the palace, the streets outside — all the city round about was suffused with her loveliness. Between her cheeks' roses, her lips' coral and the pearls of her teeth shone forth in their beauty.

When I came in, my wounded arm in a sling, the queen rose from her throne and came forward to meet me. Kissing my cheek's rose as though I were a son, she said, "You need not look for any enemy now!" I was given a place near to them, where I wished to be. She for whom my heart ached, my sun-fair lady, sat just before me; no words passed between us, but glances were stolen. Whenever I wrenched my eyes from her all things became hateful.

A banquet was held that was worthy of such a mighty king; such joy was there then as has been seen by no mortal eye; all the goblets and bowls were of turquoise and ruby. The king's hospitality would not allow even the drunk to depart.

Rapture filled me; the looks exchanged began to soothe the fires in my breast. But I brought my wild heart to prudence there in the sight of men. . . . What is sweeter than to gaze into the eyes of the loved one?

On a word from the king the singers fell silent and stood with their heads bent. "Tariel, my son, how can we tell you of the joy that fills us?" said Parsadan. "Delight is ours, while sorrow is the lot of our enemies. Not without cause are your praises so loudly sung! It would be fitting to clothe you, proud one, in a rich robe of honor, but we will not take from you this tunic which so well becomes you. — Now, radiant hero, a hundred treasure-chambers are yours; garb yourself as you choose,[67] take whatever may please you."

A hundred keys for the hundred treasure-chambers were given me; I made obeisance and called down blessings upon the heads of the royal pair. Splendid as two suns, they rose up and kissed me. . . . How can I tell you of the gifts that they bestowed on the host!

Joyful in heart, the king now sat down again. Yet more freely did the wine flow; song followed song. The feast wore on, to the strains of harp and of lyre: the queen withdrew when day turned to dusk: great joy was ours until evening.

We made an end when we could no longer drain the great goblets. My mind in a daze, I withdrew to my chamber. I could not quell the fires within my breast; I was captive — yet much did the thought of my lady's glances rejoice me.

How Nestan-Darejan wrote to her lover

A slave came in with some news that had nothing of falsehood: "A woman is asking to see you; she is wearing a veil." I knew who it must be and leaped up with a trembling heart. The woman came in, and it was indeed Asmat.

I rejoiced, for the sake of her for whom I run thus distracted. I would not let her make obeisance but kissed her and, taking her hand, placed her on my couch by me. "Has she of the cypress-form gone to her bower?" I asked. "Tell me how she is — speak of her, and her only."

"I will tell you the plain truth," Asmat replied to me. "Today you saw each other, and delight was your portion: now she has once more bidden me bring you intelligence." With that she gave me a letter; I looked at it; it was from the hand of her who brings light to the earth. She had written:

"I have beheld you, like a gem in your beauty. Fair did you appear, riding proudly, when you came back from the battle. No unworthy spring is that which my tears have flowed forth from!

"Though God has given me a tongue to praise you when you are far from me, I can now hardly speak, I am dying for you: live without you I cannot. I, the sun, have made of my countenance a garden of roses and jet for you, the lion. Never shall I be another's; that do I swear.

"You have wept torrents of tears, but no more of this vain flow. Shed no more henceforward, let all grief be put away. Those who have looked on you mock them that speak of my beauty. — Send me that fabric you had about your head and which so well became you; give it to me, that you may have the joy of seeing your token adorn me. Put this bracelet on your arm, if still you have love for me: night's shadows have passed away and daylight has come for you!"

How Tariel wept and swooned

[*Here Tariel wept, his grief increased a full thousandfold: he was like a brute beast, he was lost to all reason. Saying, "I still have that bracelet that once was upon her arm," he loosened it and took it off — it was of worth beyond telling! He pressed it to his lips and then swooned away, lifeless. Stiller than a corpse at the door of the tomb he lay, his breast bruised all over by the blows of his fist. Once more Asmat sought to revive him with laving, while blood poured from her rent cheeks;*[68] *the sound could be heard of water running away.*

Avtandil too groaned bitterly as he gazed at the senseless prince. Asmat wailed and wailed again; her tears wore through the very stones. But she succeeded at length in bringing Tariel once more to consciousness; the fires that burned within him were extinguished with water. "So I yet live!" he said. "But Fate has been drinking my blood!"

Pale and wild-eyed, he sat up; his cheek's rose was now saffron; for a time he did not speak, did not even look at the others. Great was his grief to find he was still alive! . . . Then he began to speak once more to Avtandil.]

Give ear! For all that my mind is distracted, I will finish my tale — my tale and that of her who is bringing me to the grave. Although my beloved is unknown to you, your comfort supports and sustains me. — I marvel that I am still alive, still whole in body!

I was glad to see Asmat, whom I trusted as a sister. When I had read that letter she gave me this bracelet, and I put it on my arm there and then. I took off my headgear: strange and rare it was, of a strong fabric black in color.

How Tariel wrote in answer to his lady

"Sun-fair lady," I wrote, "my heart has been struck by the shafts of your radiance: all my boldness is brought to nought, all my audacity. Your beauty fills my soul and I am now as one mad. With what service can I repay the debt that I owe for a life spared?

"Once before you had mercy when you might have destroyed me: this hour appears to me even another such. I have received your bracelet, and it is now upon my arm — too great for words is the rapture that fills me!

"I make haste to send you the veil that you asked for; also a mantle of the same stuff — nowhere in the world is the like to be found. Do not leave me to distraction — come to my aid, help me! There is no one save you who can command my obedience."

Asmat rose and went away: I lay down and fell into a sleep at first peaceful, but my lady came to me in a dream, and I trembled. I awoke — she was gone, and life was affliction. The night passed away. . . . But the sound of her voice was not borne to me.

How they took counsel concerning the marriage of Nestan-Darejan

A summons to the palace came with the first light of morning; I rose and, having learned what was required of me, went off without delay, to find the king and queen with three councillors. They bade me be seated, and I took my place then before them. "God has burdened us with years, old age is upon us, youth has passed away," they said to me. "Yet we do not grieve over the lack of a son, since we have a daughter of a dazzling loveliness. Now we wish to find a husband for her — but where are we to find one whom we can have sit on our throne, whom we can mold in our own image and make the realm's defender and ruler, that we may not suffer destruction, that our enemies may not sharpen their swords for us?"

"Heavily," I replied, "must the lack of a son weigh; but from your daughter, the sun's peer, we have much to hope for. Greatly will he whose son you ask for as a bridegroom rejoice. . . . What can I say more? You yourselves can best judge as to what to do."

There was deliberation on the matter. Though stricken to the heart I kept self-command: "There is nothing," I told myself, "nothing at all you can do to prevent this!" Presently the king said, "If the Khvarizm-shah,[69] the ruler of the Khvarizmians, would give us his son, he would in truth be the best of all matches."

It was clear that the matter had been settled beforehand; the king and queen exchanged glances; what one said was in harmony with the words of the other. I could not raise my voice to thwart them; my heart trembled; I was as earth and as ashes.

"The Khvarizm-shah," the queen said, "is a most puissant monarch; what better husband than his son could we desire for our daughter?" What could I say, since it was this that they wished for? I gave assent; and thus it was my soul became the prey of a torment.

An envoy was dispatched to the Khvarizm-shah with this message: "As we have no son to succeed to our place on the throne, we cannot let our only daughter, who is our heir, wed abroad. — You will be free of all care if you give us your son as a bridegroom." When he returned the envoy was heavily laden with veils and with fur cloaks. Great indeed had been the rejoicing of the Khvarizm-shah: "Now has God granted what we desired above all else! What better match could we have sought for our son?" he had said.

Other men were sent off now to act as an escort: "Do not

delay," they were charged to say, "but answer our call and come quickly!" . . . I went to my chamber to rest, fatigued after ball-play; grief had entered my heart, and a sorrow had gripped me.

How Tariel and Nestan-Darejan took counsel together and made a plan

I was about to plunge a dagger in my heart in my wretchedness when Asmat's slave appeared, and I strove for self-mastery. The slave put in my hands at once a message in writing: "She who is like a cypress bids you come with all haste," it read.

You can conceive of my joy! I mounted and rode off, passed through the garden and went up to the tower. At its foot I found Asmat: it was plain she had been weeping — the tears lay on her cheeks still. She seemed to have been looking for my coming impatiently. Disquieted now, I did not say anything to her; sorely did it grieve me to see this sadness upon her. She did not greet me with her usual smile; she only shed tears; she spoke not at all. No healing had she, only more wounds to give! My mind was filled with thoughts that were troubled and anxious.

She led me into the tower and then lifted the curtain up. When I had entered I beheld the moon-fair lady, and all grief fell away from me. My heart was filled with light by her loveliness; but I was not bereft of my senses.

Yet a displeasure shadowed the radiance that fell on the curtain. The peerless lady was wearing, in a careless fashion, the gold-worked veil I had given her: attired in the green robe she had worn when we first talked together, she lay on her couch, her cheek bathed in tears. Like a panther crouching in a rock-cleft was she; her face flashed forth fury. In nothing did she now resemble the sun, the moon, or a cypress growing in Eden!

Asmat placed me, my heart pierced as by a lance, at some distance from my lady: then the princess sat up; she was angry, her brow frowned. "I wonder," she said, "you have dared to come — breaker of oaths — faithless, treacherous, forsworn one! But the day will come when high heaven has you answer

for this!" "What reply can I make," I responded, "when I do
not know what I am charged with?" Then I went on, "Until
I am told this I cannot defend myself. In what have I wronged
you — pale, bewildered wretch that I am — how have I
offended?"

"What words," she said, "are fit for one who is so false and
so treacherous? Why did I let myself be deceived, after the
fashion of womankind? A torturing flame now consumes me
for this! — Do you not know they are bringing the Khvarizm-
shah's son here to marry me? You sat in the council and agreed
to the plan — breaking the oath you had solemnly sworn to
me! But with God's help I will have you and your treachery
thwarted!

"Do you remember when you sighed and drenched the fields
with tears, when physicians and surgeons came in crowds
with their cures? — What is there like the ill-faith of a man?
But since you have denied me, *I* will deny *you;* we shall see
which of us suffers the more!

"Listen to me: whosoever may reign here in India, by hook
or by crook I will hold the power in my own hands: your
thoughts are as false as your soul — you have made a false
reckoning!

"No place shall there be for you in all India, by heaven,
while still life remains in me! Soul and body shall be parted
unless you are quick to flee. . . . But though you stretch your
hand up to heaven, you will find none to compare with me!"

[*Here Tariel wept and groaned; and then he continued.*]

When I heard her speak thus, hope sprang up once more
within me; and again I found strength to turn my eyes on her
radiance. . . . Do you not wonder that, now she is lost to me,
I should still live — to be crazed? Alas, faithless Fortune, why
would you drink of my blood?

I looked round about me: upon a cushion there was a Koran
lying open; I took this in my hand, stood up and then, having
uttered praises first of God and then of my lady, said, "Sun-
like one, you have burned me; let me now be consumed utterly!
Yet, since you have not slain me, I will venture some answer.
May heaven turn its wrath on me if what I now say is false,
may I be cut off from the light of the sun! I have done no ill —

if you will but hear me." "Say what you have to say," returned
the princess, with a sign of assent.

"If, sun-fair lady," I went on, "I have broken faith, may God
in his anger strike me with a bolt from the heavens! None save
you in my eyes is sun-fair, has the form of a cypress. . . . How
can I live if a lance pierces my heart through?

"The king and queen did indeed summon me to a solemn
council in the palace, but they were in truth already resolved
to have this prince marry you: to seek to oppose them would
have been no more than vain folly. 'Give your assent and keep
your heart steadfast!' I said to myself. — How could I have
spoken out against the plan, when the king is blind? . . . Does
he not understand that India is not going to want for a lord?
None can dispute Tariel's claim to the royal inheritance! — Who
is this they are bringing, who has been thus deceived?

'There is nothing,' I told myself, 'that I can do here and now;
I must devise some plan to act on at a later time.' And then I
went on, 'Do not let a crowd of fearful thoughts overcome
you!' My heart grew like a wild thing; I was filled a thousand
times with the longing to fly to the plain. — To whom should
I surrender you, how can you cast me off?"

That tower became a market; I bartered a soul for a heart
then. The tears raining on her cheek's rose began to fall now
more gently; those pearls that were her teeth appeared within
her smiling lips' coral. "How could I doubt you?" she said to
me. "I do not believe you to be treacherous and faithless, un-
grateful to God and a rebel against his will. Now boldness must
win for you both me and the Indian realm! You and I shall
reign together; that will be the best of all matches."

She who had lately been so enraged now became tender and
loving; it was as though the sun or the moon at the full had
come down to earth. Granting more than she had ever done
before, she made me sit down beside her and spoke to me
sweetly, soothing the fire in my breast.

"The wise man does not act in haste; he will do what is best
and leave the rest to Fate," she said. "If you bar the way to the
prince, the king will be angry; there will be conflict between
you and all India will be laid in ruins. But if you let the prince
come here and marry me, you and I shall be parted; we must

change our gay purple for the dark garb of mourning. He will rejoice in good fortune, but a hundred sorrows will be ours — ah, never must it be said that the Persians lord it here at our court!"

"God forbid," I replied, "that you should have this prince for a husband! Let but the news of their coming to India reach me, and I will forthwith give proof of my courage and valor; such destruction will I work among them that they will be good for nothing thereafter!"

"A woman should bear herself like a woman; I cannot have you shed much blood, I will not become a wall of division," my lady said. "Kill the prince when he comes, but spare those in his following — even a dry tree is made green by an act of true justice! This is what you must do, my lion, first among heroes: take him off secretly — but do not butcher his escort like cattle or asses; can a man bear the burden of innocent blood? — Then, the deed done, speak to your lord, my father, saying, 'I cannot let the Persians devour all of India; my inheritance it is, and not one jot will I yield of it! I will raze your city to the ground if you do not make peace with me.' Keep your love for me hidden; the justice of your deed will so seem much greater. The king will beg for peace humbly, imploringly, and surrender me to you. Thereafter we shall reign together in the highest felicity."

This counsel pleased me well, and I began to boast how my sword's sweep would slaughter my enemies. Then I rose to depart, but the princess besought me to stay with her. I longed to take her in my arms, but did not have the daring. . . . I remained for a little and then, mad at heart, took my leave; shedding hot tears, I was led forth by Asmat. A thousand griefs flooded in now and all my joy fled away: I went off with slow steps, for it was against my desire.

How the Khvarizm-shah's son came to
India to be married, and how Tariel killed him

A messenger brought the news that the bridegroom was close at hand: little did the unhappy wretch know what God had ordained for him! Well pleased, the king uttered words

(540-57)

filled with gladness. Nodding his head, he bade me come and sit by him. "For me," he said, "this is indeed a day of the greatest joy; we must give the wedding a splendor befitting your sister. Let us send men to bring treasure from every store, and let us scatter it generously; avarice is for fools!" And I saw to the sending.

The bridegroom did not dawdle: he appeared before long, and our men went out to meet the Khvarizmians as they drew near the city. The ground could not hold the vast numbers of warriors. — "See that some tents are put up on the maidan; the prince must rest for a while," the king presently said to me. "It will suffice if the other lords go out to greet him; you will see him here later." And so I had pavilions of red satin erected.

The bridegroom rode up and dismounted; there was as much bustle and stir as at Easter.[70] The lords went out in crowds; province by province, the warriors assembled in companies.

I betook myself home to sleep, fatigued as men are by duty; but then a slave came from the sweet Asmat to deliver this message: "Come quickly; she who resembles a cypress has summoned you!" Obedient to the command, I did not dismount, but rode off in haste. Asmat met me in tears: when I asked her why she wept she replied to me, "What else can I do, since I have *you* to deal with? Must I be always seeking to justify you, always an advocate?"

We went in; Nestan was reclining on a cushion, with knitted brow — the sun itself is not possessed of more dazzling radiance! I went forward: "The hour to strike has come," she said: "what are you waiting for? — Or have you forsaken me, played me false once again?"

I turned on my heel, angered, without reply — but then shouted back, "You shall soon see if I do not love her who has given her love to me! I must be urged on to fight by a woman — have I turned such a coward!" Returned home, I made ready at once for the killing: the call to arms was received then by a hundred men, and we mounted and rode unobserved through the city. . . . Alas that I must tell how I broke into the tent of a sleeping man! No blood was shed at the time of his slaughter, but better far would it have been had it flowed, in fair fight!

I cut through his tent's side, rent it, tore it in tatters, seized
him by the feet and dashed his head on the pole: then, while
the guards lying at the door cried out and made loud lamenta-
tion, I leaped into the saddle and made off as I was, in the mail
I was wearing. — A hue and cry was raised and they came in
pursuit of me, but all those who followed met their deaths
at my hand. I rode for a stronghold where I could laugh at
my enemies, reached it in safety and then sent out messengers
with this call to the warriors: "Rally to me now, all those who
are for me!" All through the dark night pursuers came riding up;
but when they saw me and knew me they took good care to
keep whole heads.

I rose and put on my armor at daybreak: when it was light
three lords brought this message from the hand of the king:
"I have been like a father to you, God is my witness: why have
you now changed my joy into sorrow? Why have you laid upon
my house guilt for the blood of the innocent? If you wanted
my daughter, why did you not tell me so? You have darkened
the life of your old foster-father, you have cut yourself off
from him for the rest of his days!"

This was the reply that I sent back: "O King, were I not
stronger than brass the fire of shame would destroy me! But
you know for yourself that a king should always deal justly.
I do not want to have your daughter, by heaven! — But you
are lord of the realm of India and of all the lands that lie therein,
and there is no heir save me: the other kings' lines are no more,
the whole heritage is yours; and the crown can go in right to
me and none other.

"There was no justice in what you did — I tell you this
straightly. God gave you no son, he gave you only a daughter;
and had you surrendered the realm to the Khvarizm-shah,
where should I have looked for my recompense? Is another
to rule in India while I can still use my sword?

"I do not want your daughter; marry her to whom you will —
away with her! But India is mine, and I will let it fall into the
hands of no other. On him who disputes my right I will bring
down destruction — and, by heaven, I shall not need to ask help
of any man!"

(558-74)

How Tariel learned of the carrying-off of Nestan-Darejan

After I had sent off the envoys my spirit was darkened; having no word of my lady, I was consumed as in a flame by my anguish. At length, to look out over the plain, I went on to the castle's wall. . . . Fearful news was I soon to hear, such as might kill a man.

Perceiving two figures approaching on foot, I went out to meet them. One was a woman, the other a slave. Then I saw who was coming; it was Asmat, her hair wild, her cheeks torn and bleeding. Gone was the laughing word, the smile of her greeting! As soon as I knew her I fell into the grip of fear: "What has happened?" I called out. "What new grief has come upon us?" "God's wrath has brought the heavens down on our heads!" she replied, weeping piteously, scarcely able to utter words.

I went up and said again, "What has happened? Tell me the truth!" Once more she wept bitterly, once more the flame of sorrow leaped up within her: for a space she could not speak a word nor tell a tenth of her woes; the blood from her cheeks ran down red to her breast. Then she said, "I will tell it to you: why should I hide it? But let my reward be a match for the joy that it brings you: have pity on me, I beg you, let my life have its ending, set me free from the world, do your duty to God!"

"After you had killed the prince," she continued, "the news spread and soon came to the ears of the king. Enraged, he started up: 'Bring him before me!' he thundered. They went to your mansion, but were unable to find you; and the king stormed the more. — 'He has gone,' they told him; 'he is no longer within the gates.' He said, 'I know, I know; too well I understand! He loved my daughter, and blood was the end of the business: when they were met they could not take their eyes off each other.

'Now, by my head, I will have the life of her who takes rank as my sister! I charged her to instruct my daughter in the things of God, but she has caught her in the Devil's net! What did they give her, those wantons, what were their promises? To let her live longer would be a denial of God: she must die for this.' "

Rarely did the king swear an oath by his head, but his word was never broken when once he had done so; nor was there any delay before his pledge had fulfilment.

Asmat went on: "Someone who had heard of the king's wrath told Davar the Kaj of it, Davar whose arts pierced heaven's mysteries:[71] yes, some enemy of God said to the king's sister, 'Your brother has sworn by his head that you shall die; this is known already to everyone.' Davar's words came: 'The good God knows I am innocent — never shall she who has brought death to me be joined to her lover!'

"My mistress was still wearing, as when you left, the veil you had given her; that veil which had been such an adornment of beauty. — Now Davar screamed words such as I had never heard: 'Harlot! Harlot! You have killed me! But now you shall pay for it!

'Wanton! Harlot! Why did you have your bridegroom taken off? Why should I have to give my blood for his in atonement? — For my brother indeed does not lack cause now to take my life. — What have I done to you, what have I made you do? — But, please God, never again shall you see him you worked on to compass this deed!' Her face contorted with fury, she seized hold of the princess, dragged her over the floor, tore her long hair and beat her most cruelly. The princess made no answer, she could do no more than sob and moan. I was powerless, unhappy wretch; I could not go to tend her.

"When Davar had had her fill of beating, two slaves — as hideous as Kajes were they of feature — appeared, with a great chest. Inside this they put the sun-fair lady, with many a rough word: thus they made her their prisoner. 'Take her,' Davar said to them, 'and lose her far out to sea, where she will find no fresh water, either frozen or flowing!' They laughed aloud in their glee. I saw this, and yet lived — I must be harder than any rock, truly!

"They passed the windows, making for the sea, and in an instant were lost to sight. Davar said, 'Who would not stone me for this? All is over now: come, death, before my brother claims my life as a forfeit!' With that she stabbed herself and fell dead: forth gushed her blood then.

"Do you not wonder that I still breathe, that I am not struck

(575-91)

dead by the lance of affliction? Now reward me according to the deserts of one who comes bearing such tidings: deliver me, in the name of heaven, from a life that is beyond my endurance!" And on flowed the piteous stream of tears, never drying.

"Dear sister, why should I kill you, what wrong have you done?" I said. "I know what my part is, I know what I now must do: wherever there is rock or water, there will I seek her." I became like stone then and my heart grew as hard as flint: maddening grief made me tremble. "Act!" I now told myself. "To lie here idle avails nothing; better far to go and look for her, to scour the world's spaces. — Now is the time for every man who is willing to follow me!" With that I went in and armed quickly and mounted. Eight score valiant warriors long in my service mustered and, rank after rank, we rode out through the gate. I made for the coast and, finding a vessel all prepared for departure, I embarked, put out to sea and began to cast about on the waters; never did a ship from any port escape without questioning. But nothing did I learn in all the time of my watching, and I grew ever more maddened: I seemed hated of God, cast off by him utterly.

Twelve months passed, then twenty. Not even in a dream had I met with any who had set eyes on my lady; and those who had been my companions had perished. "I cannot defy God," I said at length; "let it be as he wills." — Wearied of sailing the seas, I landed upon the shore: my heart had become like a wild beast, I was heedless of counsel. Those who had survived all the hardships now went from me. . . . But God does not abandon a man who has been brought thus to extremity!

Only Asmat and two slaves remained to advise and give comfort; no shred of intelligence had I gained touching the fate of my lady; no solace save torrents of tears was now left to me.

How Tariel met Nuradin-Pridon[72]

I made along the shore in the dark, and after a time saw

gardens before me. I thought I could see a city, and then as we drew near it we came to some rock-caves. I dismounted to rest under some tall trees: my wounded heart shrank from seeing any of humankind.

While the slaves had a meal I fell asleep beneath the trees. Then I awoke to wretchedness, my heart as black as night with the soot of my sorrow: in all this time I had learned nothing, neither truth nor false rumor! Tears poured from my eyes and flowed forth to soak the ground.

Suddenly I heard a cry and saw a warrior galloping along the shore, shouting fiercely. He was wounded, and blood flowed; his hand held a sword that was reddened and broken; he was uttering threats to his enemies, cursing in rage. Astride a black horse — the steed that is mine now — wrathful and furious, he swept along like the wind. I wished to have word with him and sent one of my slaves with the message: "Hold, lion! Tell me who it is that has aroused you to anger." But he did not give the slave any answer or heed what he said. Leaping on my horse, I rode after him, overtook him and then got in front of him. "Stop! Listen!" I said. "What are you about now?" He turned his eyes on me and, pleased with me, reined in his steed.

These were the words he addressed to God after scrutiny: "In him you have made one who is like a tree[73] in his splendor!" Then he said to me, "I will tell what you wish to know: enemies I had despised as goats became on a sudden fierce lions and fell on me treacherously, when I was not in my harness for battle."

"Be calm," I replied; "let us dismount under those trees that stand over there: no warrior worthy of the name will shrink back from sword-cuts." He came with me; we rode off like father and son together. — Marvellously fair was this stranger to look upon!

One of my slaves was a surgeon: he bound up the wound and drew out an arrow-head gently. Then I asked, "Who are you, and what man gave your arm this hurt?" And he agreed to tell me the tale of the wrong that had been done to him.

"I do not know who you are," he said first, "or to what I can liken you. You are a wasted moon. . . . But for whose sake? Who brought you once to the full? Who has taken the rose and jet out of your countenance? Why has God put out the candle he himself lit?

"I am the lord of Mulghazanzar,[74] a city not far away; Nuradin-Pridon is my name, and I rule as a sovereign. The bounds of my realm lie here, just by your halting-place. The land is a small one, but it is of the finest. — When my grandfather made division of his domain between my uncle and my father, a certain island off-shore was to fall to my portion: but my uncle, the father of those who have wounded me, made himself master of it. The hunting was theirs to enjoy, but I would not give up my claim, and quarrels arose.

"This morning, in quest of sport, I rode out along the shore: as I was flying my hawk, I had no more than a few men to flush the birds with me. Telling my guards to await my return and taking only five falconers, I went by boat to the island, which lies in a bay. I had no care at all for my neighbors — what need to be on guard against kinsfolk! I recked nothing of them or their following. . . . And so, with many joyous cries, I went after the game.

"Sorely were they galled by the disdain that I showed for them! My cousins themselves at their head, the warriors stealthily closed in and cut me off from my boat; then they engaged with my escort in combat and fought hand to hand. I heard the shouts, saw the flash of the swords, begged a craft from a boatman and cast off with a cry. Warriors came crowding in like waves and strove to overwhelm me; but in vain.

"Other great companies came pressing in from the rear: from one side alone they were unable to vanquish me, and so they attacked from this quarter and that. When those to my front could do nothing against me, the soldiers behind loosed the shafts from their bows. The sword I trusted in broke, and my arrows too gave out.

"Still they came in upon me, and, unable to do more, I made my horse leap from the boat and swim through the sea — truly amazed then were all who beheld me! My companions were all slaughtered; there on the ground they lay. But no pursuer dared close with me; whenever I turned they would stand back.

"Now may God's will prevail! — May I have my revenge for the blood shed! Night and day will I harry them! I will summon the crows and the ravens to make a feast of their flesh!"

My heart went out to him then and there. "There is no need,"
I said, "to be off in hot haste now: I myself will go with you,
and your enemies shall meet with destruction. What can two
men of might such as we have to fear?" I went on, "My own
story has not yet been made known to you; but I will recount it
when we have the time and the ease." "What joy could equal
this?" he replied to me. "Until my last day I will give myself to
your service!" We rode off to his city; though small it was very
fair. His warriors came running with all haste out to meet him:
tearing their cheeks, they pressed round him to kiss the hilt
of his sword.

On me, their king's companion, they looked with great rap-
ture; fair did they think me, they gave me much praise. "Sun-
fair lord," they said, "you bring clear skies and radiance!" And
so we entered Mulghazanzar, the splendid, the wealthy: the
people were all clad in rich, costly brocades.

How Tariel gave help to Pridon

As soon as Pridon's wound was healed and he could fight,
take up arms and ride a horse again, we made ready some war-
galleys and put soldiers in them. Such strength would have
made any onlooker marvel! Now I will tell you of Pridon's
victory, of the vengeance that he took on his enemies.

I perceived his foes' design, saw them donning their helmets.
Boats — about eight of them — bore down upon me, but I
made all speed towards them, and they turned to make off. I
struck one with my heel, and so overturned it; the crew shrieked
like women. Then, making for another, I seized hold of its
prow, flung it into the water and drowned all on board. No
more fighting was there with them! The rest fled before me,
all seeking for safety; those who beheld me were amazed, and
were loud in my praises.

We crossed the water and landed then; horsemen came charg-
ing and we once more joined battle: there was war, with its
losses. Greatly did I admire Pridon's valor and ardor. A lion
in battle, he was as fair to look on as the sun, and in form
like a cypress! With his own sword he struck down both of the

(608-25)

sons of his uncle; then he cut off their hands. Thus did he
mutilate them. After that he took them away captive, in bonds:
while their followers wept his own were rejoicing.

Their warriors fled, but we pursued them and scattered them:
and then, without loss of time, we captured their city. Our
prisoners' legs were broken with stones and their skins tanned
to leather then. — The riches that we found there, upon my
oath, could never all have been packed up! After Pridon had
examined the treasure-chambers and sealed them he led away
his two vanquished cousins and had their blood flow in revenge
for his own. . . . Of me they said, "Thanks be to God, to him
who created this hero with the form of a cypress!"

We returned to Pridon's city, to the sound of rejoicing;
jugglers were there, entertaining the people. All sang the praises
of Nuradin and me, saying, "Thanks to your mighty arms,
our enemies' blood is still flowing!"

To Pridon the warriors gave the acclaim befitting a king;
me they hailed as king of kings, declaring themselves liegemen
and me the lord of them all. Yet my melancholy did not leave
me; I was never to be found culling roses. My story was known
to none; it was no matter of common talk.

How Tariel received word of Nestan-Darejan from Pridon

One day when out hunting Pridon and I rode to the crest
of a headland that jutted out into the sea; and there Pridon
said to me, "I will tell you something: I saw a marvel from
this promontory once when I was out after sport." I asked him
to make on with his tale, and he did so:

"I rode out one day to hunt on this horse of mine — it is like
a duck in water, on dry land, a falcon — and drew rein here to
watch the flight of a hawk in the distance. As I made up this
slope I would look now and then out to sea; then presently,
far out, moving at a speed beyond all belief, I saw a speck on
the waves. But what it might be I was unable at first to distin-
guish; my mind was cleft through by doubt.

'What can it be?' I asked myself. 'A bird, or some kind of
beast?' Then I made out a boat covered over with a fabric lying
in many folds; in the prow men were plying oars. I kept my

eyes fixed on it. . . . Seated in a chest there was a lady as fair as the moon; worthy was she, I thought, of the seventh heaven![75]

"Two slaves — as black as pitch they were — got out and put the maiden on shore: and now I could see her hair; thick were its tresses. To what can I liken her dazzling loveliness! The light that she shed over the earth and the heavens was brighter by far than the rays of the sun.

"Joy made me tremble: love for that lady, for her who was fair as a new-sprung rose, filled me. Down through the rustling rushes I spurred then: my black steed could overtake any creature that lives, I knew. But, use my heel as I would — they were gone, I could not win to the maiden! I reached the shore; looked about; like the last ray of the setting sun was her beauty. She was far . . . then gone utterly; and fires burned in my breast."

When I had heard Pridon's tale the flames leaped up within me: throwing myself from my horse, reddened with blood from my torn cheeks, I cursed Fate. "That it was given to another," I said, "thus to see her who has the form of a cypress!"

Much amazed was Pridon; strange indeed did this seem to him: but he pitied me greatly. Shedding tears, he soothed me: like a father he comforted me, entreated me to be calm and was kind to me: hot tears like pearls burst forth from his eyes. "Alas," he cried, "what have I said — fool, dolt that I am!" "Do not grieve or feel any sorrow," I answered him. "For the sake of that moon-fair lady fires burn in my breast; I loved her. — I will tell you my tale, since you would be my friend."

I told him my whole history. "How have I, miserable wretch, spoken to you in my ignorance! That you, the mighty king of the Indians,[76] should come here to me! A royal throne, a splendid palace, would better befit you!" he said then. And he went on, "From one he made like a young cypress God must surely withdraw the lance that dealt him a heart-wound! His mercy comes down to us from heaven like thunder; he turns our sorrows to joy; he never abandons us."

With tears in our eyes, we went back to the palace and took counsel alone. I said, "None have I but you I can look to for any aid — but God has not put your like on earth; and, now I

(625-43)

have met you, what more can I desire? You will find me a true friend, if the time comes to prove me. But let your tongue and mind work to advise me: what shall I do, what will be best for my lady and me? I must strive for her rescue or part from life in an instant!"

Pridon replied, "What more could God do for me? You, the lord of India, have of your graciousness come to this land: what beyond this is there that I can hope for? I stand here before you as a slave to give service. — Ships from all regions of the earth come to this city; news is for ever flowing to us here from far-distant lands. We can surely learn the fate of her for whose sake you burn in affliction's flame. — God grant that your woes and your pains may all pass away!

"We will send forth well-tried mariners to find the moon-fair lady we grieve for; meanwhile you must be patient, maintain calm in your mind. Grief cannot last; in the end joy will vanquish it."

We took measures without delay: seamen were summoned: "Take ship; sail the seas; ease her lover's longing by finding the maiden for us; prepare to endure thousands of hardships." Such were the orders of Pridon. To all the harbors of the world he dispatched his men: "Seek for news of her everywhere!" was the charge that he gave them. I waited. . . . Pain found relief; my sorrows grew lighter. Still bereft, I knew some joy: and for those days I am still ashamed.

Pridon had me sit in the place of honor, upon a throne. "Before this," he said, "I had no understanding; I did not know that which I ought to have known. What can I do to please you, the mighty king of the Indians? What man would not become your slave eagerly?"

To make an end: from this quarter and that they returned, those who had been sent out to gather intelligence; empty-handed were they, and weary of profitless places. They had learned nothing at all, they brought no reports with them. And once more torrents poured forth from my eyes without ceasing. — "God is my witness, this day I am stricken with grief; to speak is hard," I said to Pridon. "Gone from you, night and day will be of one darkness. I am made a stranger to joy, my heart is bound now to sorrow. But, since I can no longer hope to hear news of my lady, I cannot remain here; I beg you for leave to depart."

When Pridon heard this he began to weep tears of blood: "Brother," he said, "all my joy this day has gone from me!" Hard did they strive to turn me from my purpose, but all in vain. The warriors came and knelt before me; pressed round me and kissed me; wept, and drew tears from me. "Do not go," they said; "while we live we will serve you."

"For me too, parting will be very hard," I replied to them: "but my heart can never know rest while my lady is lost to me. I cannot forsake my captive loved one — you yourselves greatly pity her. I will not stay for any man — let none seek to detain me!"

Pridon brought this horse and with these words presented it: "Sun-fair hero of the cypress-form, you would I know accept no other gift: this steed will delight you with its speed and its schooling." — He set out with me after that: we both shed tears as we rode along; and we embraced with cries of grief when the time came for parting. All the warriors made lamentation; not with their mouths only, but in their hearts. It was like the separation of father and son.

After taking leave of Pridon I turned to my quest once more; nothing on land or sea was unreached by my searching. But nowhere could I find a mortal man who had seen aught of my lady; and I grew like a wild beast, distracted in heart.

"An end to vain roamings and voyagings!" I said to myself at length. "Perhaps the company of brute beasts will clear the grief from my heart." Then I spoke a few words to my followers[77] and this Asmat: "You have good cause to reproach me — much grief have I brought upon you. Go now, leave me, take thought for yourselves: do not look any longer on my scalding tears pouring forth." "Alas, what is this? Spare our ears!" came their answer. "May we never know another master, another lord! May God never take us from the track of your horse's hooves! May we look on you always, you who are fair beyond all others!" Fate wears a man down, however valiant his spirit: I could not send them away, but let them do as they had a mind. — I forsook now the world of men; deeming the haunts of goat and deer fit refuges for me, I trod low-lying

(643-61)

plain and lofty mountain-side. Finding these caves, unknown to man, I fought and slaughtered the Divs who had hollowed them out.[78] Against me they could do nothing, but they killed my men; chain-mail did not suffice to protect them. The treachery of Fortune once more brought me grief. The shouts and cries of the Divs rose up to the heavens; the whole earth shook and trembled under the blows of their clubs; the light of the sun was obscured by the dust. My arms were moving branches, I was a cypress to look upon! A hundred attacked from one side; I tore their bodies asunder.

Since that day, brother, I have dwelt here, and here I await death. Distracted, I roam the plain; weeping sometimes, sometimes swooning. This maiden will not abandon me; she too burns in affliction's fires for the sake of my lady. My hope is in death; in death and in death alone.

Since the beauty of the panther speaks to me of my loved one, I hold its skin dear and wear it about me: with moans and with sighs Asmat sews the pelts into coats for me. — My sword has been whetted in vain, since I have not turned it against myself!

The tongues of all the sages would not suffice for my lady's praise! Enduring and suffering, I think of my lost one. Since I came here I have kept the company of beasts, reckoning myself of their number: I ask nothing of God now save my life's speedy ending.

Tariel beat his face with his fists, rent the rose on his cheek; the ruby hue of his countenance was turned into amber; the fair crystal was shattered. Tear after tear dropped from Avtandil's lashes. Asmat knelt, soothed the young lord and implored him to calm himself. Brought to quiet by her words, he said to Avtandil, "I have given you what you desired, I who am denied all I long for; now you have heard my woeful life's history. It is time for you to return to your lady, the sun-fair."

"Hard will it be to part from you," Avtandil replied to him; "tears will flow from my eyes if in truth I must leave you. . . . Now I will speak straightly; take no offence at my words, I beseech you. — Your lady is getting no help at all from this pining!

"When a physician falls sick, however skilled he may be, he calls in another who is versed in his art to tell him what manner of illness or fever it is that afflicts him: a man will judge of what touches another better than he can of his own concerns. Attend to me now, for I speak with sense, not as one out of his mind; you must give ear like a hundred men, and not as one only! — None as crazed as you are can hope for achievement. . . . I am going to return now to her for whose sake fire burns in my breast. I shall gain new assurance of her love when I see her, and I shall tell her, too, of what I have learned here. That is all that I have to do. — Now give me a pledge, I beg you, as God is God and heaven, heaven; let us swear oaths to keep faith, one with the other. Give me your word you will not depart from here; I will make a vow I will never abandon you: I will come back ready to journey anywhere, or to die, for your sake. With God's help I will dry the tears you now shed for your lady."[79]

"How can a man," Tariel replied, "give such friendship as this to a stranger? You will part from me with such sorrow as does the nightingale from the rose. — How could I forget you, let the wind take your memory? God grant that I may look on you again, O hero formed like the cypress! If you, who resemble a great tree in your splendor, return to me, my heart will not draw me away to run with the deer and the goats: if I break faith with you, may the wrath of the Lord overwhelm me! — The darkness will pass from my mind when you have come back to me."

And so they made exchange of their oaths, those true-hearted friends. Jacinth and amber in hue were they, wise of word, wild in spirit. Dear did they hold each other; the flame in their hearts was unfailing. That night those two glorious heroes passed as companions: Avtandil wept with Tariel, they shed tears together. — At dawn they embraced, and then the two parted. So distraught was Tariel that he did not know what to do; Avtandil wept likewise as he rode down through the rushes.

Asmat went down with the young lord and spoke to him imploringly, urgently. On her knees, hands clasped in entreaty, she besought him with tears to return soon. Like a faded violet was she then in her pallor. "Dear sister," he said, "you will be in my thoughts always. I will be back before long; I will not forsake you or dally at home. Do not let him roam meanwhile; there must be an end to his wandering. If I am not back within two months, hold me caitiff and recreant. — Be assured that my spirit will not know an instant's rest."

How Avtandil returned to Arabia

Sorrow, as he set out, fastened its grip on Avtandil: his nails were like thorns; they rent the rose on his cheek. The blood that trickled down was licked up by the wild beasts. — The long journey was shortened by riding hard all the way. He reached at length the place where he had parted from his warriors, and they saw him and knew him and rejoiced as was fitting. Swiftly was the good news borne then to Shermadin: "He has returned — he whose loss plunged us all into bitter woe!"

Shermadin came out to meet his lord; he embraced him and pressed his lips to his hand. The ground was soaked with the tears of his joy as he kissed him. "O God," he said, "is this truth that I see, or a phantom? — That it should be given to me to behold you, returned thus in safety!" Avtandil returned his greeting fondly and kissed him. "Thanks be to God," he said — "all has gone well with you!" The lords made obeisance, and those of most account in their turn kissed Avtandil. Great was the rejoicing among high and low alike.

They went off to the palace, and the whole city assembled to look on the hero. The mighty and proud one sat down to feast in great joy — the tongue cannot tell of that day and its gladness! All that he had seen was related to Shermadin; how he had found the young lord, whom he compared to the sun in its splendor. Tears troubled his story and blinded his eyes as he spoke. "Without him," he said, "palace and hut are as one to me!" — Shermadin recounted then all that had passed at home: "I have done," he said, "in all things as you bade me; you might never have gone from us!"

That day Avtandil feasted and took his ease without going forth again. But he was in the saddle at daybreak, off with the first light of the sun: feasting was done with, there was no more

sitting at home. Shermadin went before with the good news
of his coming; he covered the distance of a ten-days' journey
in three. The lion Avtandil rejoiced: he would see the sun's
rival[80] soon!

Thus did his message run: "O King, proud in might and in
majesty, in most humble duty do I send this intelligence. —
While I could learn nothing of that stranger lord I deemed my-
self worthless; now I have knowledge which I will impart to
you: I come safe and rejoicing." To Rostevan the king, mighty,
proud and imperious, Shermadin with his own lips uttered
the words he was charged with: "Avtandil has found the
stranger lord," he said, "and is coming before you." The king
spoke: "My prayers have received an answer from God!"

Shermadin said to Tinatin, the lady of radiance, "Avtandil
is coming, and with him he brings good news!" Her eyes shone
more brightly than the rays of the sun: on Shermadin she be-
stowed a gift, and on his following, raiment.

The king mounted and rode out to greet the approaching
Avtandil; well did the hero understand the greatness of the
honor then done to him. Joyful and loving were the two at their
meeting; some of the crowd of lords seemed drunk with delight.

When they had drawn near each other Avtandil dismounted
and made his obeisance. Filled with joy, Rostevan then ad-
vanced to embrace him: thereafter they rode off with glad hearts
to the palace. The young lord's return brought delight to all
who were gathered there.

Avtandil, the lion of lions, made obeisance to her who was
of all sun-fair ladies the fairest. The crystal and rose of her
cheek, the jet of her lashes, were suffused now with tenderness;
her face shone with a radiance brighter than the light of the
heavens. — No dwelling upon earth would have been a worthy
abode for her; the vault of the sky itself should have served
as her palace!

They sat down to feast; the table groaned and wine flowed:
the king looked on Avtandil as lovingly as though on a son.
Like fresh snow were the two then, like dew on the rose.
Lavishly did they bestow gifts; pearls went like drachmas.

When the drinking was done, all went home, save for the
great lords, who were kept by the king. He had Avtandil sit

(679-95)

by him, and bade him tell his tale. The hero told of the hard-
ships he had endured, then of what he had seen and learned of
the stranger lord: "Do not wonder if groan follows groan when
I speak of him; to nought can I liken his face save the sun!
All who behold him are bereft of their wits straight away. A
wilted rose is he, set deep among the thorns of sorrow. . . .
Alas, he is far away!"

When the harsh ways of the world make a man suffer grief,
he is like a reed turned into a thorn; his fair crystal is changed
into saffron. Tears covered Avtandil's cheeks while he was
speaking of Tariel: he told the whole history that he had heard
from him. "He lives," he said, "in a cave that was an abode of
Divs before he won it in battle; for companion he has a maiden
who once attended his lady. Despising silks and brocades, he
goes clad in a panther-skin. For the world he cares nothing;
in his breast there burns a fire that is ever new."

When Avtandil had finished his story of endurance and hard-
ship, the sight of his sun-fair lady's beauty rewarded him. —
They praised his strong arm, his unfaltering steadfastness:
"This is prowess enough," they said; "there is no need for more!"
Joyful was Tinatin's heart as she listened; blithe was Avtandil
that day at the banquet.

When he went to his chamber he found that a slave of his
lady's — the bearer of words that were precious — was await-
ing him. He was commanded to go to her! The tongue cannot
tell of the joy that was his then. A lion that had roamed, pale
of cheek, among the lions that dwell in the wastes; the world's
fair ornament; a diamond of the first and rarest water, he went
off, filled with gladness. Heart had he given for heart in the
traffic of love.

Tinatin the sun-fair was sitting on a throne, proud and regal;
as fair was she as a cypress fed by the waters of the Euphrates
in Eden. The loveliness of her eyebrows and her hair's jet made
the crystal and ruby of her countenance yet more fair — but
who am I that I should presume thus to praise her? That were a
task for the tongues of ten thousand Athenian sages!

She had the joyful Avtandil sit down before her; their hearts
filled with gladness, they conversed as was fitting; flowing
and gay were the words that they spoke then. The lady said,

"And so, after enduring many hardships, you found him!"

Avtandil replied, "When Fate grants a man his desire it is not for him to dwell on griefs that have passed away. — I have indeed found him who recalls a cypress the world's waters have nourished: I beheld the cheek that resembles a rose — but the color is gone. I looked on the hero who is like the rose and the cypress; in the grip of despair, he told me how he had lost his crystal-fair lady. I was moved to pity; he burns in just such a torturing flame as consumes me." Then once again he told the story recounted by Tariel. Of the pains and perils that had been his on the quest did he speak too, and of how God had granted it to him to find what he sought in the end. — "The world, life and humankind all appear to that lord as they do to a brute: distracted and weeping, he roams with the beasts of the field. Do not ask me to tell of him — what could I say, how could you understand? The man who has seen him holds all else of no account; those who behold him are dazzled, as by the rays of the sun; his cheek's rose is turned saffron, the violets are gathered."

He told of all that he had learned, seen and heard. "Like a panther," he said, "he has a cave for his home, and for companion he has a maiden who cares for him fondly and comforts him. — Alas, men are put in this world but to shed tears!"

When the lady had heard this story, content filled her spirit; her face shone with the radiance of the moon at the full. "What can I say," she said, "that would help to sustain him, what would serve as a balm, what would heal his deep wound?"

"Who would put trust in a breaker of faith?" answered Avtandil. "He — may the thought perish — would give himself to the flames for my sake: I took my oath too and set a time for return; I swore by that sun-fair one who is to me as the orb of day itself.

"For the sake of a friend a man should shrink from no sorrow, but give heart for heart, love as a road and a bridge. The woes of one lover should be a great grief to another, too. . . . Ah, severed from him I can know no joy, I deem myself worthless."

The sun-fair lady said, "The desires of my heart have now all been fulfilled: first, you have found him you went forth in search of and have returned safe and unharmed; then, the love that I planted in your breast has grown greater. I have found balm for a heart that has long been aflame.

"The life of each man changes like the skies; sometimes the sun shines, sometimes the heavens thunder in wrath. The sorrow I have known is now turned to gladness: since the world has such joy in it, why should any despair?

"You are right in your resolve to keep the oath you have sworn: love for a friend must be proved with deeds, a cure for his sorrows sought with diligent searching. But what shall I do in the shadows while you, my sun, are hidden from me?"

"With my return to you," replied Avtandil, "my woes grow yet greater! Vain to blow upon ice to melt it to water; vain is the love, the kiss from beneath, of the sun at its setting. — To be with you brings one sorrow; to go from you, a thousand.

"Alas, wherever I may be, when I have departed three flames will consume me. This day has shortened my life to a third, my heart has become a target for the arrow of grief. I long for a refuge, but no hope is there now of a shelter from pain.

"I have heard your words, I have understood what you said to me. There is no rose without its thorn; must my fingers then bleed? — Sun-fair lady, become a sun to me in all truth and give me some gage now for life and for hope!"

Tenderly, in sweet-sounding Georgian,[81] did he speak to his sun-fair lady: he was like a gentle teacher addressing a pupil. She accorded him his desire with the gift of a pearl. . . . God grant that their present joy may be made fully perfect!

What better fortune for a man than to be with his loved one, with her who is as fair as crystal and rubies in countenance, to be like an aloe planted in a garden by a cypress? Joy is aroused then in the heart of the beholder, sorrow in the man who is unable to look upon them. — But grievous is the lot of the lover parted from his lady, endless are his lamentations!

To gaze on each other was then joy indeed to them. Avtandil, bemused in heart, took his leave and withdrew at length; he shed tears of blood that would have caused an ocean to over-flow. "Alas, will the world never weary of drinking my gore?" said the sun-fair hero.

And so he went off in grief; he struck his breast cruel blows. . . . Love draws tears from a man, drains the strength from his heart. When a cloud covers the sun the earth is surrendered to darkness; a parting from the loved one denies morning its light. — Tears mingled with blood coursed down the cheeks of Avtandil. "While I am far from my sun-fair lady my heart knows no peace," he said. "Strange, the power of black lashes over a heart diamond-hard! Until I see her again, Fortune, no joy can be mine. Once I was like a cypress sustained by the waters of Eden; Fate strikes with its lance today and stabs with its dagger. My heart is caught in a net of unquenchable fire now: I know that this life is but an idle tale, nonsense."

Thus did he lament; tears gushed forth from his eyes; he trembled and shuddered; sighs and groans shook his frame. Parting from the loved one always brings bitterness. . . . The paths of this world lead but to the grave, alas!

He went to his chamber: there he wept and he swooned, but still in his thoughts he remained with his lady. His face lost its hue, was like the green of leaves under frost. — How soon, denied the sun's light, will the rose lose its beauty!

"Accursed is the heart of man, in its greed never sated! It strives after pleasures, yet must needs endure all woes. Blind is it, untrue of vision, heedless of measure: no power is there that can master it, not even death itself!"

Having spoken such words to his heart as the heart understands, he took the pearl which had gleamed, white as her teeth, upon his sun-fair lady's arm and pressed it to his lips, kissed it: his tears flowed like Pison.[82]

When morning had broken he was called to the palace; forth he went — proud and splendid, for all that sleep had not come to him. A host of onlookers stood eagerly jostling; the king prepared for the chase; the drums and trumpets were sounded.

Rostevan mounted — how is the pomp of those times to be told of? Not a word could be heard for the sound of the drums: the hawks darkened the sun: the dogs ran this way and that: the ground was dyed red with the blood of the slaughtered beasts. They rode far out over the plain and then returned, blithe of heart: all the lords, captains and warriors were bidden to come to the palace. The king sat down; the chairs there were all richly adorned; harp blended with lute; the song of the minstrels was sweet.

Avtandil sat by the king and replied to his questioning: their lips' ruby shone forth, their teeth flashed like lightning. The great men sat close by and gave ear to their converse; a crowd stood at a distance. All the talk was of Tariel.

Sad at heart, Avtandil rose and went forth at last: the ground was all soaked with the tears that he shed then: the inward eye of his mind had his lady always before it. He would rise to his feet, then lie down on his bed again. . . . How can one who is crazed sleep, what heart ever heeded a call to be patient?

"How can I hope for joy in my heart?" he said as he lay there. "Lady of the reed-like form, you who resemble a tree growing in Eden — Fate has severed us! Joy to those who look on you, cause of woe to all others, since I may not behold you in truth, would that you might come in a dream!"

Thus did he lament, his tears ever flowing. Then once more he said to himself, "Patience is the source of wisdom: if we do not command it, what can we achieve, how can we school ourselves to sorrow? If we hope for happiness from God we must accept grief when it comes to us." And he said again, "O heart, however much you may long for death, it is better to endure life and devote yourself to the service of your lady. — But keep hidden the flame that consumes you, do not let it be seen by any: ill does it become a lover to betray the passion within him."

How Avtandil dispatched a request to King Rostevan, and how the vizier gave utterance

Avtandil made ready to go forth early as soon as morning had come. "I must contrive," he said to himself, "to keep my love close concealed." And he begged his heart to be patient, saying, "You must consent to be schooled now!" Then the moon-fair lord mounted and rode off to the abode of the vizier.

Told of his coming, the vizier went out to receive him. "The sun has risen upon my house," he said: "a portent of joy comes this morning!" He advanced to give salutation and addressed the splendid hero with eulogy: a welcome guest, a joyful host.[83]

He held Avtandil's stirrup — full of good will was he, and eager to show hospitality. A carpet of Cathay was stretched out for the lord's feet to tread upon; his presence filled the house with light, as the sun's rays illumine the earth and the heavens. "The scent of the rose," they said, "has been borne down on the wind!"

Avtandil sat down: those who beheld him were all bereft of their wits; they deemed it an honor to swoon for his sake; the whole air was filled with a thousand soft sighings. Then the folk of the household were told to retire; and when they were gone the lord addressed the vizier, saying, "Nothing that is done at the palace is kept from you; in every affair the king accepts gladly your guidance. Now listen to my sorrows' tale, and give me what cure you may.

"The fire that burns in Tariel's breast is consuming me also; parted from my dear friend, I am drawing ever nearer death. He would lay down his life for me; a debt must be paid — one must love a friend generous of soul and ungrudging.

"My heart was caught in a net as soon as I saw him; with him it remains, with him is content of mind. God made him indeed a sun, since he burns the hearts of all near to him! Then Asmat has become a sister to me, more than a sister born.

"Before I departed from him I swore an oath solemnly: 'I will return and strike terror into the hearts of your enemies; I will seek light to dispel the dark shadows within your soul.' It is time for me to be gone; a slow fire burns within me: what I have told you is true; not vain, empty boasting. He is waiting for me, but I cannot set out — and flames are consuming me. I cannot break my pledged word; I, a lover, cannot abandon another love has driven distracted. — And when did a breaker of oaths ever prosper?

"Go to the palace, tell Rostevan for me what I have said to you. My lord vizier, my lord chamberlain, I swear to you by his head that I will stay here no longer unless I am held as a captive; and what will it profit him to keep me a prisoner? — Help me, do not let fires destroy my heart utterly.

"Say: 'Let every tongue that is not without speech give you praise! May God, the source of light, reveal to you the awe you inspire in me! But that lord of the cypress-form has lit a flame in my breast; he won my heart in an instant, I could not have denied it. Parted from him, O King, I cannot live long, assuredly: valiant of heart, he has won my devotion. — Distracted in mind, of what use can I be here? If I can do something to aid him, yours will be the chief glory; if I fail, my heart will be able to rest at least, for I shall not have dishonored the oath that I swore to him.

'Let not your heart be angered or grieved by my going. As for my fate, let that be as God wills. May he prosper you; may he send me, your servant, back here to you. If I do not return — may you reign in great glory, may all of your enemies be brought to the dust!' "

The sun-fair lord continued, "Enough of words! Go to the king with this message before any other has speech with him. Summon up all your courage, beg him with smooth phrases to let me depart from here — and a hundred thousand pieces of red gold shall be paid to you."

The vizier replied with a smile, "Keep your bribe for yourself; that you should have come here to this house of mine is enough for me. . . . Were I to tell the king what I have just heard from you he would heap gifts on me surely — and oh, the delights that accompany worldly goods!

"He would slay me on the spot, by his head, without losing an instant! Your gold would be yours to keep — and for me there would be no more than a hole in the ground! What can a man hold as dear as his life? I cannot and will not speak as you would have me do — and I care not at all who may choose to reproach me! So far will a road go, so far and no further — am I to sacrifice my very life for you? The king would fall upon me, perhaps he would kill me: he would say, 'How can you speak to me in such fashion? Have you lost all understanding, have you taken leave of your senses?' Better to live than to perish, there is no doubt as to that in my mind!

"Even if the king gave you leave to go, how could you hope to get away from the warriors? Would they let you depart, would they say farewell to one who is as a sun to them? Why should they let themselves thus be deceived? If you go from us, our enemies will raise their heads and take vengeance — sparrows will turn into hawks before such a plan can succeed!"

Avtandil wept: "A dagger for my heart, this!" he said through his tears. — "My lord vizier, you can know nothing of love or of friendship, or yet of a sworn oath: if you did, you would not think without my comrade any joy could be mine. The sun[84] — how I know not — has strayed from his course; we must help him; in return he will bring warmth to our day. No one can know as well as I myself what grieves, what delights me. . . . Great, truly, is the sorrow that flows from the words of a man mean of soul!

"What use can the king or his men, pray, make of a madman? My tears flow without ceasing, as from the eyes of one out of his wits. There is no choice but to go — I will not be forsworn; a man is proved by his oath. What can any know of a grief he has not himself suffered from? My lord vizier, how can your cruel heart remain thus unsoftened? Iron would turn to wax were it here in my place. Were all the waters of the Oxus to flow from my eyes,[85] my tears would not match those that my friend sheds in his weeping. If you would ever have me aid your cause, help me now!

"Should the king refuse me leave to depart I will make off with none knowing; I will give my heart to the flames, I will follow its urgings. . . . The king, rest assured, will not make you suffer on my account — or at worst he will banish you. But promise me you will face even torture if need be."

The vizier replied, "Fire burns in my breast now even as in yours; no longer can I look upon your tears; the world seems at an end. Sometimes speech is better than silence, sometimes harm is done with words. No matter if I die, since it will be for your sake — I will speak for you."

When he had said this the vizier rose and went off to the palace: and there, as splendid to look on as the sun, he found the king in his royal robes. He felt afraid and, not daring to give utterance to news sure to anger, stood still in perplexity, thinking thoughts that were full of fear.

"What ails you?" the king asked him, seeing him thus silent and ill at ease. "What news do you bring? Why do you come here with such a dolorous countenance?" "All that I know is that I am most wretched," the vizier answered: "if you kill me when you hear the strange tale I bear, you will do only justly. My brow's gloom gives the measure of my grief: an envoy should be free of fear, but I am filled with dread. — Avtandil

(746-63)

humbly begs leave to depart from here: while he is sundered from his friend, life and the world are as nothing to him."

With quavering tongue he then delivered his message: "But how," he said further, "can you understand by such words as these the case that I saw him in, or how his tears flowed? . . . And now in all righteousness can your wrath break upon me."

When the king had heard all he fell into a mighty rage. "Madman!" he shouted, livid and fearful to behold, striking terror into the hearts of all those about him. "What is this? What other would have spoken thus? — But a bad man always delights in being the first with bad news!

"You have come hastening here to tell me this as though it were something to give us joy! What greater wrong could any have done me, save for a killing by treachery? How could you put your tongue to such a use as this, madman? One so crazed as you is not fit to be a vizier — not fit to be a vizier, not fit to be anything!

"A man should think, should he not, whether foolish chatter may give pain to his lord? — Why did not my ears lose their hearing before these words reached them? If I kill you, mine will be the blood-guilt — so be it!" And then he said further, "Did you not come at his bidding, upon my oath, I would have your head off your shoulders — of that you can be sure! Go, out of my sight, vile wretch — evil, insensate, witless and crazed! Splendid speech, splendid fellow, splendid the deed done!"

Bending down, he seized a chair and hurled it; it was shattered upon the wall. For all that it missed its mark, the force behind it was great indeed. "So you would tell me he is going," he cried, "Avtandil the cypress-formed!" Hot tears seared the pale cheeks of the vizier: not daring to utter one trembling word more, the unhappy wretch fled away — crept off, sick at heart, like a fox. He had arrived like one high at court; now he went off full of fears: such was the injury his tongue had done him. A man can do such hurt to himself as he can to no enemy.

"Assuredly," he said, "I have plumbed the depths of misfortune! How could I be lost in darkness, how could I be so deceived? Oh, for light! Any so bold with his lord must surely suffer as I have, what good can he look for?" Heavy of heart, the miserable vizier made his way homeward: gloomily, with clouded brow, he said to Avtandil, "Small cause have I to thank you — a fine figure I cut at court! Alas, I have brought all my greatness to ruin!"

Although his tears were not yet dry he solicited his bribe now, playing the merry fellow — strange that he could make jokes then, had his heart not been stricken! — "He who does not give what he has promised is soon called to account by authority! As the proverb has it: 'Even in Hell a consideration will settle things.'

"I cannot tell you how the king treated me, what he said to me, what manner of knave, fool and madman he called me. I am quite out of my wits — no longer, indeed, can I reckon myself a man at all! I marvel he did not kill me; God must have given him patience!

"Yet I knew what I was doing; I did not act in mere blindness. I foresaw he would be angry with me — the greater my grief now! Who can avoid the wrath of heaven? . . . But for your sake I would gladly die — and a fig for my suffering!"

"I cannot stay here," Avtandil replied; "it is not to be thought of. When the rose withers, the nightingale comes near to death; he must fly hither and thither in quest of a drop of dew. If he cannot find it, how is he to soothe his heart, what can avail him? Parted from Tariel, I can neither sit still nor lie down to rest: better to roam like the beasts and run wild in their company. The king would have me ride out to give his enemies battle! Better no man at all than one discontented . . . . In spite of his anger, I will approach him once more; surely he will yet understand the fires that consume my heart. But if he still will not grant what I ask I will make off by stealth, in despair. If I die — let my inheritance crumble to ruin!"

After their talk the vizier ordered a banquet of fitting magnificence and played the host, bestowing fine gifts upon the fair lord and lavishing presents too upon all, old and young alike, who were in the company. They made an end at length and Avtandil took his leave: it was as though the sun had gone down below the horizon then!

Generous and ever true to his word, the sun-fair, the cypress-formed, gathered together a hundred thousand pieces of gold, three hundred lengths of satin and sixty rubies rich and rare in their color: then he dispatched a man with all this wealth to

(763-80)

the vizier. He sent too this message: "How could I give you all that you deserve, with what could I discharge the debt that I owe to you? But if I am spared I will be ready to lay down my life for you, I will serve you with faith as your slave: in equal measure I will repay love with love."

How can I sing fitly the praises of the noble-hearted lord without rival? An act such as this was in full accord with his nature. Thus should one help another, even to the uttermost: when a man is in straits, then has he need of brother and kinsman.

How Avtandil talked with Shermadin

The sun-fair hero, Avtandil the radiant, spoke to Shermadin, saying, "This is a day of hope, and has brought joy to my heart; now you can give proof of the devotion you feel for me." (May those who read and listen give their story good heed!) And he went on, "Rostevan will not give me leave to go; not a word would he hear on the matter. He does not understand what afflicts me, or who it is that I live for. Life is not life to me, at home or abroad, without Tariel. . . . Then, when did unrighteousness fail to bring down God's punishment?

"I am resolved not to forsake him; every breaker of oaths offends God. While we are parted my heart weeps, sighs, groans and trembles; grown wild and savage, it shuns all of humankind.

"Three ways does a man have of giving proof of his friendship: by longing to be with his comrade, fretting when distance divides them; by ungrudging bestowal of gifts, unwearied heaping of presents; by care and assistance, help in the hour of need.

"But to the purpose: to find healing for this bruised heart I must now steal away. Listen to what I have to ask of you before I depart from here; keep in your remembrance clearly all that I tell you.

"Be ready to serve the king, first; let your valor and worth shine forth. Watch over my domain, with command of my warriors; show the same zeal in service as you have hitherto; hold my enemies back beyond the bounds of the march-lands; let your strength never falter; be generous of hand to the loyal, but bring the false to destruction. If I return, your due will be paid to you richly; service to a master can never go un-requited."

Hot tears burst from Shermadin's eyes when he heard this. "I am not afraid of being left alone here, but what shall I do?" he said. "Darkness will fall on my heart when you are gone from me! Take me with you as a servant, and I will do whatever you want of me.

"Who was ever known to journey so far through foreign lands all alone? Who ever heard of a liegeman not at his lord's side in a time of sore trouble? What shall I do here in my dis-honor when you have thus fled away — am I only to think of you?"

"However many the tears you shed," Avtandil replied, "you cannot come with me. I do not doubt your devotion, but it cannot be; Fate is working against me. To what other could I entrust my domain; what man, save you, could take my place? Calm your heart and believe my words: take you with me I cannot! I am a lover, and must go alone on my distracted way: he who sheds tears of blood must travel without a companion. Questings are the lot of lovers, they cannot grow old in idleness. Such is the way of the world; of that you can be assured.

"Think of me fondly when I am gone. — I have no fear of foes, I shall be my own servant. A brave man should keep his heart up, should not give way to gloom in times of trial. . . . For him who does not set his face against dishonor I have only scorn. I am not one to harvest this world's over-ripe cucumbers; joyfully would I lay down my life for a friend. I have said fare-well to my sun-fair lady, and she has approved my departure; why then should I linger? If I can leave *her*, can I not leave my home?

"I will give you a testament for the eyes of King Rostevan, and in it I will beg him to treat you in a manner befitting my liegeman. — Do not kill yourself, do not do Satan's work, if I perish; but let the flood-gates give then of their tears."

How Avtandil wrote a testament for the eyes of King Rostevan

Avtandil sat down to write his testament; well might its words rouse pity! — "O King, I have fled away to return to the friend whom I cannot abandon, from whom I cannot endure to be parted, for whose sake fires burn in my breast. Forgive me and, even as God is, be merciful.

"I know that in the end your displeasure must pass away; a wise man will never forsake a comrade he holds dear. I will venture to cite one of the precepts of Plato: 'Falseness and duplicity do injury first to the body and then to the soul.'[86] Falseness is the source of all ills, indeed — how can I forsake the friend who is more than a brother to me? If I will not act, how can the wisdom of the philosophers, the knowledge that should unite us with the Heavenly Harmony, avail me?

"You will have read how the Apostles write of love; how they speak of it; how they give it praise. Learn this and mark it: 'By love are we exalted!' Thus, like a sounding bell, their message comes.[87] But if *you* have no faith in it, how will simple men give belief?

"He who created me, who gave me power to vanquish foes, who is Might Invisible, the aid of every earthly being, who has fixed creation's bounds, who reigns as God till everlasting — he can in an instant change a hundred into one and one into a hundred. Everything in this world comes to pass as he wills it. . . . The violet fades, the rose withers, if it cannot gaze upon the sun: the eye longs always to behold what is fair. Denied my comrade's companionship, how could I endure to live longer?

"Great though your anger be, let my disobedience have pardon: I was a captive, I could not obey your commands. Only by going forth were the flames in my breast to be quenched. It matters nothing to me where I am if I can have what my heart desires.

"Sorrow will avail nothing, tears will not help you; what heaven has ordained cannot be avoided; it is the part of a brave man to endure grief uncomplainingly; no creature that breathes can thwart the purpose of Providence.

"Let God's will be done: when I return, may my heart be in ashes no longer; may I find you happy and prospering here in all splendor. For me there will be glory and riches enough in what I have done for my friend.

"O King, no man will censure my resolve! O King, can then

my going cause you grief? I cannot play the coward, break the word I have sworn — shamed should I be when I met him face to face in eternity.

"Ill can never come from our care for a friend; falsehood I hold in scorn, with dishonor and treachery; I must keep my faith with that prince, with the sun-fair one. What is baser than a warrior slow to set forth? Miserable indeed is the wretch who, face contorted with terror, fearful of death, will shrink back in battle! In what way is a coward of more worth than a weaving-woman? Better to win glory than all else beside.

"Death is not to be kept back by a narrow road, nor yet by a rocky; it brings all to a level, the weak and the strong. The earth receives in the end boys together with greybeards; better a glorious death than a life without honor!

"O King, I scarce dare address words such as these to you. . . . Mistaken, mistaken is the man who does not look for death every instant; the stroke which cuts all to one measure falls by day and by night. . . . If I do not return, be assured I have found a grave before due time.

"If Fate, the destroyer of all, cuts short this life of mine I shall die a stranger in a strange land, with no parent to weep for me, no friend to give me a shroud. Let your heart show its mercy then, let it pity me!

"I am possessed of wealth that is boundless, beyond any man's reckoning. Give my treasure to the poor, let my slaves have their liberty. Let every orphan and beggar have riches, that they may think of me, remember me, bless me. With what is not found worthy of a place in your treasury, build bridges and make provision for the shelter of travelers. Do not be sparing with the wealth that belonged to me: none but you can quench the fires that burn in my breast.

"No more will you hear from me; I commit myself to your mercy. In this letter I tell you the truth without flattery. The devil's lures will not prevail; mine will be the victory. Forgive me and pray for me — for what can be got from a dead man?

"Shermadin, my most trusted servant, I commend, O King, to your favor: this year has brought to him more than his share of grief. Show him such kindness as he has always received from me, that blood-mingled tears may not flow from his eyes.

(797-814)

"My testament, written by my own hand, now reaches its ending. My dear lord, I am gone from you, and my heart is distracted. Do not grieve for my sake, do not wear garb of mourning. — May your power strike terror always into the hearts of your enemies!"

When Avtandil had done he put the testament into Shermadin's hands. "Give this to the king," he said, "choosing the moment with judgement; there is no one like you to discharge any duty." With that he embraced him, and shed blood-colored tears.

How Avtandil prayed

Avtandil prayed, saying: "Great God, ruler of earth and of heaven, thou who sometimes chastisest, sometimes sendest blessings; unknowable, ineffable lord of righteousness — give me patience in my longings, master of passions!

"God, God, to thee who rulest the skies and lower realms alike I pray. Thou hast created love and decreed its law: Fate has severed me from my sun-fair lady, the peerless one; do not uproot the flower of love she has planted!

"God, merciful God, none have I save thee to lean on. Aid me, I beseech thee, on my road, however long it be. Protect me from the might of foes, the ocean's storms, the evil of the night:[88] if I survive I will serve you, I will offer up sacrifice."

His prayer ended, he mounted and slipped unseen through the gates. Then he sent Shermadin back: the unhappy wretch wept as he beat his breast; his blood flowed away to wear channels deep in the rocks. What can bring joy to a vassal when his lord has gone from him!

How King Rostevan learned of Avtandil's flight

Now to begin another chapter; I will follow the hero on his journey. — Such was Rostevan's wrath that he gave that day no audience: the next morning he rose at dawn, his face still aflame with rage, and summoned his vizier: they brought him in, his face pale with fear.

"I cannot well remember what you told me yesterday," Rostevan said to him when, with a hangdog look, he entered the hall: "you roused in me an anger that took long to calm: much did I abuse you — you who are close to me! Can you recall why you were treated so hardly? Truly do the wise say: 'Wrath is a net for sorrows!' One should never act thus, but always reflect and consider. Now once again put the matter before me."

The vizier then repeated his words of the day before: and when he had heard him Rostevan replied very curtly, "I am Levi the Jew[89] if I do not think you have taken leave of your senses! No more of this, if you would hope for forgiveness!"

The vizier went now to look for Avtandil the crystal-fair, but he could not find him: there were only weeping servants to tell of the flight. "I dare not return to the palace," he said; "too well do I remember yesterday. Let him who will raise his voice — sorely do I rue words that have already been spoken!"

When the vizier failed to return, the king sent a messenger on the same errand after him. The man learned what had happened, but did not dare to go back: no one, indeed, had the courage to tell of the flight. But suspicion entered the king's mind, and great did his grief grow. "He must have stolen away," he said; "he who vanquishes hundreds unaided!"

Head bent, he brooded; heavy was he of heart then. At length, looking up with a sigh, he gave an attendant this order: "Go and summon the wretch; he must tell me the truth now!"

The vizier returned, pale and ready to watch his words carefully: when he entered the hall he was deep in dejection. The king asked him, "Has the sun-fair one then departed and gone from me; is he as inconstant as the moon in its wanderings?" The vizier told him all, how Avtandil had fled away: "The sun shines upon us no longer; the fine days are past and gone."

When the king heard this a great cry broke from him, and he made lamentation. "Alas, my son," he said, "no more can these unhappy eyes look on you!" He rent his cheeks and tore his beard — amazed were all who beheld him. "Where have you gone," the words came, "where have you taken the light of your countenance? With your own self for companion you cannot know loneliness — but what shall I do, my son? Now I have woe for a dwelling. You have left me, abandoned me, whose heart, alas, longs for you! Till you return I shall live in torment the tongue cannot tell of! No more shall I see you coming back gay from the hunt; no more shall I see you, full of grace and jewel-fair, after a ball-game; no more will your voice give delight to my ear. Without you, what do I care for my throne or my palace?

"However far you may go, you will not perish from hunger; arrows and bow will win you your sustenance. . . . Perhaps God in his mercy will lighten your load of grief — but if I die, who will there be, my dear son, to weep over me?"

There was noise now and stir; a crowd gathered; the great men of the court tore their beards, rent their cheeks and beat their breasts so that the air was all filled with the sound. "The sun is gone from the sky!" they said. "This cursed day has brought darkness upon us!"

When the king saw his lords he said, weeping and groaning, "Our sun has withdrawn his rays now — how have we offended? What wrong have we done him, why has he thus forsaken, abandoned us? Who could command the host for us as he did?"

They all wept and lamented; then, when at last they had regained their tranquillity, the king said, "I would know whether he set out alone, or whether he has taken any to attend upon him." — Shermadin appeared, shamefaced and fearful: weeping and sick at heart, he proffered the testament. "I found this," he said, "the work of his hand, in his chamber; his servants were standing by, shedding tears and tearing their beards and their hair.[90] He has fled away, all alone, with never a follower, young or old. It will be only just if you kill me; I do not deserve to live."

When the testament had been read through they wept again for a long time. And then the king said, "Let my warriors put aside all their bravery; let the crippled, the orphans and the widows say prayers for him; let us make supplication to God, that he may give him paths of peace!"

How Avtandil set out to rejoin Tariel

When she is far from the sun, the moon shines with brightness; but when she draws near, his rays burn her, and she must

needs retire. Denied the sun, the rose withers and loses its color.
. . . By severance from the loved one old wounds are reopened.

Now I will tell how Avtandil went forth bitterly weeping;
many indeed were his tears. He kept turning round, praying
that a gleam of his sun-fair lady's beauty might reach him: he
could not force his eyes to look down the road he was going;
if he tried to remove his gaze, he would swoon. Near to faint-
ing was he, and bereft of the power of speech; but tears flowed
from his eyes like the waters of the Tigris.[91] Ever and anon
he would strive to steel himself to endure. . . . When he rode
forward, he had no notion where his horse might be taking him.

"My own," he said, "accursed were he who could know peace
when he was far from you! My thoughts remain with you, may
it be given to my heart to return! My eyes long to look on you,
eyes full of weeping — the lover should never weaken in his
service to love!

"What can I do while we are parted, in what can I look for
joy? I would kill myself did I not fear it would grieve you,
that the news of my death might cause sadness: I can but live
and shed tears."

He wept, then went on thus: "My heart has been pierced by
ten lances of meancholy: my lady's lashes, an army of Indians,[92]
are seeking to slay me. Her jet eyes lend her beauty, but why
must they take my life? Her hair, lips, teeth, eyes and eye-
brows — they all of them torture me!"

He said further, "O sun, image of him who gives light even
as the darkness, of him who is one in unity from everlasting to
everlasting, and whom the heavenly bodies obey even to the
smallest particle of time — let not evil fortune, I beseech you,
keep me and my lady parted! You whom the sages of old called
the image of God, help me, for I am held captive by fetters of
iron! In my quest for my lady's crystal and ruby hues, the coral
and jet have left my own countenance! Her presence once
brought to me pain past enduring; now to be sundered from
her is a torment!"

Consumed like a taper in the flame, thus did he make his
lament: fearful of being late, he rode hard now upon his way.
When night fell he found solace in the coming of the stars, for
they spoke of his lady. Rejoicing in heart, he looked up and ad-

dressed them: to the moon he said, "Declare in the name of God that it is you who give the plague of love to lovers, and that yours too is the balm that helps in the bearing of it. — Let me, I beseech you, look once more on her whose face is even as fair as yours."

Night brought joy, day torture; and he longed for the sunset. When he saw a stream he would dismount to gaze upon the rippling waters and swell them with rills of blood from the lake of his tears:[93] then he would hasten once more upon his way. The cypress-fair hero would weep and lament in his solitude: he killed a goat on a rock-slope, roasted and ate it; then rode onward, fair as the sun and valiant of heart. "My cheeks," he said, "have lost their roses; they have, alas, turned to violet!"

I cannot write down here all the words that he uttered — tell what he said and how he lamented, or evoke his great eloquence: sometimes the snow on his cheek was turned rose-red by his nails. . . . Then the cave came into view at length; and he rode up towards the entrance, rejoicing.

Asmat came to meet him as soon as she saw him: her tears were falling, her heart was overflowing with joy. Avtandil dismounted, embraced her and spoke to her: happy indeed is the moment of a friend's long-looked-for arrival!

Avtandil asked the maiden, "Where is the prince, and how is he?" Shedding tears of blood that flowed to swell the seas, she replied, "After your going he too departed, for he could not endure to remain here in the cave. That is all that I know; I have seen nothing, heard nothing since."

Avtandil grieved as though his heart had been pierced by a lance. "In this he did wrong, dear sister!" he said. "How could he break his oath? I have not been false to him, how could he betray trust? If he could not keep troth, why did he make a promise? Having given his word, why has he deceived me? I do not care a fig for the world when we are parted — how could *he* forget *me*? . . . Why did I leave him? — Could he not have had patience, what was it that troubled him? How could he dishonor the faith he had plighted? — But why should I marvel at a blow dealt by Fate!"

The maiden said, "I do not blame you for the turmoil that troubles your spirit, but listen to the truth, and believe that I speak without guile. Does a man not need a heart to keep faith, to make good his promises? Tariel's heart is no more, and he waits for the close of his days. Heart, thought and understanding depend one on another; when the heart goes, the others must follow soon after. A man bereft of his heart is no longer to be accounted a true man; he is one cut off from his fellows. — You were not here, you know nothing of the fires that consumed him. You can justly complain because your brother is gone, but how can I speak of his plight to a man in his senses? My tongue would fail, my aching heart would ache yet more cruelly. This do I believe; for, born to misery, I was here as a witness.

"No one has ever heard of such tortures as he has known; not men only, the very stones would crumble beneath them. The tears that have poured from his eyes would fill up the bed of the Tigris! — Yet you are right: who cannot be wise in another man's battle?

"As he was going forth, burning in the fires of his sorrows, I asked him, 'What is Avtandil to do when he comes again? I beg you to tell me, for I am now as a sister to him.' 'Let him seek for me,' he replied; 'I yearn for his coming. I will not depart from this region; I will not break my promise; I will not be false to my word; I will not dishonor my oath. I will wait for the appointed time, though my tears flow in rivers. If he finds me dead, let him mourn, let him bury me: if I am alive, let him marvel; he will have good cause so to do.'

"For me the sun has gone off from the mountain; I must water the plains with my tears all alone, tortured in madness by groaning that never ends. Death has forgotten me — thus am I dealt with by Fate!

"In China this saying, a true one, stands carved in stone: *His own enemy he who will not seek for a friend.*[94] Now is he turned to saffron's hue who once shamed rose and violet. — If you would find him, go and look for him; do what you ought to do."

"You are right to reprove me," Avtandil replied, "for the words of complaint that I uttered — but think what I, a captive of love, have done for my comrade! Like a stag seeking water I have fled from my home to find him; all my thoughts were upon him. I have left my lady, her whose face is as crystal and

(847-64)

rubies, whose teeth are like pearls. I could not stay with her, for I could neither make her happy nor myself know any joy. I have angered God's equal[95] by stealing off secretly; in return for his favor I have troubled his heart. I have broken faith with my lord, king by the grace of God, with him who was loving, gracious, even as a father to me, who was like a sky snowing mercies. I forgot all and made away; and since I have wronged him I can look for nothing from God.

"All this is because of Tariel and no other, dear sister. For my part, I have kept my word, riding by day and by night. Now he is gone, he for whom fires burn in my breast — and here I sit, wearied to no purpose, weeping and desolate.

"Dear sister, no time is there now for more talk: I will not fret over what is past, I will honor the teaching of the sages. I will go forth and look for him; I will find him or meet an early death: if Fate has ordained this for me, what complaint can I make to God?"

Avtandil made an end and then rode off weeping; down from the cave he went, across the stream, through the reeds and out on to the plain. The keen wind froze his cheek, the rose-fair, the ruby-fair: he reproached Fate — "Why," he said, "have you brought this woe upon me?"

"O God," he said then, "in what have I sinned against you, the Lord, the All-Seeing? Why have you parted me from my friend, why have you visited this fate upon me? One thinking ever of two,[96] my plight is most parlous. If death comes I will not complain — let my blood be on my own head!

"My dear friend has struck me with a rose-spray and wounded me deep in the heart: he has not kept the oath that I have made good. If you sever us, Fate, all joy is past for me; any other would be hateful in my eyes as a comrade."

He continued, "I wonder that a man of good understanding can yield weakly to sorrow; how will it help him to shed torrents of tears when he is afflicted in spirit? Rather should one take thought and decide on the best course. — I must look for that sun-fair lord, for him who has the form of a reed."

And so, shedding tears, he set out on his search. Shouting and calling, he cast about, resting neither by night nor by day. Three days passed away: many a reed-bed, forest, plain and ravine did he see; but he could not find his friend or learn anything of him. And deep was his melancholy.

"O God," he said, "in what have I sinned against you, how have I roused you to anger? Why have you brought this evil fate upon me, why have you inflicted such suffering? Judge me, O Judge, and give ear to my prayer: shorten my days and turn my woes into joy!"

How Avtandil found Tariel lying in a swoon

Thus did Avtandil lament as, pale with weeping, he rode along: at last, looking out from a hill-top over a plain filled with sunshine and shadow, he descried a black horse trailing its reins on the ground by a reed-bed. "That must surely be he!" he said. At the sight his heart bounded and was filled with a radiance: joy flooded in on his melancholy — a joy as great as a thousand! His cheek's rose reddened; yet more fair became his crystal-bright countenance; the jet of his eyes shone. His eyes fixed on the horse, he galloped down like a whirlwind.

But when he beheld his friend, he fell into the grip of fear. Tariel was lying near to death, his face torn, his collar rent, his head covered with wounds. Sense was gone; he had stepped beyond the bounds of this world. On the one hand lay a slaughtered lion, with beside it a blood-stained sword; on the other a panther that had been dashed to its death on the ground.[97] Tears gushed from his eyes as though from a fountain; the flames of a fire were consuming his heart. Understanding had fled, he could not even open his eyes; he was near to death, he had reached the uttermost bounds of endurance. Avtandil called him by name to arouse him, but failed to: forward he hastened, full of fears for his brother.

He wiped away Tariel's tears and dried his eyes with his sleeve; he sat down beside him and called him by name once again. "Do you not know me, Avtandil," he cried — "I have left hearth and home for you!" But Tariel did not hear him; his eyes were still quite closed, he was wholly bereft of his senses.

Truly, all happened even as it is told here. . . . When Avtandil had wiped away his tears and brought him to himself a little,

Tariel knew him, kissed him and embraced him like a brother. — Never, by the living God, was there mortal man to compare with those two!

Tariel said, "Brother, I have not been false to you, I have honored the oath that I swore. I have looked on you again, with my soul still in my body; thus have I kept faith. Now leave me to weep and beat my breast until death comes. . . . But I beg you to give me burial, that beasts may not eat me."

"What is this?" Avtandil replied. "Why have you surrendered yourself thus to sin? Who has not been a lover, who has not been consumed in the furnace of longing? But which among humankind has ever acted like you? Why have you fallen into Satan's clutches, why would you destroy yourself?

"Remember, if you are wise, that all the sages are agreed upon this; that a man should bear himself like a man, and weep as seldom as may be.[98] In grief we should strive to show the strength of a wall of stone; it is the workings of their own minds that bring sorrow to mortals.

"You have a good understanding, but do not let the sayings of the wise give you guidance. Shedding tears on the plain, consorting with the beasts of the field — what can this lead to? Turning your back on the world will not win you your lady; why bind up a head that is whole, why reopen your wound?[99]

"Who has not been a lover, who has not burned in the furnace, who has not suffered, who has not swooned away? What, tell me, is there that is strange in your lot — why has your spirit fled? Do you not know that the rose without a thorn has never been picked yet by any?

"They said to the rose, 'Who made you so fair? — Strange that you should bear thorns and be won only with pain!' 'The bitter leads to the sweet,' it answered; 'there is virtue in rarity; beauty, made common, has not the worth of a fig.' Since the rose, which has no soul and is but the thing of a day, speaks in such fashion, who can hope to harvest joy without struggle and sorrow? Who ever heard of devil's work without any harm in it? Why would you complain of Fate, what has it done that is strange?

"Listen to what I advise: mount now and ride quietly. Do not heed your heart's promptings; do what you ought, and not what you would. If this were not for the best I would not press it upon you — I speak in all frankness!"

"Brother," replied Tariel, "what can I say to you? I have lost the use of my tongue; I am crazed; for me your words carry no meaning. — Do you think then that my torture is no such great thing to bear? But now I am near to death, the hour of joy is at hand for me.

"The prayer of a dying man — the rest will be silence: may lovers parted on earth be reunited hereafter; may we see each other again, may we once more find joy. — Come, friends, put me in my grave and heap earth upon me.

"How can a lover forsake and abandon the loved one? I shall go to my lady in gladness; she will come likewise to meet me. I to her, she to me; she will weep, and make the tears flow too from my eyes. — Ask a hundred for counsel, but be ruled by your heart, whatever any advise.

"Give ear to what I have resolved; it is truth that I speak. Death is close upon me; leave me; only a short time remains now. What can you do if I die? If I live, can you guide my madness? . . . I am taking leave of this mortal frame to join the ranks of the spirits.

"I have not understood your words, nor have I time to give ear to them: death has drawn near my distraction, life will last but a moment more. My existence is now utterly hateful; I will go to that earth which is soaked with my tears.

" 'The wise!' — Who is wise, what is wise? Can a madman act wisely? If my mind were not darkened such talk would do well enough. But the rose cannot live without the sun, it begins to fade if denied it. You plague me — I have no time — leave me — I will hear no more."

Avtandil spoke again, trying every means of persuasion. "What good will dying do?" he said. "Hold back — this is the wrong course — do not be your own enemy!" But he was unable to move him; his words availed nothing. Then at length he said, "It seems that my tongue has spoken in vain, since you will not attend to me: I will weary you no longer. Die if you must; let your cheek's rose, already withering, shrivel up utterly. One thing only do I beg." — Here the hot tears came. — "I have left her whose lashes, dusky as a host of Indians, border with a hedge of jet her cheeks' rose and crystal. In haste did I come away, without any dallying; the king could not hold me with his fatherly words. Now you repulse and reject me — there is no joy remaining. But there is one thing you must grant me, do not send me off desolate: mount once more and let me see you, dear friend, in the saddle. It may be that then my bitter grief will go from me. After that I will leave you, you shall have your desire."

Eight times did he implore Tariel to put his foot in the stirrup; he knew that despair would fall away from his mind as he rode, his body would sway like a reed, his jet-lashed eyes open wide. Then at last he won consent; the sighs and moans ceased, to his joy; and in a steady voice Tariel said, "I will mount; bring my horse to me!" Avtandil fetched it and gently, unhurriedly, helped his friend into the saddle; then he took him out on to the open plain, Tariel's graceful form swaying from side to side. They rode on for some time, and the motion brought benefit.

Avtandil entertained his friend with agreeable converse, moving in speech lips that were the color of coral; old ears might have grown young again could they have heard him! Banishing Tariel's melancholy, he schooled him to patience.

When Avtandil, healer of grief, became aware of the mending, his rose-fair countenance was illumined by a joy beyond words: a physician to clear the sick mind of its darkness, he spoke words of wisdom to him who had so lately been raving.

After some talk had passed between them Avtandil said straightly, "Listen, and then tell me the truth of the matter: this bracelet that she who dealt you your wounds gave you[100] — how much do you treasure it, how much do you prize it? Answer me that; I shall then be content."

Tariel replied, "How is the value of a thing beyond price to be measured? It is my life; and it is, too, the giver of sorrow. It is dearer than all the world, than earth, water or tree. — But words that offend are more bitter than vinegar!"

"That," Avtandil said, "is the answer I looked for; now it has been given, I will speak to your plainly. — It were better by far to lose this bracelet than Asmat! You have chosen an ill course that I cannot commend. This gaud that you wear is a thing of gold only — smith's work of yesterday, without speech, understanding or soul: yet you would leave Asmat — oh, there was fine judgement! She was your lady's companion and became like a sister to you; she was your link with your loved one; you *called* her your sister; she contrived your meeting with the princess; she was worthy of the trust that you placed in her; she was your lady's companion from childhood; she gave all her devotion. And now you would forsake her, will not even see her — oh, this is judgement indeed!"

"What you say is most just and true," Tariel answered. "Asmat thinks of Nestan, and sees me in my madness — her lot is most pitiful! I thought death was upon me, but you have returned in time to quench the fire in my breast. Now, since I am still alive, let us go back to the maiden, although my wits are still wandering."

Avtandil agreed, and the two set off: truly, to praise them according to their deserts is beyond any powers of mine! Their teeth were like pearls, their lips like the opened rose. . . . The very serpent will be charmed from its lair by words used with skill!

"I will serve you with mind, heart and soul," said Avtandil; "but do you take a different way, do not reopen your wounds. If you will not follow the teaching of the wise, learning profits you not at all; of what value is hidden treasure if you do not make use of it?[101] Grief will not help you, sorrow is fruitless. Do you not know that no man dies until Providence so decrees? Three sunless days will not wither the rose. — Good fortune, hard striving — and success will be yours, if God wills it so!"

"Your words," Tariel replied, "are worth the whole world to me. The good counsellor is loved well by the man of sense, although the fool's heart is troubled by him. But what shall I do, how can I stand firm against the griefs that come crowding in? Strange if you, suffering the same woes, have nothing but blame for me! Wax may be set alight, for it and the heat of fire have an affinity. With water the case is otherwise; a taper is quenched if it falls in. A man will be touched by another's woes when he endures the same sorrows; well should you understand the pain in my heart!"

(898-913)

How Tariel told of the killing of the lion and the panther

"I will tell you of all that has happened to me; you can judge in your heart's wisdom then. — I fretted, waiting for your return, and at last, unable to bear the cave any longer, I made up my mind to ride out on to the plain. After I had passed through those reeds I made up the hillside; and then I saw a lion and a panther meet, come together. They were like lovers, and within me my heart rejoiced as I looked at them. But what they did to each other filled me with horror, astounded me!

"They seemed an enamored pair as they came towards me together, and the sight of them soothed the fires that burned in my breast. But then they turned on each other and fought, struggled fiercely. The panther turned and fled soon, and the lion pursued it — sorely displeased was I!

"They played gaily together at first, then closed in cruel combat; each dealt blows with its paws, caring nothing for death. The panther lost heart, as the way is with womankind: and, mad in its fury, the lion went after it.

"The lion moved me to anger: 'Shame!' I cried. 'Are you out of your senses? Why are you treating your lady thus cruelly? The deed of a felon, this!' Then I charged with my sword drawn and freed it from this world's sorrows, struck it dead with a head-blow.

"Throwing away my sword, I leaped from my horse and caught up the panther — I longed to kiss it for the sake of her who kindled fires in my breast.[1] But it tore at me with its claws, roaring, so that the blood ran. This was over-much to endure; filled with rage, I did it to death too. — Try as I might, I could not soothe it; and in the end, seized with fury, I raised it above my head and dashed it to the ground so that its bones were broken in pieces. Then I thought of the day there had been unkindness between me and my lady — my soul did not burst forth at that hour; why do you wonder I now weep!

"Brother, I have told you of the woes I have suffered. I am not for this world; how can you marvel to find me thus? I am parted from life, but death itself does not want me." And then, his tale ended, the young lord sighed and shed tears.

For a space Avtandil wept with him; and then he said, "Take courage and hold to life, do not rend your heart utterly! God will have mercy, although sorrow has thus fastened upon you: had it been his design that you and your lady should be for ever apart, he would not have had you meet at the outset. Fate pursues the lover and makes his life bitter, but to him who endures affliction it gives joy in the end. A thing grievous indeed is love: it brings us near to death, it renders mad the instructed, and it schools the simple."

How Tariel and Avtandil returned to the cave and found Asmat

After they had wept for a time they continued on their way to the cave. Great indeed was the joy of Asmat when she beheld them; shedding tears that wore channels in the rocks, she came forward. There were kisses and tears, and they exchanged news again eagerly.

"O God," Asmat said, "thou whom the tongues of men cannot speak of, thou art the fullness of all, thou fillest us with light like the sun's. How can I magnify thee, what can I say — thou art not to be praised by the mind! To thee be glory, for thou hast not condemned me to die of the tears I have shed for them!"

"Sister, herein lies the cause of my weeping," said Tariel. "Fate first gives us laughter and then makes us pay with our tears for it — an old rule of the world, that; no new discovery! . . . Death would be joy to me, were it not that I pity you.

"What sane man, parched with thirst, would pour water away? Truly, I marvel that I am soaked thus with tears! I am dying, panting for the spring, while these waters flow without ceasing! Alas for the lips' unfolded rose, alas for the teeth that shone once like pearls!"

The thoughts of Avtandil too turned to his lady, the sun-fair. "O my own," he said, "how can I live longer without you? When we are parted my life is but wretchedness. Who can tell you how I suffer, how fierce is the fire in my breast? Without the orb of day, the rose cannot think it will bloom; and what, alas, will be our lot when the sun goes down behind the hill? . . .

(913-30)

But take strength, my heart; turn yourself into rock; you may
see her again, do not yield to an utter despair."

The heroes grew calmer, and silence descended; inward fires
burned them both. Consumed by the same flame, Asmat fol-
lowed them into the cave and in her wonted way spread out
the panther-skin.[2] Tariel and Avtandil sat down then, and
talked as they would.

They roasted some meat and prepared such a meal as they
might: there were not over-many dishes, and they did not have
any bread. Avtandil and Asmat begged Tariel to eat, but he
could not: he spat out what he chewed, swallowing hardly a
dram's weight.

That is a good hour when a man talks at ease with his friend,
listening to what the other says, not letting it go for nothing.
Then will the fires in his breast burn more gently. There is
much comfort in speaking of our woes, when we may.

That night those lions, those heroes, spent as companions;
they talked, and each of them spoke much of his sorrows. Their
words began to flow again with the coming of morning; each
heard the other give his oath for a second time.

Tariel said, "What need for so many words? God will reward
you for what you have done for me. Oath against oath is
enough — these are not like the words of a drunkard! We have
each sworn to cherish the memory of the friend who is far away.
Show me mercy, do not rouse the hottest fires to rage here
within my breast. You cannot quench the flame that consumes
me; it is one never struck from steel. Rather will you yourself
burn in it, such is the law of the world. Go now and return
home, to the side of your sun-fair lady.

"My cure would be hard even for him who created me: dis-
tracted, I roam abroad — let all who hear comprehend! I too
used to bear myself like a man of sense, but now my wits have
clouded to madness, and I am utterly crazed."

"What answer can I give you?" Avtandil replied to him.
"You have spoken like a man well instructed in mind — but how
could the cure of your wound lie beyond the power that is
God's? It is he who makes grow all that is planted and sown.
Would he create two such as you and your lady, not to unite
but to part them, to drive them to madness through the weeping

of endless tears? Misfortune pursues the lover — be in no doubt of this! — but if you do not once more find your lady, let my soul and body be rent apart! What kind of man is he who cannot endure sorrow? Are we to bend under grief? — Enough of such talk! Fear nothing; God is generous, if the world be hard. Learn the lesson I have to teach: the man who will not learn is an ass and no better, I tell you!

"Give heed to my words; here is all that you need to know. I have left my sun-fair lady to come back here to rejoin you. 'Since he has set my heart aflame,' I told her, 'I am good for nothing here; longer I will not stay — what need I say more?' 'I am well content,' she replied; 'you are proving yourself now a true man; I will count your care for your comrade as service received by me.' I came away with her sanction — I was not drunk, not in liquor! What answer could I make to her 'Why have you slunk back like a coward?' if I were to return now?

"Enough of this! Listen rather to what I am now going to say to you: a difficult task demands clear understanding; the rose that is denied the sun, that cannot bloom, has no hope of continuance. Since you cannot do anything to help yourself I will give you my aid; a brother must act like a brother. Live where you choose, in your accustomed way, meanwhile; with a wise heart or a distracted mind, as you will. Take strength, fair hero of the graceful form, do not die; do not let the fire that burns in your breast wholly consume you.

"This is all that I ask of you: in a year's time from now you shall see me here in this cave again, with news from all parts. As a sign of the time, take the season of roses' abundance; the sight of the blooms in the dog-days[3] will tell you the hour is approaching. If I do not return then, you can be sure I am dead, and no more with the living. Shed tears for a space; thereafter be gay or mourn, as best pleases you.

"It may be that you will be saddened by these words I have just said; I am going from you, and do not know but that my horse will throw me or my ship founder. Yet I cannot keep silent, I am not as the dumb beasts. . . . I do not know what may be designed for me by God, or by the heavens in their eternal revolving."

"I am not going to irk you with long speeches," Tariel answered him: "you would not listen, indeed. If a friend will not follow you, *you* must follow *him* and do what he wills: every hidden thing will come to light in the end. When you have a greater understanding, you will enter into my sorrows. For me it is all one whether I stay here or go away: however my madness may torture me, I will do as you bid me. But what, alas, if my days should reach their ending while you are still far away?"

Their talk finished thus, with promise given against promise, they mounted their horses and rode out to kill game. Then they turned back; tears welled up again from their tearful hearts; the thought of morning and parting added grief now to grief.

Tears are standing in your eyes too, you who are reading these verses! What, alas, is a man to do when his comrade goes from him? To part from a friend is to enter the house of death; he who has never done it cannot know the full bitterness.

When day had broken the friends mounted and took leave of Asmat: tears flowed from the eyes of all three, their cheeks were like banners of scarlet.⁴ As wild in heart themselves as any brutes, the heroes rode off to the wild beasts; down from the cave and away they went, uttering cries, shedding tears. Asmat wept and lamented: "Where, O my lions, are the tongues that should mourn for you? Stars of the heavens, the sun has burned and consumed you! Alas for my weight of woe, alas for life's sufferings!"

The heroes set out and, companions for the day, journeyed down to the sea-coast: when they had reached it they halted. That night they remained together, two sharing one sorrow; and sorely they bewailed the parting now come upon them. — "Enough of tears!" Avtandil at length said to Tariel. — "What caused you to part from Pridon, the man who made a gift of this horse to you? His city is the place to get news of your sun-fair lady: tell me how to reach it, for I have resolved to go to see the hero with whom you exchanged oaths of brotherhood."

Tariel gave directions to set him upon his road, making as clear as he could all that he said to him: "Keep riding eastward and hold close to the sea-shore: if you find him, give him news of me — he will surely ask after his brother." They went off and killed a goat, and dragged it back after them: kindling a fire on the shore, they ate and drank as best they might in their sorrow. Stretched out under a tree, they passed the night side by side. — Curses on this treacherous world, by turns generous and miserly!

At dawn they rose to part; but first they embraced each other. The words that they uttered then would have melted the heart of any man who had heard them! Like waters from a spring did the tears gush forth from their eyes. Long did they stand clasped together there, breast to breast; but, shedding tears, rending their cheeks and tearing their hair, they parted at last. One going upward, the other down, they rode off through trackless rushes. As long as each could see the other, shouts passed between them. Pain contorted their faces: the clouds on their brows made the sun too withdraw into darkness.

How Avtandil set out for Pridon's city

Alas, O world, what would you? Why do you whirl us round — what is it that ails you? All who put their trust in you must weep unceasing tears, even as I do. You uproot, you carry off — whence? Aye, and whither? . . . But the man abandoned by you is not forsaken of God.

Avtandil wept over the parting; his plaint reached the heavens. "Once more," he said, "does my heart's blood come gushing forth! We met at the cost of much sorrow; parting brings us now no less pain. . . . Men are not all alike; one differs much from another."

The beasts of the wild drank their fill from the blood of his tears; he could not quench the flames of the furnace within his breast; the thought of Tinatin made his grief yet more bitter. The light of his countenance, crystal and coral, shone over the rose of his lips. The rose on his cheek was faded; his frame, that fair cypress-branch, was shaken by sobs; his face of crystal and ruby turned livid, turned blue. But bravely he steeled his heart now to contempt of death: "Why should I wonder at darkness," he said, "since I have left you, who are as the sun to me?"

He addressed then the orb of day: "I would compare you to my lady's cheek: there is resemblance between you; you both of you bring light to valley and mountain. I keep my gaze fixed

closely upon you, for the sight of you comforts my madness —
but why have you left my heart all cold and unwarmed? If
lack of one sun in the winter can chill us, how could my heart
escape harm, since I am parted from two?[5] Only a rock has no
feeling and never knows hurt: a knife cannot cure a wound; it
will deepen it, make it more angry."

As he rode he made his plaint thus to the heavens: "O Sun,"
he said, "mightiest of the mighty, thou who exaltest the humble
and givest thrones and good fortune to whomsoever thou wilt,
reunite me with my lady, do not turn day into night!

"Zual,[6] add tear unto tear, sorrow unto sorrow; dye my
heart deepest black, give me over to darkness; let me be loaded
with grief as an ass is charged with its burden — but say to my
lady: 'Do not forsake him; he is yours, and for you he weeps.'

"Mushtar,[7] divine judge, fair judge, come now, I beseech thee,
and mete out true justice. Heart makes complaint against heart;
do not let right be distorted, do not bring thy soul to destruc-
tion! Judge me — my cause is good. . . . Why add yet more
wounds to those that my lady has given me?

"Come, Marikh,[8] let thy spear strike without mercy and
stain me, dye me red with my blood; let thy tongue tell my
lady of all of my torments. Thou knowest what my plight is,
how my heart is parted from joy.

"Come, Aspiroz,[9] lend me aid; she whose pearl-like teeth
are enclosed by lips of a coral hue has burned me in flame. The
fair thou adornest with graces that are like thine own beauty;
but one such as I, alas, thou drivest right out of his wits!

"Otarid,[10] thou and thou alone hast a fate that resembles
mine. She who is my sun makes me turn about and will not let
me go; drawing me to her, she gives me over to burning. Sit
now and write down the tale of my woes. For ink I will give a
lake of tears; my frame, worn thin as a hair,[11] may serve for
a pen.

"Come, Moon, take pity on me, for I have waned and wasted
after thy fashion. She who is as a sun to me first brings me to
the full and then wears me away; at times I am rounded, at
times I am meagre. Tell her of my torments, of my pains, of
my swoonings. Go, bid her not to forsake me; I am hers, and
for her I am dying.

"The stars bear me witness, the Seven[12] confirm my words:

Sun, Otarid, Mushtar and Zual swoon for my sake; Moon, Aspiroz and Marikh have come with their testimony. — Tell her that unquenchable fires are consuming me."

Then he said, "Though my tears flow without ceasing, why should I kill myself? I must have taken the Evil One for a brother assuredly! I know that my enchantress has hair like the raven's wing, but — all can be steadfast in joy — can I endure weight of sorrow? Best to live, if I can (for he thought life was doubtful); perhaps I shall indeed see my sun-fair lady once again, and not mourn for ever." And then, although his tears flowed still, he raised his voice in sweet song — he made the note of the nightingale sound like an owl's hoot!

When they heard his song the beasts all came up to listen. Its sweetness drew the very stones out from the water; all gave ear to it, marvelling. When he shed tears they did likewise; for sad were the songs from the river of his weeping.

All the creatures of the earth were soon thronging to praise him; beasts from the rocks, fishes from the waters, crocodiles from the Nile, birds from the air. Men came too, from India, Arabia and Greece; from the East and from the West; from Russia, Persia, Egypt and the lands of the Franks.[13]

How Avtandil journeyed to Pridon's city

For seventy days Avtandil traveled, shedding tears, along the coast road; then, looking out to sea, he saw a vessel making in to the shore. He waited, and then asked the sailors, "Who are you, I pray you? Whose realm is this, whose voice does it obey?" "You fill us, fair lord, with delight," they replied to him; "greatly do we marvel as we speak these our words of praise. — The Turks' border[14] runs here; beyond it lies Pridon's realm. If we do not swoon, beholding you, we will tell you of him whom we own as lord.

"Nuradin-Pridon is king of our land. A valiant warrior is he, generous of soul, strong of arm and quick to horse: none is there who could do hurt to him, to the sun-fair one. He who is like the morning's rays commands our allegiance."

"Brothers," said Avtandil, "in you I have met with some honest fellows. — I am seeking your king; tell me where I must go. Which way should I follow, when shall I reach him, how long is the road?" Standing there on the shore, the sailors gave him directions. "This," they said, "is the road to Mulghazanzar; there you will find our king, the hero whose arrow flies swiftly, whose sword is sharp in its cutting. Ten days will bring you to the city, lord of the ruby cheek, the cypress-form. But alas, why have you burned us, O stranger, why have you consumed us like fire?"

Avtandil replied, "Much do I wonder, brothers, that I should thus delight your hearts, that the faded winter rose can afford you such pleasure! You should have seen me in my pride, before I was struck by misfortune; I rejoiced then the hearts of all who beheld me!"

The sailors departed, and the hero went forward upon his way: in form like a cypress, he had a heart that was iron. Putting his horse into a gallop, he spoke aloud and chanted to cheer himself: a storm broke from his narcissus-eyes; the tears came down upon his cheeks' crystal like rain.

Eager to do him some service, those he met on the road came up to gaze and admire him; they saw him go with reluctance and found parting hard to bear. They gave him guides for his journey, and they answered his questions.

He drew near Mulghazanzar after a long journey done quickly, and then on a plain he saw a host of warriors engaged in the slaughter of game: formed in a ring round the chace, they were loosing arrows with shouts and mowing the beasts down like corn. He made inquiry concerning this host of a man whom he came upon: "Whose command has caused all this noise and this stir?" The man replied, "That of the lord of Mulghazanzar, King Pridon: he is hunting, and the plain's reedy verges are filled with his warriors."

Rejoicing in heart, Avtandil rode towards the soldiers. Peerless was he in bearing — how can I find words to tell how fair he was to behold then? Those far distant were frozen, those near him were burned as by the rays of the sun. His body had the grace of a reed in its swaying; rapture filled the souls of all those who looked on him.

From the middle of the ring of warriors an eagle rose, soaring. Boldly Avtandil spurred forward, and brought it bleeding to the ground with an arrow. Dismounting, he cut off its wings;[15] and then, calmly and without haste, he got on his horse again.

As soon as they saw him the bowmen ceased shooting and, breaking their ring up, came hastening towards him. Their souls filled with delight, they pressed in and surrounded him; but they did not dare to ask who he was or to say anything to him. The mass of the warriors following after, Avtandil rode off towards Pridon — who, with forty chosen companions of the chase, was on the top of a knoll. Annoyed and puzzled, Pridon sent off a slave, saying, "Go and find out what has come over my warriors, why they have broken their ring, and where they are going, like so many blind men." The slave made his way over to Avtandil with all speed; but when he set eyes on the cypress-formed hero he stood like one bemused, and could not recall what he had to say. Avtandil, however, had no doubt that he came as a messenger: "Take this," he said to him, "to you lord with my humble duty: 'A stranger, a wayfarer from a far country, I come to you on a mission; I am a sworn brother to Tariel.' "

The slave went back with the message. "The sun has surely come among us — he brings light to the day!" he said. "Even the wise, if they saw him, would be bereft of their wits! He sends this: 'I am Tariel's brother, come to find Pridon the glorious.' "

When he heard Tariel's name Pridon's mood changed to joy. His eyes filled and his heart beat faster; his cheek turned pale, like a rose caught by an icy blast; tempests of tears were unloosed from his lashes. Now they advanced to meet and exchange words of greeting and eulogy. Pridon came down in haste from his knoll; when he had looked on Avtandil he said, "This is the sun's very self!" What he had heard from his slave fell far short of the truth, indeed. The two dismounted and, weeping for joy, embraced; they cared nothing for being strangers. Pridon thought that Avtandil was beyond all compare, while Avtandil for his part was delighted with Pridon. Those who beheld them thought the sun was as nothing — such as they were, by heaven, are not to be bought or sold in the bazaar!

Where is the hero to be set beside Pridon? — But none could

(980-97)

deserve greater praise than Avtandil. When they have drawn near the sun we see the planets no longer; a candle gives no light in the day-time, but by night it shines brightly.

They remounted, turned their horses' heads towards Pridon's palace and rode off. An end was put to the hunt and the slaughter of beasts. From all sides the warriors came thronging to gaze on Avtandil: "That such as he could be created!" they said. — "What a wonder!"

"I know that you wish to hear my story," said Avtandil to Pridon; "so I will tell you who I am and where I come from, also how I met with Tariel and how I can call him my brother: for brother he holds me, though indeed I am hardly worthy to be as much as a servant to him. — I am King Rostevan's vassal, a lord bred in Arabia; my name is Avtandil, and I am captain of the host. I come of a great house and was brought up like a king's son. Valiant and proud am I, and none dares to dispute with me.

"One day when the king was out hunting we came upon Tariel: he was weeping — the ground round about him was soaked with his tears. Amazed and astonished, we sent him a summons: he did not come, and — for we knew nothing of the fires in his breast — we were angered at this. In wrath the king called on his attendants to seize him, but Tariel slaughtered them easily — no hard battle that for him! Some had their bones broken, others gave up the ghost: thus did they learn that the moon was not to be turned from its course!

"When the king saw his men worsted his rage grew yet greater; he mounted himself, bold and fearless, and made after the stranger. But Tariel did not stay to meet his sword when he saw this: he gave his horse a loose rein, and in an instant was gone from our sight.

"Search as we would, we could find no tracks, and had to suppose him a demon. The king fell into a melancholy, and would have no drinking or feasting. I had to learn what was the truth of the matter, and slipped away swiftly to search for the stranger lord; hot were the fires that burned then in my breast.

"When I had sought him for three years without even the solace of sleep, I met with certain Cathayans who had suffered wounds at his hands, and these gave me direction. I had speech with him, the rose withered and wan, and he made me welcome and loved me like a son or a brother. He has his abode in caves he won from Divs after much bloodshed; Asmat is his sole companion, no other is with him. Still, without ceasing, the old fire consumes him. Alas for the poor wretch from whom Fate has parted him! A black stone would fitly serve such a one for a pillow!

"Alone with her tears, the maiden sits there in the cave: Tariel goes out hunting, as a lion does for its whelp, and brings her back game for food. Stay in one place he cannot: save for Asmat, he has no desire to look on any of humankind.

"For all that we were strangers, he told me his wondrous tale; he recounted his history and that of his lady. To speak of the woes he has suffered would be beyond my distracted tongue! He is dying for the love of her who is lost to him.

"He is never at rest, but wanders like the moon, riding that horse you gave him, never out of the saddle. He will approach no creature endowed with speech, but shuns all men like a brute beast. Alas for me, who have remembrance of him; alas for me, for his sake distraught!

"Even such a fire as his burns here in my own breast; I shed hot tears, grew mad and distracted, so greatly I pitied him. I resolved to search by sea and land for balm for his spirit; but first I returned home, and there I found the king and his daughter in sorrow. When I sought leave to go forth again the king was angry and troubled in spirit; but, deserting my warriors — bitter were the lamentations they made then — I slipped away, and so put an end to my tears of blood. Now I am casting about this way and that, in quest of a cure for my friend's wounds.

"He told me how you and he had exchanged oaths of brotherhood; and now I have found you, a peerless hero, worthy of highest praise. — Tell me where to look for that sun-fair lady, the joy of those who behold her, source of woe to those denied the sight of her loveliness."

A flame was kindled in Pridon's breast by these words of Avtandil's; the two gave sorrow its utterance in words of great beauty. They sobbed, wept together from the depths of tumultuous hearts; hot tears came rushing from their lashes' dense

(997-1015)

thickets down over the roses that bloomed on their cheeks. Loud too was the lamentation made by the warriors; some tore at their faces and some rent their raiment. Amid the flow of his tears Pridon bewailed the seven years gone by since he and his friend had parted. "Alas," he said, "how false is this world, and how faithless!" And then he lamented, "How can we laud one far beyond the reach of our praise? Sun to us here on earth, you can change the course of the sun in the firmament! Giver of joy and of life to all those who are near you, light of the heavens, you burn and engulf all! Life, since we parted, has always been hateful to me; you never think of me, but I long for your company. You are happy without me, but I know desolation. Life is a desert, denied you, the world but a place of woe." In these words of beauty did he make his lament.

They grew calm and fell silent, and rode off without song. Fair indeed did Avtandil seem to those who beheld him; the inky lakes of his eyes were covered by the jet of his lashes. Presently they entered the city and arrived at the magnificent palace, where all the great officers of state were assembled and richly-clothed slaves stood in perfection of order. Avtandil filled the hearts of all with delight and with rapture.

They went in: great was the gathering there that day. On this hand and on that ten times ten great lords were ranged. Avtandil and Pridon — who could give them their due of praise? — went and sat down together; enamel and jet adorned the crystal and ruby hues of their countenances. A banquet was held then, and the best wine flowed freely. Pridon entertained Avtandil as he would have a kinsman: fine vessels, all new, were brought out for the feasting. A flame seared the hearts of all who looked on Avtandil. That day they ate and drank, quaffing deep of the wine: then when dawn had come Avtandil was led to a bath, brought satins and clad in raiment worth many thousands of dinars. Round his waist they put a girdle of a price beyond reckoning.

Although the loss of time chafed him he stayed there for several days, going out hunting with Pridon and taking part in diversions. No matter the distance, he brought down all the beasts that he shot at; his skill with the bow put every marksman to shame.

He addressed Pridon thus at length: "You must give me your

ear now: parting will be like death to me, a most grievous injury; but, alas, I cannot stay any longer, for a fire burns in my breast that is past all enduring. A long road stretches before me, and I must be gone, for time presses. Well may tears flow from the eyes of the man who must part from you, but I leave here today, for another flame is burning within me: the traveler should be on his guard against lingering. — Now take me to that place on the shore where you saw that lady, the sun-fair."

Pridon replied, "I will not try to hinder you; I know that you cannot stay, that there is another lance which is piercing your heart. Go, God be with you, may your enemies come to destruction! — But what shall I do, tell me, after you have gone from me?

"You must not go unaccompanied; I will provide you with servants, also armor, some bedding, a mule and a horse. If you will not take these, it will surely go hard with you; tears will come coursing down over the rose on your cheek."

He furnished Avtandil with four slaves who were true of heart; a whole suit of armor, with brassards and greaves; sixty pounds of red gold to a full weight; and a magnificent courser with a complete set of trappings. A strong-legged mule was loaded up with the bedding. — When Avtandil set out Pridon mounted to ride with him. Fires burned in Pridon's breast as he thought of their parting, and thus he lamented: "No winter could freeze us if the sun would but stay!"

The news of Avtandil's going plunged all deep into sorrow. Traders in silk and fruitsellers alike, the townsfolk came flocking; the sound of their cries rose aloft, loud as thunder. "The sun," they said, "is about to depart from us; come, let us now give our eyes over to grief!"

Avtandil and Pridon passed out of the city and rode to the shore of the great sea, to the place where Pridon had once beheld the lady who resembled the sun in her beauty. There they shed torrents of blood from the lake of tears, and Pridon told how he had seen the captive, like a star in her loveliness: "The black slaves brought the sun-fair maiden to this spot in their boat — ruby were her lips, white her teeth, black her eyes! I put spurs to my horse, resolved to win her with the strength of my sword-arm; but they saw me while I was still at a distance

(1015-31)

and made haste to escape — their boat moved like a bird, skimming over the water."

Shedding fast-flowing tears, they embraced one another; the fires in their breasts burst once more into flame. They had sworn oaths of unbreakable brotherhood, those two, and like brothers they parted. Pridon turned; Avtandil, the delight of all who beheld him, rode onward.

How Avtandil departed from Pridon's realm to search for Nestan-Darejan, and how he met with a caravan

Fair as the moon at the full, Avtandil rode forward upon his way: the thought of Tinatin gave him strength and sustained him. "Cursed Fate and its treachery," he said, "have, alas, parted us! You have in your keeping the balm for my wound! Truly, my heart, tempered by fire come from three heroes' ardor, has turned as hard as a rock now; the thrusts of three lances would show never a bruise on it. And you are the cause of the world's turning bitter!"

With the four slaves following, he journeyed along by the sea-shore, bent on doing all that in him lay to bring joy back to Tariel. Day and night his tears poured forth to form pools; the whole world seemed to him to be worth no more than a straw. For a hundred days he went onward, seeking news of the sun-fair lady from all the travelers he met with on the coast: then from a hill-top he caught sight of camels laden with merchandise and of a crowd of traders who were standing on the shore, silent, disconsolate. A vast caravan it was, resting there by the sea; cast down were the merchants and troubled in mind, at a loss whether to continue their journey or to stay where they were. Avtandil gave them greeting, and they replied with words of eulogy. "Good merchants, who are you?" he asked; and they began then to talk to him.

The leader of the caravan was one Husam, a man of discernment. He addressed Avtandil with courtesy, praising him and calling down blessings upon him, then said, "Light of the world, you are assuredly come as a comforter: dismount, and we will tell you our story and how things now stand with us." Avtandil got out of the saddle, and then Husam began:

"We are merchants of Baghdad — followers of Muhammad's faith, abstainers from wine — on our way to the city of the king of the Seas[16] to sell our goods: costly are our wares, and we do not deal in mean quantities.

"Here on the shore we found a man lying senseless: we gave him care, and then, when he had got back the use of his tongue, we asked him, 'Who are you, stranger, and what was it that brought you here?' He replied, 'If you put out to sea you will quickly be slaughtered! — Can I be still alive?' And then he went on: 'We set out from Egypt under guard in a caravan and took ship with a cargo of rich merchandise of many sorts. But pirates rammed our vessel, there was killing, and all were lost; how I come to be here passes my understanding.'

"That is why, sun-fair lord, we are standing here in this fashion: if we turn back we shall suffer a loss beyond measuring; if we take to the water they may butcher us, for we are no fighting men. We cannot stay, we cannot go — we are utterly helpless."[17]

"Only those without spirit grieve," said Avtandil; "no good ever comes of it. What is sent down from on high to us may not be avoided. I will answer for your lives, I take them into my care; those who attack you shall feel the weight of my sword."

Joy filled the hearts of the men of the caravan. "Without doubt," they said, "he is a hero of prowess who knows nothing of fears such as those which assail us, and has trust in his strength; we need no longer be anxious." And then they embarked and put out to sea.

With Avtandil, the bold of heart, to lead and protect them, they sailed under kindly skies. Then a pirate-craft, flying a large flag and armed with a ram, came into view; with much yelling and blowing of trumpets it bore down upon them. Terror gripped the merchants at the sight of the vast swarm of armed men, but Avtandil said, "Do not let their sound and fury dismay you! I will either slaughter them all or this day meet my death. Though the armies of the whole earth should come marching against me, I can suffer no harm that is not decreed. If I am fated to die, the spears are now ready for me; no stronghold, no friend, not even a brother can save me: the man who

(1031-48)

understands this is stout of heart, even as I am. — You mer-
chants are cowards and know nothing of fighting: close the
hatches upon you, that you may have shelter from arrows.
You will see me give battle alone, you will see how a hero makes
use of his arms, you will see the blood flow from the wounds
of this pirate-crew!"

Swift as a panther, Avtandil put on his armor, then went and
stood in the prow, holding an iron mace in one hand. Valiant
of heart was he! His beauty vanquished those who beheld him,
as his sword did his enemies.

The pirates drew near to ram, their yells never ceasing; in
the prow Avtandil stood, fearless and calm. He shattered the
ram with a mace-blow — his arm was unfaltering: with the
stroke that he dealt then he saved his own vessel. The pirates,
stricken with terror, tried to escape now, but Avtandil had
leaped on them before they could make away, and was cutting
them down to right and to left; of those with life still in them
there was soon not one unwounded. Like goats did he slaughter
them in his valiance of heart: some he threw down on the deck,
some he hurled into the sea; one on another he flung them,
eight upon nine and nine upon eight. Trying to stifle their
moans, the wounded crawled away to hide among corpses. —
The victory, indeed, was all that his heart could desire. Some
begged him for mercy in the name of religion: he spared them;
all who were not dead of their wounds he made captive. . . .
Truly does the Apostle say: "Love comes out of fear."[18]

O son of Adam, do not make a vaunt of thy strength like a
drunkard! Nothing will it avail without the help of the Lord.
Great trees can be brought down and consumed by a tiny spark;
a stick can cut as clean as a sword if God wills it so.

Great were the treasures that Avtandil found on the pirate-
craft; he brought the two ships alongside each other and called
the merchants of the caravan to him. The heart of Husam was
now filled with rejoicing; he sang the hero's praises like a man
seeing visions.

We should need a choir of a thousand tongues to hymn the
deeds of Avtandil! And not even these could tell how fair he
was to behold after the sea-fight. The merchants cried aloud,
saying, "Thanks, O Lord, be to thee! The sun has shed its rays

on us, dark night has turned into morning." Coming up, they kissed his head, hands, face and feet, and offered unbounded praise to him who deserved it so richly. All who beheld him were lost to reason, wise men and fools alike. — "You have saved us," they said, "from the jaws of disaster!"

Avtandil replied, "Thanks be to God, to him who is the maker of every creature that breathes, by whose celestial power all that passes here below is decreed. By him alone is all done, in the open or secretly. All men must believe; the wise man accepts destiny. It is to the grace of God that you all of you owe your lives. What am I, alas? A poor clod of earth, and no more. What can I do through my own power? — Now I have slaughtered your enemies and made good my promises; and I have won too this ship and the treasure that fills it."

Sweet is the hour of a brave warrior's triumph in battle, when he outshines his comrades, all those who went forth with him! — They bless him, they praise him, they feel humbled before him; and there is maybe some slight hurt to make yet greater the glory.

There and then they went over the pirate-craft: past any reckoning was the treasure contained in it! When they had carried these riches into their own ship they broke up the vessel. Flames made an end then — it was not in their minds to sell the timbers for drachmas!

Husam addressed Avtandil thus on behalf of the merchants: "We know that in ourselves we are helpless; it is in you that our strength lies. All that we have is yours by right, of this there can be no doubt: it is for you to give us for our own what you choose. Thus have we decided, talking among ourselves."

Avtandil gave this reply: "Brothers, it is not long since I told you the truth of the matter. God saw the tears pouring down from your eyes, and he and none other it was who preserved you. What am I — what, alas, have I done for you? And what could I do with whatever you gave me? I have myself and my horse! All the wealth I could want lies stored in my treasure-vaults, I am possessed of the greatest, the most splendid of riches — what could I do with yours? Enough, I am your companion and nothing more: a different concern is mine, a matter of danger.

(1048-65)

"Let each take what he will from this vast treasure I have won; for myself I make no claim. Only one thing do I ask, and it need cause you no alarm: I want to pass myself off as being one of your number. Speak of me as your chief, call me 'our leader': do not let it be known that I am a man of arms nobly born. I, for my part, am going to put on merchant's garb and set myself to play the trader. Do you keep close my secret, by the brotherhood now between us."

Delighted at this, the merchants came up and saluted him then as commander. "This," they said, "is what we had been hoping for; this that you ask of us is what we ourselves would have wished to be. — We will obey in all things this lord whose countenance is as fair as the sun."

Without waste of time they continued their voyage; the weather was fair, and they sailed on with nothing to trouble them. Avtandil delighted them all, they were lavish in their praise of the hero: they bestowed on him pearls that shone as bright as his teeth.

How Avtandil arrived in Gulansharo[19]

And so Avtandil, the fair of form, voyaged across the sea. At length they arrived at a city surrounded by rich gardens filled with wondrous flowers of many colors — how can I picture for you that land and its splendors!

They moored their ship by those gardens with three ropes; then Avtandil donned a cloak and sat down upon a bench. They hired men as stevedores and paid them with drachmas; the hero played the trader and caravan chief to hide his true quality.

Presently the man who tended the garden by which they had landed approached them; with delight he gazed upon Avtandil's countenance, as bright in its beauty as lightning. Avtandil called him over and put probing questions to him: "Who is your master, who are you, and what is the name of the king who rules here? Tell me with care too which goods fetch the best prices, and which ones go cheap." The gardener replied, "In you I behold one as fair as the sun; I will tell you truly all I can, with no lying, crooked words. — This is the kingdom of the Seas; ten months are needed to travel across it. The city is Gulansharo, and it is filled with treasures of the richest and rarest: ships that sail the broad seas bring all manner of splendid things. Melik-Surkhav[20] is our king; he is wealthy and smiled on by Fortune.

"Even greybeards, when they come here, find that their youth is restored to them; there is no end to the drinking, sports, song and diversions; in winter and summer alike we have flowers of many hues in bloom. Our lot is envied by all who know us, by friends and by foes. Nowhere are there richer profits to be won by great merchants; they buy, they sell, they gain, they lose. Within a month wealth may be acquired by a poor man; goods flow in from all quarters; even a beggar after a year here may hold rich stocks in a warehouse.

"I am gardener to Husain, first among the merchants; and I will tell you of the rules he has laid down for observance. This garden you are now in is his, and the first thing traders must do is show him all the finest of the wares they have brought with them. Great merchants, when they arrive here, all go to see him, bestow gifts upon him and show what they have; they may not have their bales opened up in any other place. The choicest of their goods are put aside for the king, and the purchase-money is paid over on the spot, there and then. After that Husain allows them to sell as they please.

"Husain has the duty of receiving strangers of note, such as you, and of ensuring their fit entertainment. Just now he is not here, so I need say no more of him; but it would fall to him to come to meet you and to give you a welcome. Fatima, his wife, is at home however; she is a good hostess, and her temper is cheerful and amiable. When I have told her of your coming she will welcome you like a kinsman assuredly; before night falls she will send a man to bring you into the city."

"Go," said Avtandil, "and do as you think best." Rejoicing, the sweat pouring down, the gardener hastened off to give his news to the khatun:[21] "Listen to this wonder! A stranger has come here who is as fair as the sun to behold. A merchant is he, the chief of a great caravan; like a cypress in form, he resembles a seven-days' moon in his beauty. Splendid indeed does he look in his tunic and a turban of the color of coral. He

(1065-80)

called me to him and put questions, asked of the prices wares fetch here."

Well pleased, Fatima Khatun sent ten slaves to Avtandil: the caravanserai was made ready and she had the bales placed in it. And now he whose face was like the rose, with crystal and jet, came into view: those who looked on him thought him the peer of the lion, the panther.

There was noise and excitement; pressing in from all sides, the townsfolk came flocking: "Let us," they cried, "oh, let us but look on him!" Some gazed with rapture, some were near then to swooning; and wives turned away with contempt from their husbands.

Fatima, Husain's wife, came out to welcome Avtandil; her pleasure was plain to see in the warmth of her greeting. Courteous words passed between them, and then they went indoors and sat at ease: it was clear enough that the lady did not find the stranger's arrival displeasing.

This Fatima Khatun was a woman who had her attractions, and she was none the less lively because her first youth had now passed away. She had a good figure and dark coloring, and her face was well-rounded. She was a great one for singers and minstrels, and was fond of her glass of wine: many were the fine gowns and head-dresses possessed by her.

She entertained the newcomer that evening with lavishness; he for his part filled her with delight through the presents he gave her. Happy indeed was Fatima then, playing the hostess! — When they had eaten and drunk, Avtandil withdrew for his night's rest.

He had all his wares unpacked and laid out in the morning: then, when the finest had been set aside for the king and their price paid over, he told the merchants to take the rest off, and saw them loaded up and carried away. "Sell them as you will," he said, "but do not let any man know my true quality."[22]

He still kept to his trader's garb, leaving aside his own raiment. Sometimes Fatima visited him, sometimes he went to see her: pleasantly conversing, they would often sit together. And soon Fatima found his absence as cruel as did Vis that of Ramin.[23]

How Fatima conceived a passion for Avtandil

Keep clear of Woman, if you have the strength and self-mastery! She will play with you, she will charm you, she will build trust up between you and her — and then suddenly she will betray you and do you what harm she can. . . . Never should a secret be told to a woman in confidence![24]

The heart of Fatima Khatun was filled with love for Avtandil: ever greater grew her passion, and it burned her like fire. She strove to keep it concealed, but her woe was not to be hidden. "What am I to do, what will become of me?" she said at length, shedding torrents of tears. "If I speak he may be displeased, alas, and seek to avoid me; but if I stay silent the flame in my breast will burn yet more strongly, beyond all enduring. — Come what may, live or die, I will declare myself to him! How can a physician cure one who will not tell of his malady?"

How Fatima wrote Avtandil a love-letter

And so Fatima wrote Avtandil a most piteous letter that told of her sufferings and of her love for him; a letter such as moves and wrings the heart of a reader, such as deserves to be kept, not lightly torn up and then tossed away!

"O sun — since it has pleased God to make you the peer of the orb of day — source of woe to those sundered from you, with your fires you consume all those who would draw near; the planets delight in gazing upon you, they make it their boast! All who behold you are smitten with love, swoon in wretchedness; you are the rose — I wonder the nightingales do not cluster upon you! Your beauty withers the flowers, and I am fading even as they do: if your rays do not reach me I must be reduced to a cinder.

"I take God to witness, I tell you this fearfully; but what can I now do to help myself, unhappy wretch that I am? For I have been driven past the bounds of endurance; not for ever can my heart suffer your black lashes' piercing! Give me aid if you can, else I shall lose all my wits!

"Until an answer comes, and I know whether you are going to kill or be kind to me — until then I will steel myself to bear

(1081-95)

woe, however grievous my tortures. But oh for the moment when I shall know whether I am to live or die!"

As soon as she had written this Fatima Khatun sent it off to Avtandil. . . . It might have been a letter from a sister or a kinswoman for all the thrill that it gave him! "What does she know of my heart," he said, "and who is she to court one who is already a lover? In what way could she be compared with my lady?" And then he went on, "What has the crow to do with the rose — are they two of a kind? . . . This when the sweet-voiced nightingale has yet to sing on the rose! . . ."[25] Monstrous acts are never lasting, they must always be fruitless — but what nonsense is this, what a letter is penned here!"

Such were the censures that passed through his heart then. But this was the turn that his thoughts began to take presently: "I am alone here, with no one to help me. I can flinch from nothing that might aid me in my quest for the lost one — that is the thing I must bear clearly in mind! — This woman has to do with many men here in this city, keeping open house and befriending travelers from all quarters. If I let her have her way she will tell me anything she knows — though I must suffer tortures of flame for it! She may be of use to me . . . and I shall know how to settle the score!"

And then: "When a woman loves, binds herself close, gives her heart away, she cares nothing — accurst one — for shame and dishonor. She will tell what she knows, blab out any secret. . . . Best to do what she wants of me; perhaps I shall come then upon what I am seeking."

And again: "A man is powerless against the stars: what I desire I do not possess, what I possess I do not desire. The world is a kind of twilight, here all is dusky; one can pour from a pitcher only that which it holds."

How Avtandil replied to Fatima

"I have read your letter," wrote Avtandil, "and all that is said there in praise of me: you have moved before me, but love's fires are burning me yet more grievously. You would have me with you always, as your constant companion: that is my wish too, and, since we are of one mind, let us find joy in each other's arms."

How can I tell you of the transports of Fatima! "Farewell to tears and solitude!" she wrote in a second letter. "You will find me alone here, I shall have no one with me: let no time be lost, but come when the darkness falls."

Avtandil received this summons, and set out in the half-light that evening; but on the way he met another slave who gave him this message: "Do not come tonight, I cannot now see you." But he only said, "What foolery is this!" and went on, for he felt annoyed: although no longer a bidden guest, he would not retrace his steps.

But when he entered, the sapling-fair hero, Fatima was sitting sorely troubled in mind. He perceived her unease at once; but, fearful and anxious to please him, she would not speak openly.

They sat down together, there was kissing and love-making — but then suddenly at the door there appeared a lord, handsome and nobly formed. He entered, a slave bearing sword and shield following; but when he beheld Avtandil he was daunted; the road ahead seemed to him full of rocks. Fatima began to tremble with fear as soon as ever she saw him, while he looked with wonder upon them, lying there in each other's arms. Then he said, "I will not raise my hand now, woman, to stop your flutterings among the flowers; but when morning comes I will make you repent of your hours with this gallant! You have dishonored me, wanton, you have made me a thing for scorn; but tomorrow you shall learn what the cost is to be for you! I will have your teeth rend the flesh of your children! Spit on my beard if I do not make good these words — may I run mad through the fields!"

As soon as he had said this, he touched his beard[26] and withdrew. Fatima now began to beat her head and to tear her cheeks. Forth gushed her tears; they came gurgling like rivulets. "Let them," she said, "bring their stones here to stone me!" And then: "I have killed my husband!" she moaned, "I have slaughtered my children! I have lost all our wealth, with those jewels no man could price! I shall be torn away from all those, old and young, who are dear to me! I have brought destruction upon my house, my tongue has worked my dishonor!"

All this Avtandil heard in the most utter bewilderment.

(1096-1112)

"What ails you," he said, "why these strange words, lamentations? Why did he make you such threats and revile you? Calm your mind, and then tell me who he is, and what brought him here."

"O lion," replied Fatima, "I have been driven by my tears to distraction. Do not ask questions, for I can frame them no answers. By my own act have I now killed my children — all joy is gone! On fire for your love, I have given myself to destruction: such is the fate of the chatterer, witless, raving, besotted, who cannot hold a secret secure in his keeping! — Of your pity, weep, groan for me! You were here and you saw, so I will make everything known to you — how can he who drinks his own blood be cured by any physician?

"One of two things you must do, for there is no other choice. You can go and kill that man under cover of darkness; thus you will save me and all my house too from death and from ruin: and when you return I will tell you why these tears fall from me. But if you will not, then have asses loaded this very night, pack all your gear up and be gone straight away! I fear that my sins may bring suffering likewise on your head. . . . Let him but get to court, and he will have me eat my own children!"

When Avtandil, the noble-souled, the great of heart, heard this, he rose and picked up a club — how fair he was to behold, and how valiant! "My honor," he said, "would be stained were I to stand aside from this business!" Truly, his like is nowhere to be found upon earth!

"Give me," he said to Fatima, "a guide to show me the way; that is all the help I shall need — I do not think that that man is a match for me. I will return and tell you how I have dealt with him; wait for me here and do not let your spirit be anxious." Fatima gave him a slave as a guide, and then came her parting cry: "Since you would soothe the fires in my breast — if you manage to kill him (oh, the joy for my heart then!), I beg you to bring back a ring of mine that he wears on his finger."

Avtandil, the peerless in grace and form, was led through the city then. On the sea-shore stood a palace of red and green stone; floor upon terraced floor it rose, lofty, magnificent, over a hall of great splendor. To this the sun-fair hero was brought by his guide: "That is the abode of him you are seeking," said the man in a low voice. And, pointing, he went on, "Do you see that terrace there, that one just half-way up? If he is not sitting below, he will be lying asleep there."

Two guards lay stretched out before the door of the ill-fated lord. Without a sound Avtandil crept up and seized them both by the throat; they were dead in an instant, head dashed against head; brains were mingled with hair. Bloody of hand, the mighty one then entered the chamber where, with a heart full of anger, the lord was lying alone. He gave him no time to rise but, quicker than thought, killed him in silence — seized him, flung him to the floor and made an end with his dagger. Fair as the sun to those who might look upon him, terrible as a wild beast to his foes was Avtandil! — He cut off the ringed finger and then threw out the body, hurled it forth from the window, to be lost in the sea's sands. No tomb did that lord have, no spade dug him a grave. . . . None heard sounds of slaughter. . . . Calm and untroubled, Avtandil the rose-fair went forth again — that he could put his hand to a deed of blood such as this! — and made his way back by the way he had come.

In Fatima's house once more, the sun-fair hero, the master of eloquence, said, "I have killed him; no more will his eyes see the light of day. I have your own slave for a witness, let his oath give you assurance. Here is the ring, with its finger, and here is my dagger, all bloodied. — Now tell me the meaning of your words, tell me why you were distracted, quite out of your mind, and why he made threats to you: I am eager to know." Fatima clung to his feet: "I am not worthy," she said, "to look on your countenance! The wound in my heart is healed, the fire in my breast is extinguished. I, Husain and our children are all born anew! How can we, O my lion, praise you as is fitting? Since your word has been made good with that lord's blood, I will tell you the story from its very beginning: now give me your ear."

How Fatima told of Nestan-Darejan

On the first day of the year[27] no trading is done in this city, nor does any man ever set out on a journey: we all put on fine clothes, and at the palace the king and queen hold a great banquet. It is the custom for us of the great merchantry to take gifts to court; in return they bestow on us presents that are even as splendid. Cymbals and harps are for ten days heard everywhere; in the maidan there are contests, ball-play and the thunder of hooves.

My husband, Husain, goes at the head of the merchants; I lead their wives — nor do I need to have any invite me! Rich and poor alike, we give our presents to the queen and pass the time in diversion; then by and by we return home — all is joyful.

At this festival we offered our gifts to the queen; we gave and were given, bestowed lavishly and received in abundance. Filled with great gladness, we withdrew at a fitting time and repaired to my house, where we sat down to pursue further our pleasure. When evening had come I conducted the ladies, guests of my table, out into the garden; sweet-voiced minstrels came after. Gay as a child, I changed my veil for another and decked out my hair anew.

In the garden there are lovely, high-built bowers that command a prospect upon every side and look out over the sea: I took my companions to these, and we sat down to feast again; all was joy and delight. I laughed then, I entertained the merchants' wives like a sister; but, as we drank there, a strange distress came upon me. When they perceived this my guests rose and took their leave: I was left alone; and like soot a black sadness fell down on my heart.

Trying to cast off the melancholy that was growing within me, I opened the window and looked out over the sea. Presently I descried a small speck in the distance moving over the water that I thought must be either a bird or a beast. I could make out nothing at first, but as it drew nearer I perceived it was a boat: on this side and on that two men, black of face and of body, were standing, watchful, alert. Straight in to the shore it came, and out got the negroes. Great was the wonder this sight so strange roused in me.

Looking carefully round to see if any observed them, the men beached the boat and drew it up by the garden. Not a soul did they spy, there was nothing to trouble them: quiet and still in my bower, I watched them unseen.

They lifted a chest from the boat and then opened it; out stepped a maiden of most marvellous loveliness. A black veil covered her head, for the rest she was clad in green. — Happy would the sun be, were it possessed of such beauty!

When she turned her face towards me the rocks were bathed in her radiance; her cheeks flashed their lightning too through the far highest heavens. I shut my eyes — as soon could I have gazed on the sun itself! — and, closing the window, unnoticed still, summoned four slaves who attended me and showed them the maiden. "See," I said, "what loveliness those Indians[28] hold captive! Go down — but quietly, not bounding in hustling haste. If they will sell her, you can give them whatever price they may ask for; if they will not, do not hold your hands, but seize her and kill them, and then bring the moon-fair here. Do what you can, show address in the matter!" The slaves slipped down, swift as though they were winged, and sought to make purchase. But they met with denial; I could see that the blacks' faces were scowling.

When I saw the negroes would not sell, I called out from my window, "Kill them!" My slaves fell upon them and cut off their heads; then they threw the bodies into the sea; they secured too the maiden. I went down and took her from them — it was all but the work of a moment.

How can I praise her fitly, how can I tell of her loveliness? I swear that *she* is the true sun — not the orb in the heavens! What eye could look on her undazzled, who could hope to depict her! Would that I might be consumed, alas, in the flames she has kindled!

[*Here Fatima tore at her face: Avtandil too wept, shedding hot tears. Heedless one of the other, they surrendered to a grief close to madness; the tears coursed down their cheeks like torrents rushing through melting snow. "Tell me the rest," said Avtandil, when their spirits were calm again: and Fatima continued her story.*]

I gave her my heart at that moment of meeting; wearied was she by the kisses that I showered then upon her. I placed her upon a couch, and I softly caressed her. "Tell me, sun-fair

(1130-47)

lady," I said, "who you are, and of what people; from where did those negroes bring you, the empress of the clustered stars?" But, ask as I would, no answer could I win; I only saw tears that flowed forth from a hundred springs. Under my talk, with all its questioning, soft sobs welled from her heart: from eyes like the narcissus tears flowed through jet lashes on to her cheek, on to the crystal and ruby. I gazed and gazed, and fire burned in my breast.

She said, "You are like a mother to me — no, more than a mother; but what would it avail if I were to tell you my story? You would not believe it! — I am a waif from a far land, overborne by misfortune. Ask me nothing, lest the wrath of the All-Seeing is turned on you."

I thought, "I must not vex this sun-fair lady with more ill-timed questioning; it would end in my madness and utter distraction. Every request should be made in due season; I should have known that this was not the right moment for talk!"

I led away that sun-fair one who must in truth win the praise of all. . . . Hard indeed did it prove to conceal the light of her beauty! I kept her always behind curtains, heavy and hanging in many folds. Her tears hailed down without ceasing, to freeze the rose on her cheek; tempests blew from her lashes.

I took that sun-fair maiden, the cypress-like, to my house; and there I prepared a bower for her, and lodged her in it very secretly. I did not make her presence known, but kept her carefully hidden, with a negro for servant. When I went to see her I was always alone.

Alas, how can I tell you of her most strange demeanor! By day and by night alike she shed tears that were ceaseless. When I begged her to calm her spirit she would quieten for only an instant. — Alas, alas, now she is gone, how can life still remain in me?

Whenever I went in I saw great pools of tears there before her; in her eyes' inky abysses the lashes were like lances of jet; streams came pouring forth from those lakelets of darkness; between her lips' coral and cornelian teeth shone bright, like pearls.

There could be no questioning, so constant the tears' flow. If I asked, "Who are you, and what brought you to such a pass as this?" tears of blood would gush forth from the eyes of her whose form resembled the cypress. . . . Who could have endured it save one who was made of stone?

Neither blanket nor bed would she have to lie down upon; she had a long veil that she would never put from her; when she rested, an arm under her head was her pillow. A thousand entreaties would hardly bring her to eat the least morsel.

I must say something now of that veil, and the wonder of it: I have seen rare and costly things of every kind, but it was made of some stuff that was strange, quite unknown, to me. It was woven, fabric-like, but strong as the best tempered steel.

Long was that lovely lady here with me; but, fearful lest he should make my secret known, I said nothing to Husain. "I have but to speak of her," I thought, "and he will be off hot-foot to the palace to betray me, the villain!" Such were my broodings, going to the bower or coming back again. But then at length I said to myself, "What can I do, what can I hope to achieve, if I do not confide in him? I do not know what she wants, or how any might aid her. If my husband discovers my secret he will assuredly kill me — and how can I keep a light hidden that shines as bright as the sun? What can I do without help, on my own, alas? The fires in my breast are burning ever more fiercely. No, I will not do Husain wrong, I will give my full trust to him. I will make him swear an oath not to betray me: he will not break faith, once his word is pledged, to give his soul to damnation!"

I went and saw him alone; and then, after I had caressed him and played with him, I said, "I have something to tell you; but first swear to me that you will not speak of it to a living soul; promise this solemnly." He then swore a fearful oath: "Let my head crash upon rocks! I will not reveal what you tell me until death; to old or young; friend or foe." Then I told the kindly Husain all, ending, "Come, follow me, and I will show you the sun-fair one."

Husain rose to come after me, and we went to the gate of the bower and passed through it. When he beheld the radiance he trembled and marvelled; then, "What is this you have shown me," he said, "what do I see before me, what is she? If she is a creature of flesh and blood, may God turn his anger upon me!"

(1147-64)

"Nor am I sure that she is a being of this earth," I replied to him;
"I know no more of her than what I have told you. But let us
ask her who she is, and who has caused her distraction: per-
haps if we beseech her to speak she will consent, in her
graciousness."

Respectful of demeanor, we stepped forward and said, "Sun-
fair lady, for your sake we are consumed in a furnace: tell us,
how can the pale moon be cured of its sickness? What has
turned your cheek's hue from ruby to saffron?"

Whether she understood what we said, whether she even
heard, I cannot tell. The rose of her lips remained closed, we
could not see those pearls that were her teeth; her locks were
serpents tangled in an utter disorder. She turned her face from
us — that garden of beauty; the dragon of eclipse darkened
the sun of her countenance;[29] morning's light was denied us;
our words drew no answer. Like a panther, like a leopard, she
sat there with darkened brow; but we could not divine the
cause of the anger that filled her. When once more we dis-
tressed her with our importunity, tears sprang from her eyes:
"I can tell you nothing," she said; "go — leave me!" And no
more came from her.

We sat down and wept with her; many were the tears that we
shed then. We wished unsaid the words we had spoken, re-
gretted them bitterly. It was a hard task to quieten her, but at
length we succeeded. . . . We pressed fruit upon her, but to no
purpose; she would not eat any.

"A thousand cares," said Husain, "have fallen away with
the sight of her; those cheeks should receive the sun's kiss, not
the caress of a mortal's lips! Well may he who cannot behold
her suffer a hundred fierce torments! — May God give my
children to destruction if I hold them more dear than her!"

We gazed long upon her, then went out, sighing and moan-
ing. . . . To be with her was joy for us, parting — grief, misery.
Affairs of trade were neglected so that we might go and look
on her; our hearts lay enmeshed in her net, helpless captives.

After some time had passed, after nights had gone by with
days, Husain said, "I have not seen the king of late; if you think
well, I will go with an offering of gifts and attend at court."
"Go by all means," I replied, "since you wish so to do." He set

out pearls and rubies on a tray, and then I besought him thus: "You will be seeing that crowd of tipplers there at the palace; keep your mouth shut about the maiden, or you may as well strike me dead here and now!" And once again he swore, "Not a word, though swords cut at me!"

So Husain went to the palace, to find the king feasting. The king — Husain is his boon companion, always sure of a welcome — had him sit down before him, and accepted the gifts he brought. . . . Behold the merchant in his cups now, false, faithless and thoughtless!

Or ever Husain had come the king had emptied many a goblet: now they drank and filled up again; bumper followed hard upon bumper. Husain forgot all the oaths he had sworn — what were Korans and Meccas! Well is it said: "The rose is not for the crow, nor yet horns for the ass!"

Presently our great king said to Husain, the besotted, the drunken, "Where you get these jewels that you bring is to me a great mystery. How do you find such huge pearls and such wonderful rubies? By my head, I could not give you one tenth in return!"

Husain replied to him, after making obeisance, "O mighty monarch of the shining rays, O sun, sustainer of created things — to whom, if not to you, does all I have belong, my gold and my treasure? What came with me forth from my mother's womb? From you have I received all my earthly possessions. No, by your head, there is no call here for gratitude. But I have something else as well, a bride for you to give to your son. When you see before you the maiden who is as fair as the orb of day you will assuredly thank me and declare yourself blessed, not once but many times."

Why should I lengthen the story? He broke his solemn oath, broke the bonds of religion, and told of her whom all likened to the sun, and her finding. The king heard him gladly, his heart overflowed with joy; and forthwith he gave commands for her to be brought to the palace, that all might be done even as Husain had counselled.

I was sitting quietly at home here when, with sixty men at his back, as the court's custom requires, the chief of the royal slaves appeared at the door. "It must be some matter of moment that brings them!" I said to myself, much amazed.

(1164-79)

"Fatima," said the chief slave, saluting me, "it is the command of the Equal of God that you surrender the maiden as fair as two suns of whom Husain has this day made a gift to him, that we may take her with us; make haste."

When I heard this, the heavens fell down on my head, God's wrath struck the mountains. "Maiden — what maiden?" I asked in a stupor. He replied, "Husain has bestowed on him her whose face in its beauty resembles the lightning's flash." Helpless was I; the day had come when I must lose my soul. . . . I could neither rise nor sit still for my trembling.

I went to the bower where that fair one sat shedding tears and said, "Sun-fair lady, black Fortune has dealt with me treacherously! The heavens have shown a countenance of wrath, my life has been turned into a wilderness. My secret is out: the king has sent for you, and my heart has been broken."

"Dear friend," she replied, "hard though this be, there is nothing to wonder at; cruel Fortune has always worked evil upon me. Had some good thing come to pass you might well have marvelled, but how can disaster cause any surprise? There is no kind of sorrow that has not long been known to me."

Tears that were like pearls came pouring forth from her eyes: as brave in heart as a panther or a hero of battles she rose now: she had passed beyond the dominions of joy and of sorrow. . . . She asked for a veil to cover her face and her shoulders.

I went to our treasure-chamber — there are riches there of a worth beyond reckoning — and gathered up as many jewels and pearls as I could carry away with me: each single one of them would have ransomed a city. Then I returned and girt them round the waist of her my heart longed for: "My dear one," I said to her, "perhaps these may prove of some use to you." And with that I gave the sun-fair lady into the slaves' charge.

When the king heard they were bringing her, he went out to receive her: drums sounded, and loud was the noise and the tumult; but the maiden walked calmly, head bent and in silence. Crowds came thronging to see her, there was excitement and clamor; the guards struggled without avail to hold back the multitude; there was everywhere uproar.

When the king saw the cypress-formed lady approaching, he said in amazement, "What is it, O sun-fair one, that has brought

you among us?" And like the sun, indeed, did she dazzle the
eyes of beholders. "Never," said the king, "have I seen her
like anywhere — what hand save God's could have created
such beauty? Well might her lover run through the fields in
distraction!" He placed her at his side and then spoke to her
gently: "Tell me," he said, "who you are, whose you are, and
who are your kinsfolk." But the maiden, the sun-fair, would
vouchsafe no answer: she sat there with head bowed; she was
quiet and sorrowful. She did not give ear to the words he was
saying; her heart was elsewhere; her thoughts were on other
things; her lips' rose was closed; her teeth were like hidden
pearls. Those who beheld her were all struck with wonder;
every man there was at a loss utterly.

"What are we to think," said the king, "or what can we con-
jecture? There are two ways, and two only, in which we can
interpret her silence. Either she is enamored and, thinking
of her beloved, has no care for any other, will have speech
with no one; or, a seer beyond the reach alike of joy and of
sorrow, holding woe and happiness to be vain fables equally,
she is not here, but has her spirit in some far land where it soars
up aloft, like a dove. — God grant my son a happy return from
his battles! I will hold this sun-fair one here to await the day;
perhaps he will prevail upon her to speak, so that the truth may
be known to us. Until then we shall have here no more than a
waning moon, denied any light from the far-distant sun."

The king's son is a splendid young man and a valiant, fair
of face and of form, and noble in mind; he had then for long
been away at the wars. The star-fair maiden was to receive, it
now was decreed by his father, the high honor that would be
the due of his wedded wife.

They brought robes adorned with many jewels that shone as
brightly as stars and put them upon her; then they set on her
head a crown that had been wrought from one ruby: very fair
were the crystal and rose of her cheek.

The king said, "Let all be made ready in the princess's cham-
ber." They put there a throne of red gold from Morocco, and
then our great king, master and lord of the palace, rose and set
upon it that sun-fair lady who rejoiced all who looked on her.
He gave commands for nine slaves to keep watch at the door

of her chamber, then sat down to feast, in the way kings are wont to do. In return for the sun-fair one he showered upon Husain gifts beyond measuring; trumpet and drum were sounded to add to the joyful din; the feast lasted long, and even longer the drinking.

Thus did the sun-fair lady complain of the workings of Destiny: "What a cruel fate is mine! Where have I come from — where am I now — to whose lot shall I fall — for whom is my love? What shall I do — what shall I turn to — what could be of help to me? A very hard lot is mine!" But then she went on, "I will not sit here idle and let the rose of my beauty fade: perhaps with God's help I shall yet foil the plans of my enemies. What man in his right mind will yield himself up to death before needs must? It is when we are in straits that wit can provide its best service!"

She called to her the slaves now and said, "Come, listen to reason! You are deceived and mistaken in thinking to guard me, and in desiring to have his son wed me your lord shows himself clouded in judgement: in vain do drum, trumpet and clarion sound for me. I am not a fit queen for you, my path is quite other! May God keep this prince from me, although he be as fair as the sun and with the form of a cypress. What you would have is far removed from my destiny; I was not born to live here in this land among you. I will kill myself, make no mistake — stab myself in the heart with a dagger: your lord will put you to death then, this world will not hold you long! Better to let me escape; I will give you the riches that I have here girt about me. Let me go; if you do not, you will learn to regret it."

With that she loosed the pearls and jewels that she had tied about her, took off the crown made from a single ruby that shone in translucency, and offered all to them. "Let me go," she said; "with a burning heart I implore you: set me free, and you will find favor in the sight of your God."

Their greed aroused by the sight of the treasure, the slaves had no more care for the king's wrath than they would have had for a watchman's; there and then they resolved to aid the beautiful maiden to regain her liberty. — Ah, the power of gold, gold that comes to us as a gift of the Devil! Never can joy be known to those that lust after it; they grind their teeth in avarice until their last day is upon them. It comes and goes, their gold; and when it is lacking they are ready to rail against the very stars in their courses. It keeps the soul in chains here on earth; in its shackles it cannot soar.

When the slaves had decided to do what she asked, one of them took his coat off and gave it to her. Then, avoiding the hall, which was full of carousers, they led her out of the palace; a moon at the full was she, clear of the eclipse-serpent's jaws now! — Stealing forth at the same time, the slaves fled away.

The maiden came to my door, knocked upon it and asked for me. I went, and when I saw who it was I embraced her. — Great was my surprise! To my sorrow, she would not come in: "I have bought myself free," she said, "with the wealth that you gave me; may God reward you for this with his heavenly favor! You cannot hide me now; give me a horse and let me be off at once, before the king learns of my flight and sends men in pursuit of me."

I ran to the stable, loosed and saddled our best horse, and assisted the maiden — joyful was she of heart now — to mount it. As splendid as the sun, the most glorious of the heavens' luminaries, when it enters the sign of the Lion[30] was she at that hour! Thus was my labor lost; I garnered no harvest from what I had sown.

The alarm was sounded towards evening; pursuers mustered, a hue and cry was raised, soldiers were called out in the city. "If you find her in my house," I said in reply to their questioning, " I shall in truth have done the king wrong, and must bear a burden of guilt." They could find nothing, for all their searching, and returned empty-handed. The king and those about him have ever since that day mourned her loss; the courtiers' garb is of the hue of the violet.[31] We have lived in the dark since the sun-fair one went from us!

I will tell you of the moon-fair lady's fate in a moment, but first to explain why that man made the threats he did. — Like very goats, alas, we used to wanton together, he and I. . . . As a man is brought to dishonor by cowardice, so is a woman stained by unchastity!

(1197-1212)

I have no use for my husband; he is ugly, all skin and bone.
That man, the Cup-Bearer, was a lord who stood high at court.
No mourning will I put on for him, for all we were lovers.
Would that I had a bowl of his blood — I would drink it!

Like a woman, like a fool, I told him this story; how the
sun-fair maiden had come to me, and how, soft as a fox, she had
slipped away in the end. Thereafter he was for ever making
threats to denounce me — he was not like a lover, he bore
himself like an enemy. Now I know he is dead, oh, the weight
off my spirit! Whenever we quarrelled, alone together, out came
those menaces. . . . When I asked you to come here I thought
him away from home: but he had returned, and he sent word
that he purposed to visit me. I dispatched that message telling
you to turn back because I was filled with fear. But you did not
obey me; no, you came, you brought the light of your counte-
nance, and the two of you met here, face to face, looking over
me! I was stricken with terror, distracted — for I knew that
not only his tongue but his heart too wished me dead. He would
have gone, had you not killed him, to the palace, and there in
his anger denounced me; for his heart was on fire. In his wrath
the king would have given over my house to destruction: he
would have made me eat my children, by heaven, then had me
stoned!

May you have your reward from God, for how can I thank
you? You have saved me unharmed from the stare of that
basilisk![32] Henceforward I need have no fears for what Fate
may bring to me: I shall dread death no longer — oh, happy
am I!

"Have done with your terrors," Avtandil said: " 'The false
friend is the worst of all foes,'[33] it is written. The wise man puts
no trust in such a one: but you need fear that lord no more,
for he sleeps with the dead. Now to the maiden: tell me, since
you sped her upon her way, have you learned anything of her,
has any news reached you?" Tears streamed from Fatima's
eyes as she took up her tale again: "Alas," she cried, "those

rays that illumined the earth like the sun's beams are now darkened!"

How Fatima told Avtandil of the Kajes' capture of Nestan-Darejan

Alas, Fate, as false in your deceit as is Satan! Who can understand you, or your treachery's workings? Where have you hidden the maiden who is as fair as the sun itself? I see that in the end all is vanity, everywhere! . . .

Fatima went on.

The sun — the light of all the world — life and existence — the gain of my hands — was now gone from me. Hot fires burned thenceforward in my breast without ceasing: the spring that gave tears to my eyes never dried up. Children and home became hateful, joy was fled from my heart. I thought of her, waking; she came into the dreams of sleep. Husain, the oathbreaker, I looked on as one utterly faithless; the wretch did not dare show his accursed face near me. . . .

One evening, at sunset, I walked out beyond the guard-house and found myself near the door of a travelers' hostelry. My mind was filled with sad thoughts of the maiden: "Dishonor," I said, "sits in the pledged word of every man!" Presently a man-at-arms, a stranger from another land, came up with three companions. The man-at-arms had the garb usual in one of his calling; the other three all wore plain travelers' clothing. With them they had food and drink they had bought in the city, and now they fell to, talking gaily together. I watched; and I listened to what was passing between them.

These words were uttered by and by: "We are indeed passing the time very pleasantly; but, although we have met and made friends here, we are like strangers still one to another. None knows who his fellows may be, or where it is that they hail from: let each one of us now tell his story."

The others told tales of the sort usual with travelers: then the man-at-arms said, "Wondrous indeed are the ways, brothers, of Providence! But you have sown only millet; I

(1212-28)

will harvest you pearls, for mine is a better tale than any of those you have told here. — I was the slave of a great king, the lord of the Kajes,[34] but he was struck down by a sickness that carried him off: he was no more, he who had comforted the orphan and protected the widow. The upbringing of his children is in the hands of his sister, and better does she do the task than ever a mother could. Dulardukht,[35] though a woman, has the strength of a rock: the man does not live whose blows could draw blood from her warriors — but they give wounds to others! Two young nephews has she, her brother's sons Rosan and Rodia; she rules in Kajeti as sovereign, and they call her 'the Mighty.'

"The news of the death of her sister across the seas reached us some time since. Dismay struck the viziers; they had no more thought for affairs of state. 'How are we to tell her,' they said, 'that the light of the world is extinguished?'

"Then Roshak,[36] — he is captain over many thousands of warriors — raised his voice. 'Though I pay for it with my life,' he said, 'I am going to withdraw from the mourning! I will ride out to win plunder — and be back with my booty in time to go with the queen when she sets out to weep over her sister.' He addressed us, his soldiery, then: 'I am going; come with me!' And off he went with a hundred of us, all men he had picked himself. Each day while the light held we were busy with brigandage, and during the hours of night we were still on the watch. Many a caravan did we shatter and pillage.

"One dark night as we were riding over the plain we saw a great light shining brightly before us. Had the sun come down to the earth, we all wondered, racking our brains in an utter perplexity. Some said it was the dawn, others thought it the moon. Knee to knee, we rode forward to look more closely upon it: then we made a great circle, and so we surrounded it. And now from within that light there came a voice saying, 'Who may you be, you horsemen? I would know your names. — Give me passage; I am a courier from Gulansharo on the way to Kajeti.'

"We pressed in to draw our ring closer, on hearing this; and then we beheld a rider who was as fair as the sun. We gazed on a countenance that was like a star flashing lightning; even as the sun sheds its rays did it cast its light all around. The words uttered were few and were quietly spoken; lashes of jet were illumined by teeth of a dazzling brightness.

"We addressed the stranger, the sun-fair, with gentleness: we were sure that here was no courier, but one who was trying by all means to deceive us. Roshak perceived that we had to do with a woman, and straightway rode up to her; and then we secured her and made her our captive.

'Sun-fair lady,' we said again, 'tell us the truth. Who are you? Whose are you? And where have you come from, to lighten our darkness?' She would give us no answer, but torrents of scalding tears burst forth from her eyes now. . . . Piteous indeed is the full moon when the eclipse-serpent has swallowed it!

"Nothing would she tell us, either in plain speech or in riddling — who she was, or at whose hands she had suffered betrayal. Her words were filled with anger, she withheld her story still, sullenly; her glance was as baleful as the glare of the basilisk.

"Roshak said, 'No more questioning; we shall learn nothing from her. Hers is surely a strange tale, not one to be lightly told. But wondrous, most wondrous, is the good fortune of our queen: to Dulardukht God has sent a very great marvel; he has delivered this maiden into our hands to take as a gift to her. We shall be well thanked assuredly when we come with the lady. — If we tried to keep her hidden she would without doubt be discovered, and our queen's spirit is stern. . . . A grievous wrong would have been done her, and our shame would be great indeed.'

"We agreed without more ado and, bearing the maiden away with us, took the road to Kajeti. She was treated with honor, we did not venture to speak to her: but she wept; the bitter tears rolled down her cheeks without ceasing.

"I said to Roshak, 'Let me now take myself off for a short time; I have affairs to attend to in the city of Gulansharo.' And he granted me leave to go. I had some goods to fetch from here, and I am about to set out with them to make after my comrades."

The tale of the man-at-arms was enjoyed by his listeners.

(1228-44)

I too followed the story, and soon the ford of tears was dried up by what I heard; for everything spoke of the maiden so dear to me. This gave some scrap of comfort, a dram's weight, to my heart.

I called the man over, had him sit down before me, and said to him, "Tell that story once more; I too want to hear it." He told it again, and my faltering spirit received life anew.

I have two black slaves who possess skill in sorcery, and who through their arts can come and go unseen by the eyes of men. These I summoned and dispatched to Kajeti with this command: "Make haste — use your magic to bring me news of the maiden!"

They made good speed, and in three days they were back again. "The maiden," they told me, "was brought before the queen, who was then about to set out to cross the sea: there is none who can look on her any more than upon the sun, truly! She is soon to be given to the young prince as a wife. 'She shall be wedded to Rosan,' it has been given out by Queen Dulardukht. 'There is no time now for the marriage, and my heart is still too full of grief,[37] furthermore; but when I return I will make the sun-fair maiden my daughter-in-law.'[38] She has confined her in the castle with a single slave to attend on her, meanwhile

"The queen has taken with her all who have knowledge of sorcery, for the journey is full of dangers, and enemies stand ready for battle. But she has left behind her most valiant warriors. — Some time must pass before her return, for it is not long since she went away.

"The city of the Kajes has never been stormed yet by any foe: a mighty rock, long and high, rises within it; and inside this rock a hollowed-out passage leads up to the citadel. There, all alone, sits the star-fair lady who burns the hearts of those who behold her. Splendid warriors stand on guard at the passage's entrance: ten thousand, all of them noble, are always on watch there. At each of the three gates of the city three thousand others are posted. — O heart, the world tortures you; what keeps you still bound to it!"

The hero of the mighty brand, Avtandil the sun-fair, rejoiced over this story; but he kept his own counsel. To God he offered thanks: "Glad news indeed," he said, "is this I have just heard!" Then he spoke thus to Fatima: "Dear heart, you have shown that in truth you deserve my love; with good will you have told a tale that has afforded me much delight. But tell me more of Kajeti: the Kajes are spirits — how then have they taken flesh and blood to themselves? I am consumed with pity now for the fate of the maiden, but what can those Kajes do with a woman, when they lack any substance?" "Listen," Fatima replied, "for I see that you do not understand the matter. These are not true Kajes, but mortal men who live secure among steep rocks. They hold together as one people, and are called Kajes because they are adept in sorcery. They do injury to all men, but themselves suffer hurt from none: those who go forth to do battle with them come back dishonored and blinded.

"Wonderful are the things they can do: they render their enemies sightless; they raise fearful winds and send ships to the bottom; they pass over the ocean's bed, having dried up the waters; they turn day into night and night into day, as they will. That is why the people round about call them Kajes, although they are in truth mortal creatures even as we are."

Avtandil gave her his thanks: "You have now soothed the hot fires that burned in my breast," he said: "glad indeed am I to have heard this tale you have told me." Then, weeping, he glorified the Lord with a full heart thus: "O God, comforter of woes, all thanks to thee who wast and art in transcendence: thy mercy lies suddenly spread all around us!"

Even so did he give praise to the Almighty through his tears for this piece of intelligence: but Fatima thought it was for her sake that he had taken to weeping, and the fire of her passion leaped once more into flame. The hero kept his thoughts close concealed, but he lent himself now to love: Fatima put her arms about him, pressed kisses on the face that was as fair as the sun. . . .

That night the lady had the joy of sharing her bed with Avtandil: his neck, fair as crystal, lay upon hers — but against his will! The thought of Tinatin was death; inward shudders ran through him; away leaped his maddened heart, to run with the wild beasts. The secret tears that he shed flowed to join with the

(1244-61)

ocean: his pupils floated as jet-black ships in his eyes' inky whirlpools. "Behold me, you lovers!" he said. "You see a nightingale parted from its rose sitting, like a crow, on a midden!"[39]

The tears that he wept then would have softened a stone; bursting through his jet lashes' thickets, they formed pools amid the roses that bloomed on his cheeks. Fatima rejoiced over him, for her part, like a nightingale: when a crow finds a rose it always fancies itself the bird of song.[40]

When morning came Avtandil the sun-fair went forth to bathe himself; his radiance flooded the world. Fatima brought a great number of tunics, turbans and cloaks; perfumes of many kinds too, and shirts that were choice and fine "Do not hold back," she said, "but put on what best pleases you."

"Today," Avtandil said to himself, "I will tell her what business it is that has brought me here!" Thus far he had kept to the garb of a merchant, but now he clothed his frame's splendor in a paladin's raiment. Even fairer than before was the hero to look upon; in his beauty he resembled the sun.

Fatima made ready a meal for herself and Avtandil. When, having put on his attire, he came in with cheerful looks, she was surprised to see that he was no longer in the dress of a trader: smiling, she said, "Those who run distracted for your sake will now indeed be delighted!" Greatly did she marvel as she gazed on his beauty. He gave her no reply, only smiled as he said to himself, "So even now she cannot discern my true quality! — How absurd she is!" Fatima did all she could to please, but she got no response from him.

The meal ended, they parted: Avtandil returned to his lodging, lay down well contented, having drunk wine, and fell asleep peacefully. He awoke in the evening — the earth was suffused with his radiance — and sent off this message to Fatima: "Come now; I am all alone, no one is here with me!" She set forth, and was presently to be heard without, sighing, "I must die for love of him who has the form of a cypress, most surely!" He set her at his side on a cushion taken up from the carpet; his cheeks' roses lay within the shadows that were cast by his eyelashes.

"Fatima," he said, "this story will make you tremble as you would after a snake's bite. — You know nothing of the man

that I really am! . . . I have been brought near to death by black
lashes like trees of jet. . . . You have thought me a merchant,
the chief of a caravan; but I am in truth the captain of the host
of the mighty King Rostevan, the commander of a great army,
one that befits such a monarch. And I am the master too of
many a treasure-chamber and armory.

"Listen, for I know you for a good and faithful friend, worthy
of trust. — Rostevan has one child, a daughter, who illumines
the world like the sun; and I burn for the love of her as though
in a flame. She bade me ride forth, and to obey her command
I broke faith with her father, my sovereign lord.[41] In search
of that maiden, the sun's peer, to whom you gave shelter, I
have journeyed over the whole earth:[42] I have seen in his re-
treat the young hero who roams, pale and distraught for her
sake, wasting away, wasting in heart and in strength."

Avtandil now told Fatima his tale; also the story of Tariel,
and how it was that he came to wear the skin of a panther.
"In your power it lies," he continued, "to bring balm to this
stranger, help to him whose thick lashes are as black as the
raven's wing. — Come, Fatima, give me your aid, let us strive
to assist him; let us toil for those star-fair ones, perhaps they
may yet come to joy. We shall win praise from all men who
hear of our labors — surely those lovers will be once more
united!

"Now call that sorcerer-slave,[43] and we will send him to Ka-
jeti to tell the maiden of all that is known to us. When we have
had word from her we will act in accord with her judgement:
God grant that you may hear we have conquered the realm
of the Kajes!"

Fatima cried, "Glory be, what a business is this! Whose ears
ever heard such things as mine have this day!" Then she sent
for the sorcerer slave — he was as black as a raven[44] — and
said, "Kajeti! Let there be no delay, for the way is a long one.
Now is the time for your magic to prove its worth: make haste,
and quiet the fires that are raging within my breast. Tell that
sun-fair lady that we are possessed now of the cure for her
sorrow." "Tomorrow," he replied, "I will bring the news that
you wish for."

(1261-78)

How Fatima wrote to Nestan-Darejan

"O star," Fatima wrote, "heavenly light of the world; source of sorrow and woe to all who are parted from you; lady of loveliness, sweet of words and of tongue; ruby and crystal joined together in beauty! —

"Although you did not tell me your story, all has now been revealed to me; and my heart has been comforted. — Send news now to ease the distraction of Tariel, for he is as one out of his wits for your sake: may you both attain your desire, may he bloom as the rose and you as the violet!

"His sworn brother Avtandil has come here in search of you: captain of the host of King Rostevan is he, a hero without reproach, a lord of Arabia and of high renown in that land. Now tell us all you can, lady brave in heart and most wise in mind! We have sent this slave so that we may learn how matters stand in Kajeti. Have the Kajes come home? — We want to know just how strong is the force there. Then, who are your guards, and who has the command of them? — Set down for us all that you know of the place; and send some token as well for the hands of your lover. Put away all grief from you now and rejoice! May God help me to unite two lovers worthy indeed one of the other!

"— Go, letter, hasten, you must make all the speed you can! I envy you, for you are going to her whose countenance is as jet, ruby and crystal! You are happier than I, letter, for the eyes of her for whose sake fires burn in my breast will soon look upon you. When you have gone, understand: understand, aye, and pity me!"

Fatima gave this letter to the sorcerer, to the master of magic: "Take this," she said, "to the maiden, the sun-fair one." Wrapping himself in a green mantle, he disappeared in an instant, skimmed away over roof-tops.

Swift as an arrow from the bow of an archer of mighty arm, he sped on his way; dusk was just falling when he arrived in Kajeti. Invisible to mortal eyes, he passed through the host of warriors on guard at the gates: to give the sun-fair lady the letter of the woman who longed for her, he went through the castle's closed gates as though they had stood wide.

When the negro made his entry — black of face, long of locks and close-wrapped in his mantle — the sun-fair maiden trembled in every limb, for she feared he would do her harm: she turned deathly pale, her cheek's rose changed to saffron. "What do you think I am, why are you afraid?" he said to her. "I am Fatima's slave, and I come as a messenger; this letter will prove I am not speaking falsely. Do not wither so quickly, but await the sun's rays, rose-fair one."

Great was the amazement of the sun's peer when she heard Fatima spoken of; her jet lashes trembled, she opened her almond-eyes widely. The slave gave her the letter and, sighing and drenching it with her hot tears, she perused it. Then she said to the slave, "Tell me who this man may be who is seeking me: what man upon earth is there that knows I am still alive?" "I will tell you," he replied, "of all that is known to me. — Since you left us we have lived without sunlight, in shadow: Fatima's heart has been pierced by the lances of sorrow; the tears she has shed have flowed down to the ocean. She has never ceased to weep, I call God to witness, since the day — I have come before — when I first brought her news of you. . . . Now a certain young lord has come — splendor sits in his countenance — and to him she told the whole story of you and your sorrows. He, the hero mighty of arm, it is who would find you; they sent me here, urging me to make all the haste I might."

"I believe," said the maiden, "you are speaking the truth to me. . . . Fatima did not know the name of the lover from whom I am parted. . . . This world still holds, somewhere, him for whose sake my heart burns! I will write, but do you tell them also of me and my wretchedness."

How Nestan-Darejan wrote to Fatima

"O Khatun, you who were kinder than a mother to me," wrote the sun-fair one, "see how cruel Fate has used me, its prisoner! New griefs, alas, are added now to my woes. . . . But I have read the letter you wrote to me, and that has brought me much comfort.

"When you delivered me from those two sorcerers[45] you

(1278-94)

lightened my load of sorrow, but now I am held captive in this place by the Kajes. The might of a kingdom guards one who is all alone with many thousands of warriors: my plans and my resolves have all crumbled to ruin.

"What more can I tell you? The queen has not returned yet; some time will have passed away before they are back in Kajeti. But countless valiant men of arms here are keeping watch over me. I cannot be rescued, I am lost for ever, believe me! This young lord who has come seeking me must lose all his labor; he will suffer, fires will burn in his breast and a flame will consume him. But yet do I envy him; he has looked on Tariel, on the sun-fair, he has rejoiced in his radiance. — Parted from him I love, how bitter is life to me!

"I did not tell you my story, I kept it in darkness; my tongue could not have given it utterance, I wished to spare myself agony. — Implore my lover, I beg you, to have pity, let him not seek to win through to me: write, send him a message. I have already enough to bear, let him not double my load of grief: if I must look on his corpse I will die with a two-fold death. I am now beyond mortal aid — this is truth, not idle imagining. If he will not listen, may I be stoned, let black stones pile up over me!

"You have asked for a token: here is a piece from the veil that he himself gave to me.[46] For his sake I cherish it, black though it be in hue: black, like my destiny."

How Nestan-Darejan wrote to her lover

And now, sobbing and weeping, she penned her lover a letter: the tears that she shed quenched the fires that consumed her. The words that she wrote would pierce any heart through, like lances: her lips' rose was opened to show her teeth, shining crystal.

"See, O my beloved, here the work of my hand. My form serves for a pen, a pen steeped in gall: our two hearts, pressed together, are the paper I write on. — O heart, sad, captive heart, lie still where you are bound!

"O my beloved, the workings of this world! No matter what light shines, there is for me only darkness. The world is dis-

dained by the wise, for they know its true nature. . . . Parted
from you, how bitter is life to me!

"O my beloved, Fate and evil fortune have severed us; never
again shall we have the rapture of looking into each other's
eyes. What can avail the heart pierced by longing when you are
denied to it? — But that must be made plain which until now
has been hidden. I had believed, upon my faith, that you were
with the dead; life, I thought, had gone from me, with nothing
remaining. This news has made me praise the Creator, humble
myself before the throne of God; the sorrow that was mine
is now changed into joy. You are alive — that is enough; my
heart has something to hope for, my heart that is afire and cov-
ered over with wounds. Think of me, remember me, as one who
is lost to you; and I will cherish the love that was planted long
since in my heart.

"O my beloved, I cannot write my story down; my tongue
would tire in the telling, and none who heard would believe me.
Fatima — may God reward her! — delivered me when I was the
captive of sorcerers; but thereafter Fate once more took its ac-
customed way: to woe it added further woes yet more grievous,
for, not content with all the sorrows I was already possessed
of, it gave me as a captive into the hands of the Kajes, terrible
to meet as foes. — O my beloved, we are the sport of Fate!

"I sit in a castle with walls so high that the clouds shroud
the battlements: guards stand at their posts by the passage of
entry, and neither by day nor by night does their watch ever
cease. Any host that attacks them must meet with destruction;
they will bring it to ruin like the flames of devouring fire.

"Do you think these are warriors who fight in the common
way? — Do not kill me with a grief worse than that I already
bear! If I must look down on your corpse I shall be consumed
like sparked tinder. I am lost — but you must endure, with a
spirit stronger than hardest rock.

"Temper, beloved, the madness of your grief: do you believe
that I, the cypress-formed, would yield myself to another? I
can have no life without you, can have nothing but sorrow: I
would throw myself down on to the rocks below rather, or
make an end with a knife. No man, I swear it, shall ever be
possessed of your moon-fair one — no, not though he were

three times as fair as the orb of day! I would leap forth from here, to fall on the great crags. . . . Pray that heaven might grant then the gift of wings to my soul!

"Pray to God, that he may deliver me from this world and its travail, release me from the bondage of water, earth, fire and air. May he give me wings to fly up to attain my desire; to gaze, day and night, on the sun's flashing splendor. Without you the orb cannot shine — you furnish too much of its radiance; and you will attend upon it in all glory and honor. I shall see you, and you will dispel then the darkness about my heart: my life was bitter, but death will be sweet.

"Death cannot grieve me now; I have sent you my soul; I have laid your love within my heart, and there does it lie at rest. Wound is added to wound when I think how distance divides us; but do not weep, do not mourn, my beloved, for your lost one. — Set out, ride to India and bring aid to my father; he is beset by his enemies and has no one to help him. Comfort his heart for what he has lost in me. . . . Think of me, and of the tears that flow for your sake without ceasing.

"A just cause must make its way from heart to heart; I have railed against Fate enough. For your sake I will die, the ravens' calls will sound over me. . . . While I live you can know only sorrow and suffering.

"Here as a token, beloved, is a piece cut from an end of the veil that you gave me:[47] this is all that is left of the great hope that was once ours: the seven wheeling heavens have turned their anger upon us."[48]

She cut off a piece from her veil when she had written her lover this letter: fair were the long, thick tresses to see when her head was bared; black as the raven's wing, and fragrant with perfume.

The slave left for Gulansharo: no matter was it for him of a journey of many days — he was back in Fatima's house once again in an instant.[49] When Avtandil had received the news he had longed for, he raised up his hands and gave thanks to God reverently. Then he said to Fatima, "I have secured what I came in search of, but not a moment to lose is there. I must be gone now, I cannot stay longer, though great is the debt that I owe you: the time set last year for a tryst is approaching.[50] I must make haste to loose on the Kajes the hero who will work their destruction."

The khatun replied, "Yet fiercer, O lion, is the flame in my breast now; cut off from all light, my heart will be shrouded in darkness. But you must not delay — do not grieve for me, the mad must be left to their madness: you will have a hard task to win through should the Kajes' host be beforehand."

Avtandil summoned those slaves of Pridon's who had attended upon him and said to them, "We are like dead men who have been brought back to life anew; the joy of discovering that which we sought has been granted us; you will behold our enemies groaning in the pain of their wounds soon. Return now to Pridon and give him a true report: I cannot myself go to see him, for I am in haste and must ride hard on my own road. — Let him raise his mighty voice to sound in the field of war!

"To you I give all the booty, all the wealth, that has come to me. Great indeed is my debt to you; in Pridon's realm I will prove my gratitude in ways much more ample. — Take all that we won from the pirates' ship; I must seem mean-souled, but I have no more. My home is far, and I have no gifts here."[51]

He bestowed a vessel upon them that was filled with the richest treasures: "Set off homeward with all," he said, "and give this letter from me, his sworn brother, to Pridon."

How Avtandil wrote to Pridon

"Mighty Pridon," he wrote; "king of kings supremely blessed; hero with the heart of a lion, happy in good fortune, the sun's peer, quick to shed the blood of foes — from far off your younger brother now sends you his greeting.

"I have had much to endure, but my reward has now come to me; in the task I set my hand to success has been granted. I have gained certain intelligence of the fate of the sun-fair lady; news and comfort for the hero who lies in the abyss of despair, in the lower depths. She is held captive by the queen in the land of the Kajes: we must fight battles to reach her, but it will be all so much sport to us! Those eyes fair as the narcissus rain tears down in crystal drops, wet are the roses that stand on her cheeks. The Kajes have gone away, but they have left be-

(1312-28)

hind them a host that is countless. My heart rejoices within me now, and my tears flow no longer! Wherever you and your brother[52] go, hard things will become easy; you cannot, assuredly, fail to do all you desire. No man can stand against you — the rocks themselves, I believe, will all crumble!

"Forgive me for not myself now coming to see you; I cannot linger by the way while that moon-fair one is still held a captive. Soon Tariel and I will come to you, rejoicing; your heart will know gladness then. What more can I say? — Give your brother aid when the hour comes, the aid of a brother!

"The devotion your slaves have shown me is beyond all rewarding; well have they served me, and you can be pleased with them likewise. — But why should I give praise to men who have been long in your household? 'Like comes forth from like' is a saying of sages."

When he had finished this letter Avtandil tied it up and secured it; as fair was he to look on as the rose, as the violet! Then he gave it to Pridon's men. His teeth showing between his lips like pearls through a coral gate standing open, he charged them with a message containing intelligence of everything done by him.

He found a ship that could give him the passage he wanted and made ready for the voyage, he who was as fair as the sun, as the moon at the full. But he took leave of Fatima the unhappy with sadness; those who saw him go made a river of blood with their weeping. Fatima, Husain and their servants all shed hot tears: "What, sun-fair lord," they said, "is this you have done to us? You are burning us all in the fires of affliction. Why must you depart and plunge us thus into darkness? Let the hand that has drawn our souls forth from us now give us our burial!"

How Avtandil departed from Gulansharo and returned to Tariel

Avtandil crossed the sea in a vessel that gave travelers passage and then rode on his way alone, swiftly and gaily. Exulting in the good news that he was bearing to Tariel, he made with upraised hand a profession of faith in God.

Summer had come; on every hand the earth had turned to green, the roses were in the bloom that was to mark the time for the tryst; the sun had changed the house of its dwelling and moved into the sign of the Crab.[53] The flowers so long unseen drew forth a sigh from the hero. Thunder rolled in the heavens, and from the clouds there fell raindrops that sparkled like crystal.[54] He kissed a rose with lips that were even as red of hue: "Tender is the gaze," he said, "that I turn on you. Parted from my lady, I suffer; yet to converse with you affords solace for sorrow."

The bitter tears flowed when he thought of his comrade: wearisome was the way he had to take to rejoin him, through trackless deserts and regions all unknown. Whenever he saw lions or panthers among reeds he would kill them.

The caves came into view at last. "There," he said, rejoicing, "among those rocks is the friend for whose sake my tears have flowed. Do I not well deserve now to see him face to face, to make known my discovery! . . . But if he is not there, what shall I do? — I shall have labored in vain!

"If he has come, however, he will assuredly not have mewed himself up in the cave; he will have sallied out to roam like a creature of the wild. . . . Best to search through the reeds!" Thus did he decide after looking round and reflecting; and so now he made about and rode out on to the plain. Putting his horse into a gallop, he sang with a glad heart, and called out his friend's name in a voice that was filled with joy. When he had gone a little way, by the edge of a bed of reeds, his sharp sword in his hands, he saw Tariel, the sun-fair, in his beauty's full splendor. He was on foot; the blood of a lion he had just slain was dripping still from his sword-blade.

He looked round, startled, on Avtandil's shout; and then, when he saw who it was, he came, running and leaping: flinging his sword aside, he made straight for his brother. Avtandil, he who was fairer to behold than the sun, dismounted, and the two kissed and embraced one another. Their lips' roses parted, they exchanged loving greetings.

Tariel wept and spoke words filled with beauty; his lashes' jet thickets were reddened by rills of blood; streams of many tears watered the cypress that was his form then. "Since you have come back to me," he said, "what do I care for my pains and my sufferings!"

(1328-45)

Avtandil replied to his weeping with laughter; brightly through the coral of the hero's lips shone his teeth as he smiled: "The news that I bring will suffuse you with gladness; the rose fading upon your cheek will regain the bloom that it once possessed."

Tariel said, "Brother, the joy already come will suffice without increase: what happiness could be mine save once more to behold you? Where have you heard of a cure that was not of God's giving? How can a man hope to find in this world what heaven's will has denied him?"

When he saw that Tariel would not believe him, Avtandil was seized by impatience; there and then, eager to impart his news, he drew out the piece of veil come from her whose lip was to be compared with the rose. Tariel recognized it the instant he saw it; and he leaped on it, seized it and tore it away. Well did he know whom the letter and the veil's corner came from; unfolding them, he pressed his lips to them; then, pale as a withered rose, he fell to the ground. His jet lashes closed and he swooned right away. . . .[55] Not Qays,[56] not Salaman,[57] had woes such as his to bear!

When he saw Tariel lying lifeless Avtandil sprang forward to look to him, and spoke to him gently. But nothing was there he could do to help the young lord, consumed by the flames of affliction; he had been robbed of his senses by the sight of the token.

Avtandil sat down to weep and mourn with a voice soft and tuneful. With a hand fair as crystal he tore again and again at his raven locks. With a fist as hard as a hammer of adamant he struck his cheek's polished ruby: streams of blood came bursting forth that were coral in color. He rent his cheeks, and gore flowed while he gazed upon Tariel: "Could a fool," he said, "could a madman, have done such a deed as this? — To be in such haste to pour water on a fire passing hard to quench! . . . The heart cannot withstand a stroke of tremendous and sudden joy. — I have killed my friend; what am I to do in the shame come upon me? Fool, thoughtless fool that I was! What is worse than a dolt in a delicate matter? 'Better censured and slow,' runs the adage, 'than praised and precipitate'!"

Like one seared by a flame, Tariel lay in his swoon. Avtandil rose and went through the reeds, looking about him for water. Seeing the lion's blood in a pool, he took some to quench the fire consuming Tariel's spirit: and when he had sprinkled it on his friend's breast the countenance that had been lapis-lazuli-livid began to turn back to ruby. The lion's breast was thus sprinkled with the blood of the lion.[58] — Tariel stirred; his lashes, those ranks of dark Indians, fluttered: he opened his eyes, and found the strength soon to sit up. But the moon's beams seemed pale by the light of the sun.[59]

With the coming of winter the roses fade and their petals fall: in summer the sweet-voiced nightingale comes to sing upon them, but the sun shrivels them up, and they bemoan the drought sadly. Heat consumes, cold freezes; either way there is sorrow. Even so is it hard for the heart of man to find content anywhere; alike in grief and in joy it tends always to madness. It is for ever nursing wounds, at odds with the workings of Fortune; the man who puts his trust in this world will prove his own enemy.

Tariel looked at his lady's letter again; although it drove him to distraction, he read it through. Tears blinded his eyes, and the daylight was darkened. — Avtandil now rose and began to speak sternly: "Such weakness," he said, "is unworthy of any man with a mind well schooled! What cause have we now to weep? Rather is it a time to be gay. Rise up, let us be off to deliver that sun-fair lady, the lost one; I will bring you soon to the place where you long to be.

"Let us first rejoice together, for rejoicing is fitting, and then take horse and set out on the road to Kajeti: our swords will show us the way. We will strike our foes down as they flee, we will return without injury, we will leave their corpses behind us as a feast for the crows!"

Tariel, done with swooning now, began to ask questions: he looked up, the black and white of his eyes flashing lightning. His color grew stronger, like a ruby's in sunshine. . . . He who is worthy of it will always receive the mercy of heaven.

He gave his thanks to Avtandil: "How can I praise you, who deserve to be praised by the wise?" he said. "You have brought water to the flower in the valley like a stream from the mountain; my eyes' narcissus-pools have no longer their flow of tears.

(1345-62)

I can make no return, but may God in heaven repay you; may he reward you in place of me, may he send a gift from on high!"

They mounted and rode off towards the cave, in great gladness of spirit; and now did Fate grant to Asmat what she had so long hungered for. She was sitting at the entrance to the cave, in her shift: looking up, she recognized Tariel and the lord on the white horse who was with him: the two of them were singing as sweetly as nightingales. And, even as she was, she sprang up to greet them. Hitherto Tariel had always returned to the cave shedding bitter tears; greatly did she wonder to see him coming thus, with song and with laughter! Her head reeled like a drunkard's — she had not heard the good news yet — and a sudden fear seized her.

When the heroes saw her they shouted, their teeth gleaming through smiling lips, "Asmat, God's mercy has come down now from heaven! We have found what we sought, we have discovered where Nestan is, Nestan the lost moon! Fate has quenched the fires of our affliction, turned our sorrows to joy."

Avtandil dismounted and pressed her to him: she put her arms round the hero whose embrace was like the enclosing of a cypress's branches. "What have you done?' she said through her tears as she kissed him. "What have you learned? Let my weeping move you to pity, and tell me!" Avtandil gave her the missive her mistress — the cypress with the withered branch, the pale moon — had written. "Here is a letter," he said, "from her who has had so much grief to bear; the sun has drawn near, it will drive all our shadows away from us!"

As soon as Asmat set eyes on the letter she knew from whose hand it came. Amazed and disquieted, she trembled like one possessed; from head to foot she was fast in the grip of an utter astonishment. "What do I see, what have I heard," she said — "can it be really true?" "It is indeed true," Avtandil replied; "you need have no fears. Joy has come upon us, the bitterness of grief is a past thing; the sun has shone forth and the darkness has fled away. Good has overcome evil, for its essence is lasting."

The Indian prince[60] spoke some words gaily to Asmat; weeping for joy, they embraced one another. From their lashes, black as the raven's wing, a light dew of tears dropped on their cheeks' roses. . . . God will never abandon the man who puts trust in him.

They all gave thanks to the Almighty: "You have decreed," they said, "that all that came to pass should be for the best for us; now we understand that you did not will disaster!" Hands uplifted, the Indian prince shouted this joyously. With glad hearts they went into the cave then, and Asmat bestirred herself to provide entertainment.

"Attend to me now," Tariel said to Avtandil; "I am going to tell you something that is worth giving ear to. — Ever since I slaughtered the Divs to make myself lord of these caverns,[61] their rich store of treasure[62] has lain here inviolate. I have never examined it, for I had no desire to; but now let us open it and see what is there contained." Avtandil agreed to this; they rose to their feet to go, and Asmat went with them.

They broke down forty doors — no great matter was that for them — and found such treasure as has never been looked on by mortal eyes; pearls the size of balls, heaped jewels cut with rarest skill — and who could have made a reckoning of the amount of gold lying there! Each of the forty chambers was filled thus with riches. Stored away like victuals, armor and weapons of every kind were found in a room that had served as an armory: there was also a coffer, closed and sealed, with this legend:

Here are arms of most wonderful quality; mail, helmets and sharp-bladed swords brought from Basra.[63] Should the Kajes attack the Divs, the day will go hard with them: he who opens this coffer at any other season will be a slayer of monarchs.

They opened it, and found inside suits of armor and weapons to equip fully three warriors; mail, swords, helmets and greaves, all lying in cases of emerald much like reliquaries. Each hero donned a suit to make trial of its quality: no blow left the least mark upon mail, helmets or hauberks; the swords cleft through iron as they would have through thread. In their eyes that gear was the world's greatest treasure; nothing, I warrant, would they have taken in barter for it! "A good omen, this," they said; "we are favored by Fortune; God has looked down upon us in his mercy from heaven!" They took it all on their backs then — there was one suit for each of them, and the third they trussed up with leather thongs to take as a present for Pridon. Laying hands on some gold and fine pearls, they went forth; the forty chambers were all sealed. "My hand," said Avtandil, "from this day forward will not leave my sword-hilt; let us rest here tonight and depart with the dawn."

Now, painter, limn those brothers; brothers stauncher than brothers, lovers of star-fair ladies, heroes without a peer, paladins renowned for valor! There will be a thrusting of lances in battle when they come to Kajeti!

How Tariel and Avtandil journeyed to Pridon's realm

They set out at break of day. Asmat went with them: until they reached Nuradin's realm she rode behind one or the other; then a merchant furnished a horse — not as a gift, but for gold. Avtandil acted as guide to them: no need for another!

They rode on, and at length they saw before them Nuradin's herdsmen watching over his horses: the beasts won their praise, and they felt sure they were Pridon's. Then the Indian said to Avtandil, "The chance for a jest here; come, let us play a trick upon Pridon and drive off this herd of his. We will possess ourselves of it, and when he hears what is afoot he will ride out to give battle, to dye the ground hereabouts all red with our blood. Then recognition will come to him, and his wrath will be swallowed up in surprise. Nothing like a good joke; even the proud must unbend before it!"

And so they began to secure Pridon's finest steeds. The herdsmen took flint and steel to kindle a signal fire, and then shouted out, "Who are you, sirs, that would do such a deed? — This herd belongs to one who strikes dead at a blow!"

Tariel and Avtandil bent their bows now and made after the herdsmen. "Help! Help! We are being butchered by brigands!" these began to shriek at the tops of their voices: and they fled to tell Pridon the news in a body, all clamoring.

Pridon made ready for battle, mounted and rode out in his

harness. The noise grew, and great was the muster of warriors. Those two fair ones — suns winter's chill had no power to freeze — now rode forward, their faces concealed by their helmets. "That is the man I am looking for!" Tariel said, seeing Pridon. And, taking his helmet off, he called out with laughter, "What are you about? Why, pray, are you so annoyed at our coming? A fine host, sallying out to give battle!"

Pridon leaped from his horse at once, fell on his knees, made obeisance. Tariel and Avtandil dismounted likewise; and then they embraced him. Hands upraised, Pridon rendered thanks to God with his whole heart; and those of his lords who knew Tariel and Avtandil gave them their greeting.

"What kept you?" said Pridon. "I had looked for you earlier. — I am ready and eager to do any service." It was as though two suns and a moon were gathered together then; the beauty of each seemed increased by the other two. — They rode off to Pridon's magnificent palace now. Avtandil, his sworn brother, Pridon placed at his side; Tariel sat upon a throne that was covered with velvet and gold brocade.[64] Then the guests presented the armor they had brought to the hero of renown who now was a host to them: "At this present time," they said, "we have nothing else for you; but many are the treasures that are laid up in store." Pridon touched the ground with his forehead: "This is a gift that accords with such natures as yours," he responded.

Tariel and Avtandil were Pridon's guests that night. When they had bathed he pressed on them an abundance of raiment; they were clad in rich garments, each fairer than the one before, presently. Rare jewels and pearls in a vessel of gold did he give them too. Then he said, "And now I must speak words that will make me seem a reluctant host, as though guests with such minds as yours wearied me as might any fools: but we must not lose time here: let us set out on the long road before us; for if we find the Kajes are back again our task may be a hard one.

"A large force would not serve our turn; what we need is a small band of good soldiers: three hundred will be enough — but now let us make all haste and be off to Kajeti and battle, our hands on our sword-hilts! We shall soon win the lovely one with the form of a cypress.

(1379-95)

"I have been to Kajeti once: when you see it with your own eyes you will agree that the fortress is indeed of the strongest; all round there is steep rock that no attacker could ever scale. We must get in by stealth — there is no hope of our storming it. That is why an army would be of no use to us; it could not slip in unperceived."

Tariel and Avtandil assented: taking leave of Asmat, after Pridon had bestowed gifts upon her, the heroes set out with three hundred horsemen, all famous men of arms. . . . At the last God grants victory to those who have suffered woe!

The three sworn brothers took ship and voyaged across the seas; and then, with Pridon as guide, they pressed onward by day and by night. At length Pridon said, "We are now drawing near to Kajeti; henceforth we can travel only under the cover of darkness." The three were at one on this: when dawn came they halted; they rode hard through the night hours. Then they saw the city before them: its guards were unnumbered; all around were the rocks; everywhere sounded the calls of the sentinels; at the passage's entrance[65] watch was kept by ten thousand warriors.

The heroes surveyed the city as it lay bathed in the moonlight: "A hard matter!" they said. — "Let us now take counsel together; a hundred can vanquish a thousand if they go the right way about it."[66]

How Nuradin-Pridon put forward a plan

Pridon said: "This is my judgement, and I think it a sound one. — We are few, and an assault would demand very many.[67] We cannot offer them battle — this is no time for boasting! With the gates shut, a thousand years' striving could not gain us entry.

"I had instructors in boyhood who gave me an acrobat's training; they taught me their leaps and all manner of other tricks. I could make along a rope with such speed that the eye could not follow me; the young lads who saw me were one and all envious.

"Now let whichever of us has the most skill with a rope take a great length and throw a noose to the top of a turret. I will run up that rope just as I would over level ground[68] — and then you will have to look long to find a man who is whole and unwounded! My shield and my armor will in no way encumber me. Leaping down inside, I will fall on the guards like a hurricane and work slaughter among them. I will open the gates then — you will see them flung wide. And do you make for the spot where the tumult is rising."

How Avtandil put forward a plan

Avtandil said: "Your friends, Pridon, truly cannot find fault with you! You trust in the strength of your arms, and wounds hold no terrors: the plan of a hero, this, for the destruction of enemies. But listen — do you not hear how sentinel is for ever calling to sentinel?

"They would hear your arms' clatter, see you running — and cut your rope. Of this you can be very sure. . . . Disaster, and nothing gained! No, this scheme will not answer; we must try something more prudent. — Keep yourselves hidden, stay away out of sight. No hand will be laid on a solitary traveler who desires to get into the city: I will put on a merchant's disguise to deceive them, loading a mule with sword, armor and helmet. It would be unwise for all three to go; it might lead to discovery: I will go alone in my merchant's garb and gull them completely. In some quiet spot I will get into my harness, and before they know what has happened I will have fallen upon them: I will, with God's help, make blood flow there in rivers![69] To deal with the guards who are within will be easy; outside the gates you will meanwhile be laying about you like heroes. I will shatter the locks and throw the gates open — nought do I care for their stones and their mortar! Such is my plan; if there is a better way, let us hear of it."

How Tariel put forward a plan

Tariel said: "Here do I see valor far beyond that of other heroes; these counsels and projects are indeed worthy of hearts such as yours. I know that you are athirst for fierce fighting, not for vain, empty flourishes: when the battle grows perilous, you prove yourselves men in truth!

"But you must let me too have some voice in the matter. — The din will be heard by my lady; she will look down, like the sun in her beauty. Are you to have mortal combat while she sees me stand idle? I should be sunk in disgrace — peace, no smooth words of flattery!

"Here is a better plan, the scheme we will carry through. Let each put himself at the head of a hundred men at the break of day; we will come spurring up from three different quarters thereafter. They will sally out to give battle when they see how small are our numbers; and then will they feel the full weight of our swords! We will charge them fiercely and make round their flank to possess ourselves of the gates. One of us shall enter, while the others continue the fight outside, and there, within the walls, make the blood flow in rivers. Let us trust again to those arms we have used so well in past days."

"I grasp, I understand, I can see what lies behind this," said Pridon. "Show me the horse that could reach the gates before the steed that was mine once! Little did I think when I gave it to you[70] that we should one day have business in Kajeti. Had I foreseen that, you should never have got the beast — so far goes my meanness!"

Pridon continued to banter, gay at heart, in this fashion: and now the three heroes — eloquent of tongue were they, wise of speech — began to laugh and to joke one with another. Presently they dismounted and put on their war-gear; then they took their best horses. After they had talked the matter over again, in the best of good humor, Tariel's plan was agreed upon; and each put himself at the head of a hundred of their magnificent warriors. They got into the saddle then and put on their helmets.

I saw those heroes; more splendid were they to behold than the sun; the seven planets enclosed them in a great column of light; graceful of form, Tariel bestrode his black charger. . . . The foe was undone by their valiance, the world by their beauty.

After the cloud-burst the torrent breaks from the mountain; it roars down through the valley, and great is the tumult; but when it reaches the sea at length its waters are calmed. Here is a likeness for the three friends. Pridon and Avtandil were without their equals in valor — but where is the man who could stand against Tariel? The sun's rays darken the planets and swallow the stars' light. . . . Now give ear, you who listen, and you shall hear of fierce fighting!

The bands formed, each took one of the gates for his entry; three hundred men did they have in all, made of the stuff of heroes. Before dawn they examined the ground, quickly but carefully; then, each man with his shield, they began to advance when the morning came. Quietly did they ride at first, like so many peaceable travelers: suspecting nothing, the garrison did not stand to their arms; free of foreboding, they remained at their ease. . . . The three hundred drew near; and then in an instant they had all donned their helmets.

They put spurs to their horses; their whips cut the air; they reached the gates and broke through them; a tumult arose in the city. The Three charged through the three gateways and attacked the defenders; loudly sounded the trumpet, the drum and the clarion.

And now did the measureless wrath of God strike Kajeti: Kronos[71] looked down in anger and withdrew the sun's sweetness; the wheel of the heavens turned on the fortress in fury; the corpses were piled up high, one on another; the bodies of dead men lay thicker and thicker. Warriors dropped to the ground whenever Tariel shouted; chain mail gave in his hands, he tore armor in pieces. — No hard matter was it for the heroes to break in at the three gates; and once inside they made with all speed for the citadel.

Avtandil and Pridon caught sight of each other inside the city's walls; they had slaughtered all the foes in their paths, made their blood flow in rivers. Each at once gave a shout and then made for his comrade; and so they rejoiced together. But, looking this way and that, they said, "What of Tariel?" Neither had seen or heard anything of him. Giving no heed to their enemies, they betook themselves now to the gates of the citadel. There they found heaps of armor, shattered swords, and ten thousand guards lifeless; like men stretched out in sickness they lay cleft through from head to foot, their armor all rent in pieces. The way in was open; round about lay the gates'

(1411-27)

broken fragments. They knew it for Tariel's work: "This," they said, "is his doing!"

The mouth of the passage was now just before them: they entered and, creeping, made their way to the other end. And then they saw Nestan: like a moon was she — a moon delivered from the serpent of darkness to be joined to the sun! Tariel had doffed his helmet; and fair indeed, his locks all swept back from his brow, did he look then. There they were standing, locked close in each other's arms. Their tears flowed as they kissed — like Mushtar and Zual conjoined were they then![72] The rose is lovely indeed when it is bathed in the sun's beams; it casts back the radiance. . . . Those two had seen sorrow; they would henceforth know joy.

Again and again they kissed, holding each other close; their lips were as fair as the rose at its opening. Avtandil and Pridon advanced to give the sun-fair lady their greeting then; thus were the three brothers once more united.

Her lovely face lit with joy, Nestan the sun-fair went up to the newly-come: with a heart full of gladness she kissed those rescuers gently, and sweetly gave them thanks in words softly spoken and winning. The two responded with courtesy; and then they turned to Tariel, the hero of the cypress-form, with acclaim. Each paladin wanted to know how it had gone with the others. None had received any injury; their armor had given proof of its worth.[73] They had quitted themselves like three lions; as helpless as deer or goats had their enemies been.

Of their three hundred warriors a hundred and sixty were left to them; Pridon grieved for his men, for all the joy that possessed him.[74] — They searched, and put to the sword every foe who was still alive: the treasures that they found were beyond any reckoning.

They gathered together camels and mules — every stout beast they could lay hands on — and pearls and precious stones — all cut, rubies and jacinths — were loaded upon the backs then of three thousand animals. Nestan the sun-fair they placed in a litter; every care would henceforward be lavished upon her. And so, leaving a garrison, sixty men, behind in the castle, they bore off the maiden; hard would it have been for any man to steal her away from them! Long though the way was, they took the road for the city of the king of the Seas: "We must see Fatima," they said; "for great indeed is the debt that we owe to her."

How Tariel went to meet the king of the Seas

Tariel sent a courier to the king of the Seas with this message: "I, Tariel the victorious, am bringing my sun-fair lady, her for whose sake my heart is pierced through as by lances, forth from Kajeti: I desire to see you and to show you such honor as a son does his father.

"I have made myself master of the possessions and land of the Kajes, but for all that I have conquered I am beholden to you, O King. My sun-fair lady was rescued by Fatima, who was as a sister to her, as a mother. — What return can I make you? I hate empty promises. Come, I urge you, to see us before we pass beyond your realm's confines. I am going to give you the lordship of the land of the Kajes; it is yours to take from my hands. Send a force, hold the castle there with a strong garrison. I cannot attend upon you — my haste forbids it — so do you ride forth to see me now.

"I would have you bid Husain send Fatima, his wife, in your company; she whom she rescued will rejoice greatly to see her; whom could she more wish to see — she who outshines the sun as crystal pitch darkness?"[75]

When the king of the Seas had received Tariel's courier — startling news must always fill the heart with amazement! — he gave thanks to God and glorified him, the Just Judge of all, and then straightway took horse — he did not need to be summoned twice. There was a loading-up of gifts then to take to the wedding; jet in great quantity, and many treasures of other kinds also. The monarch set out, taking Fatima with him; and after ten days of traveling the sight of the lion Tariel and the sun-fair lady who illumined the whole earth rejoiced him.

Forward rode the three heroes to meet the great king of the Seas; then they dismounted and kissed him in greeting before the warriors, according him reverence. The king sang Tariel's

(1427-42)

praises, and the prince replied with many words of thanks. —
When the monarch beheld Nestan her radiant beauty bewitched
him.

Slow fires began to burn within Fatima Khatun when she
set eyes on the maiden. Taking her in her arms and kissing her
hands, feet, face and neck, she said, "O God, thanks be to thee
for thus lightening my darkness! Now do I understand that
evil is the thing of a moment, while good is enduring." Nestan
then embraced Fatima and said to her sweetly, "God has
brought light to my heart, that was utterly broken: I am like a
moon at the full, restored after waning; like a rose saved from
the frost by the rays of the sun."

There, in great splendor, was a marriage festival held by the
king of the Seas. He gave Tariel thanks for the gift of Kajeti;
for seven days he would not let his guests take their departure.
He made generous gifts from the treasures brought with him;
gold coin lavishly scattered was worn away with much tread-
ing; brocades, satins and silks were piled high one on another.

Tariel received from the king a crown made out of a single
unflawed yellow jacinth; no price could be put on it. A throne
fashioned from fine red gold was given him also. On Nestan-
Darejan was bestowed a mantle that was covered with jewels;
red jacinths adorned it, and rubies of Badakhshan.[76] The bride
and the bridegroom were seated together; their faces flashed
lightning; all who beheld them were burned in a new flame
of rapture.

On Avtandil and Pridon the king bestowed great gifts beyond
measure; there was a splendid horse and a costly saddle for
each, and a rich-jewelled tunic with rare colors that sparkled.
They said, "What thanks would be fitting? — May your reign
be attended by joy and felicity!"

Tariel gave his thanks then in courteous phrases: "O King,
I rejoice — first because it has been given to us to look thus
upon you, and then because you have laden us with so many
wondrous gifts; we did well for ourselves when we asked for
this meeting!"

The king of the Seas said in answer, "Prince; lion; hero; life
to those who are with you; death to those at a distance! What
could I give you that would match your deserts well, my fair

lord? What can I look for when once I have gone from you?"

Tariel said to Fatima, "On you I will always look as I would on a sister; great, beyond repaying, is the debt that I owe you. Yours is the treasure I have brought from Kajeti; take it all as a gift."

Fatima Khatun made a reverence and uttered words of great gratitude: "Prince, I am consumed by an inward fire when I look on you! What shall I do when you have gone far from me? Assuredly I must lose my wits when you take your departure! To be near you is happiness, to be denied sight of you, misery!"

At length those three radiant heroes — their lips were like mother of pearl, their teeth shone like crystal—addressed thus the king of the Seas: "We shall have no heart for revelry when we have gone from you; for pipe, for harp, or for the sound of the tambourine: but grant leave to depart, we cannot linger, time presses. Be to us as a father — all our hope lies in you: furnish a vessel, this is the prayer that we make now."

The king replied, "I would make myself earth for your feet to tread; since you are eager to set forth, what more can I say to you? Go then; you will find your best guide in the strength of your sword-arms."

The king had a vessel made ready; there it lay at its moorings. When Tariel embarked those who had now to say farewell wept; they beat their heads, rent their flesh and tore their hair and their beards. The ocean's waters were swollen by the tears shed then by Fatima.

The three sworn brothers voyaged over the sea together: they confirmed the oaths they had already given one to another. Laughter and song lent them radiance; in these things they delighted. Bright were their lips, and their teeth shone like crystal.

They sent forward a messenger to give Asmat the good news, and to tell Pridon's great lords how the fighting had gone. — "She who resembles the orb of day is approaching, like the sun when it rises to darken the light of the planets; we shall soon be released from the grip of the frost." They placed the sun-fair lady in a litter then and took their way along by the coast road, as carefree as boys and rejoicing; for sorrow was passed from them. In the land of the valiant Nuradin a welcome awaited them, and song filled the air: the lords of the kingdom all came out to greet them. The blows of an axe could not

(1442-60)

have severed Asmat from Nestan; grief had vanished, and her heart was suffused with joy utterly. Now her devotion had no further to go.

Nestan-Darejan embraced Asmat and kissed her. "Alas, dear friend," she said, "I have brought you also to wretchedness! But God has shown us his mercy now; generous indeed is he. — How can I ever make a return for your faithfulness!" "Thanks be to God," Asmat replied; "I have found you a rose that the frost has not seized upon; in the end understanding has revealed what was hidden. Since I have seen you thus happy, I could meet death itself joyfully. — Best of all friends are lord and vassal when they love one another."

The barons then made obeisance and spoke words of eulogy: "Glory to God for this joy he has granted us! Now he has let us behold you, inward fires burn us no longer; he who deals the wound has also the power to give healing." They went up to Tariel, and all of them kissed his hand: the prince said, "Your brothers have laid down their lives for our sake; they have found joy in eternity to be truth, not a dream; they have attained to communion with the One, and great is the glory that now rests upon them. I grieve for their deaths, but they have won a gift beyond our mortality."

When he had said this he wept quietly; the rain of tears fell on the snow of his countenance. Boreas[77] blew down upon his eyes, those narcissi; January's cold froze the rose on his cheek.

When they saw his tears they all wept; those who had lost a kinsman now made lamentation. At length, their grief quietened, they said, "Those who behold you, who are likened to the sun by the sages, should sing for joy; they should not for ever be moaning. Where is the man who could deserve that you should grieve thus much for him? Far better to die for you than to wander upon the earth vainly!" Pridon then lifted up his voice and addressed him: "Do not yield thus to sorrow! May a thousand joys be sent by God to reward you!"

Avtandil too spoke of the dead with great sorrow. They responded with praise, and then joined in saying, "The time has now come for rejoicing; since the lost lion-hero has found the vanished sun-fair one, let us put a swift end to all grief and all tears."

And now they rode on to the great city of Mulghazanzar:

trumpets and clarions blew fanfares; great was the noise and excitement; tambourines and copper drums sounded bravely together. The townsfolk left the bazaar and came crowding about them; merchants quitted their alleys; upon every hand there was a thronging of onlookers. The men of the city guard must needs use their arms to hold back the multitude. Begging to be allowed to gaze, the people kept pressing in; hard put to it indeed were the guards to contain them.

When they reached Pridon's magnificent palace the heroes dismounted; a host of slaves with golden girdles[78] came forward to meet them. Rich brocaded velvet was spread out before their feet; gold pieces were showered then that the crowd quickly gathered up.

How Pridon held a marriage festival for
Tariel and Nestan-Darejan

A throne white and coral in color, studded with splendid red and yellow jewels, was set in place for the bridal pair; the hues of Avtandil's were yellow and black. — When they came forward and sat down all who beheld them were filled with delight.

Minstrels appeared, and the sound of sweet song arose; in honor of the marriage they held a great festival. Many were the rich stuffs given away by Pridon, the generous-handed host, then; Nestan's dazzling smiles illumined her countenance. Marvellous were the gifts from the wealthy Pridon that were brought forth: nine pearls, each the size of a goose's egg, and a jewel that shone like the sun in its brightness — a painter could have painted a picture at night by the light of it. To Tariel and Nestan he gave collars of jewels, jacinths, each cut to a roundness. Then a tray so heavy that the hand could scarcely hold it was brought forth; a gift from the valiant Pridon to the lion Avtandil. Quite filled with pearls enormous in size was it; they were given to Avtandil with the loving words of a comrade. The palace was piled high with brocades and rich velvets. Tariel, the proud in heart, gave thanks of a gracious turn.

For eight days Pridon continued to maintain thus high festival; on each there was a bestowal of gifts that were priceless; in light, in dark, harp and lute never fell silent. Here were a bridegroom and a bride truly worthy one of the other!

(1460-78)

One day Tariel opened his heart in this fashion to Pridon: "You have shown me a love like the love of an elder brother. When I was near death you brought the balm that would give my wound healing: not my life, not my soul itself, would suffice to requite you.

"You know what Avtandil too has done for my sake. I would do something for him now in return; go to him and ask him to declare what he wants most. He has quenched the fires in my breast; his must have an end likewise. — Say for me: 'What, brother, could repay you for the sorrows you have endured for my sake! God will grant you assuredly his grace from on high; but if I cannot win the desire of your heart for you, no home will there be for me anywhere, in hut or in palace.

'Now tell me what I can do for you, how best I can render aid. For my part, I am for our taking the road to Arabia; let us set out together! We will win what we are seeking — with fair words or with sword-blows. If I cannot see you and your lady united, I will, upon my oath, be no husband to mine!' "

When Pridon had given him Tariel's message, Avtandil's face was illumined by laughter. "Why should I need help?" he said. "No man has done me hurt: my sun-fair one does not languish in the hands of the Kajes, nor does anything grieve her. By the grace of God she sits upon a throne in great majesty: she is proud, highly honored — no man does her injury. She suffers nothing from Kajes, she suffers nothing from sorcerers. What occasion for help here? — This is the truth I am telling you!

"When heaven's decree is disclosed in my destiny, my burning heart, if it please God, will receive consolation; the sun's radiance will fall then at last on my wretchedness. But until then any move of mine would be so much vain striving.

"Go and give this answer to Tariel: 'Your heart, prince, is gentle, but what have you to thank me for? It was to give you service that I was born from my mother's womb: and until you are acclaimed king, may I be as dust in the sight of God!

'You would see me united with my lady, you tell me. That is a wish indeed worthy of your heart's generosity; but the sword will not cut a way here — no more will a ready tongue. Better to leave all to the workings of heaven, to Providence. Rather do I desire to see you sitting on the throne of India in majesty, that star-fair lady by your side, her face flashing lightning, with your enemies slaughtered, with no foe left to give battle.

'When these desires have been granted I will indeed return to Arabia, once more see my sun-fair lady; and when she thinks good she will quench this fire that consumes me. I am a lover of plain words — I have no more to ask of you!' "

Pridon delivered this message: "It would not take a sooth-sayer to foretell that I would not accept this," said Tariel. "Av-tandil it was who discovered where my life's well-spring was held as a captive; in return he shall find the valor and strength of a brother within me. — Go now and give him these un-adorned words from me: 'I must betake myself next to the court of your sovereign. Many of his best warriors met their deaths at my hands once; I will ask for forgiveness and then come away.' And tell him this further: 'No more of these messages; I will set out tomorrow — the thing is decided. The king of the Arabs cannot refuse what I ask of him. I will beg for the hand of his daughter with soft words; I will beseech him, and I will gain his consent to the wedding.' "

Pridon went off and delivered the message then. "He is deter-mined to go," he added; "he is not to be turned from his pur-pose." Avtandil grieved sorely; the fires in his heart burst once more into flame. . . . Even so should a vassal hold his sovereign in reverence!

He went now and threw himself on bended knee before Ta-riel; he kissed his feet, clung to them, but did not dare raise his eyes. "This year," he said, "I have done Rostevan wrong enough;[79] do not make me sin again against my allegiance! God's justice, indeed, can give your project no counte-nance. — How can I play false the liege lord to whom I owe ser-vice, how can I raise my hand against one who has become pale through his grief for me, how can a vassal turn his sword's edge against his own master! Such a plan would create discord, moreover, between me and my lady: if she were angered, if wrath filled her heart, my lot would be truly most wretched. I should hear nothing from her, even the sight of her would be denied me; and the man does not live who could win me her pardon!"

(1478-95)

Taking Avtandil by the hand and raising him to his feet, Tariel the sun-fair said, laughing, "To you am I beholden for every good thing that has come to me; you too must know joy such as that which is mine now. For my part, I detest reserve, observance of form, between friends; and I likewise hate gloom, mighty airs and ill-temper. Let a man come to me if he be a true-hearted friend. For others, let them go their way — and me mine; it is better so.

"I know how you stand in the regard of your lady — and she cannot be loath, surely, to give your comrade a welcome. Then why should I use words of deceit with the king? I desire only to behold those whom all men desire to see. With all due reverence, I will pray the king to be graciously pleased to give you the hand of his daughter. Since you both yearn for union, how can you endure to be parted still longer? Do not waste away in your separate solitudes; let each lend to the beauty of the other new lustre."

When Avtandil saw that Tariel was fully resolved to go, he argued no further, but acquiesced in the project. Pridon selected the best of his men for an escort; he also set out himself with them, took the road in their company.

How the three heroes went to Tariel's cave, and thence to Arabia

Denys[80] the wise has revealed this arcane truth to us: "God sends good, and good only; evil is not his creation: he gives the bad but a moment, the good he wills to endure. He sustains his own excellence in its utter perfection."

Those lions, those sun-fair heroes, now set out from Pridon's realm. With them they took the lady whose loveliness dazzled all who beheld her. Her plaited tresses, black as the raven's wing, framing a face crystal-fair, her cheek's ruby adorned by the most delicate beauty, she was borne in a litter. Many were the beasts of the chase that they killed on the journey. In each place on the road they delighted all who beheld them; the people came out to greet them, to bestow gifts and to lavish praise. They were like a sun in the heavens with three moons surrounding.[81]

For many days they traveled thus onward; gladness filled their hearts, understanding their converse. At length, in those great wastes untrodden by mortal men, they drew near the rocks where Tariel had had his abode. "It falls to me to play the host now," said the Indian prince; "my habitation, this, in the days of my madness. Asmat will provide entertainment; she has a store of cured meat here. And then you will be amazed by my rich gifts, and by their diversity."

They went on to the cave among the great rocks, and there they dismounted: Asmat carved venison to make a repast for the company. One and all, they rejoiced that their woes had now passed away, and gave thanks to God for turning their sorrows to gladness. Taking their pleasure, they roamed through the caverns and examined the treasures that had been sealed up by Tariel[82] — treasures never counted or known of by any man. No cause was there for any to feel ill-contented!

Tariel bestowed many rich gifts; each received what was fitting. Pridon's men, common soldiers and captains alike, received wealth; every man who had come with them had it heaped on him lavishly. But the treasure might have had no hand laid on it, so much was there still remaining.

Tariel said to Pridon, "The debt that I owe you will be hard to repay; but it is said, 'The man who does good finds his reward in the end.' Yours are the riches that lie here or may yet be found; take away your possessions!" Pridon made profound obeisance and spoke words of great gratitude: "Prince, do not think me foolish, bereft of all understanding! A foe as stout as a cudgel is no more than a straw to you! My joy will endure only while I can look on you."

After Pridon had sent for camels to carry all the treasure back to his palace, they took the road for Arabia. Avtandil resembled the moon going, wasted, to meet the sun.[83]

After many days' travel they reached the land of Arabia. Village after village they saw, castle after castle: the people were clad in blue and in green; and all were bathed in tears for the sake of Avtandil.

Tariel sent this message forward to Rostevan: "O King, may every happiness be yours! — I, the sovereign of India, am on my way to your royal court to present to you her who is as fair as a rose of the morning.

(1495-1513)

"Once, in your dominions, I moved you to anger; but in trying to take me captive with charge and attack you did ill. — Your warriors felt then the weight of my rage! Many of your men, servants of your crown and throne, did I slaughter. But now I have turned aside from my road to come before you; pardon the wrong that I did you, let your ire be appeased. No presents do I bring — Pridon and his followers will bear me out in this; the only gift that I have for you is — your own Avtandil."

When the messenger arrived at court there was rejoicing such as no tongue could tell of. The bloom on Tinatin's cheeks was heightened threefold; the darkness of eyebrows and lashes made her countenance's crystal and ruby yet fairer.

There was a beating of drums and a thudding of feet: the warriors ran this way and that, eager to set forth to give greeting. Horses were led out and saddled; and a great company of lords, strong of arm and valiant of heart, mounted without delay.

The king took horse likewise; the captains and all the soldiery went out with their welcome. As soon as they heard the news the people came flocking from every side; all raised their voices in thanksgiving to God. "Evil," they said, "is but a shadow that passes; the Good is enduring!"

When the two companies had come within sight of each other Avtandil said in a low voice to Tariel, "Do you see the dust that is rising up over there on the plain? There is the cause of the fire in my breast, of the flame that consumes my heart. My lord is coming to meet you, I can go no further forward now. I am ashamed; my heart is burning as though in a furnace. Never was a man so dishonored as I! But do you ride up to him; take Pridon with you: you will know for yourself how best you can aid me!"

"It is fitting that you should stand thus in awe of your lord," replied Tariel. "I will leave you here and ride on and tell the king that you do not dare to enter his presence. With God's help I will soon unite you with your sun-fair lady, the cypress-formed."

The lion Avtandil went no further, but waited in a small tent erected there. Nestan-Darejan, she who filled with delight all who beheld her, halted likewise. The airs wafted from her lashes were like a soft southern wind.

The Indian prince rode forward proudly, and Pridon went with him: some time passed away while they covered the ground. . . . Then Tariel advanced alone, he of the graceful form. The king recognized him; dismounting, he made a reverence to the bold, lion-strong hero and accorded the honor befitting a father.

Tariel showed his respect likewise, and then went up to Rostevan and kissed him in greeting. The king returned the salute, in delight and in ecstasy; he lifted his voice up in praise, he was possessed by astonishment. — "You are the very sun; your departure must turn day into night!" he cried. Marvelling at his beauty, he gazed on his countenance; the strength of the hero's mighty arms filled him with wonder. Pridon in his turn gave the king salutation, bowed down low before him. . . . But impatience to look on Avtandil seized Rostevan; he began soon to falter in his praises of Tariel; his spirit was restless. "O King," Tariel said to him, "my heart is now slave to you: but I marvel that you should find so much good to commend in me. When you can call Avtandil yours, how may any other win favor? — Do not wonder that he has not come with me, that he has stayed at a distance. Let us sit down here on this pleasant greensward, O King, and I will tell you why I could not bring him into your presence. Then I shall have something to ask of you, a boon there will be to crave."

They sat down, and the warriors came up and stood round about them; a smile brighter than a candle's flame illumined the features of Tariel; the grace of his bearing made captives of all who beheld him. — He began to address the king with words wisely chosen:

"O King, although I deem myself unworthy to speak of the matter, I have come here with a prayer, I have come to make an entreaty: I bring too the supplication of her who is as fair as the sun's rays, of her who is to my eyes as the bright light of day itself; we make our submission with prayer and beseeching. — Avtandil found balm for my wounds with no thought for his own good; though his woes were no less than ours, he had no care at all for them. . . . But I will not be tedious; there is no need for a long speech.

(1513-30)

"Avtandil and your daughter are in love with each other;
he loves her and she him. His cheek is pale, he weeps; piteous
to look upon indeed is he! On bended knee I implore you to
let flame consume them no longer, but to give the maiden to
the hero whose heart is so valiant, whose arm is so mighty. I
have no more than this to say, in few words or in many." With
that he drew out a kerchief and tied it round his neck in a
knot;[84] then he rose and knelt before Rostevan like a man who
makes his lord a petition. All who had heard him were stricken
with wonder.

Dismay seized the king when he saw Tariel kneeling thus;
he started back, bent before him, and then fell to the ground.
"O King," he said, "all my joy has been reft from me; to see you
abase yourself fills me with sorrow. Who would wish to deny
you whatever you wanted? Could I grudge you my daughter,
even if it were your desire to enslave or to kill her? I should not
weep — no, not though the command were merely brought by a
messenger. . . . But were she to take wing and fly up to heaven,
she would not find the like of Avtandil!

"A better husband I could not find for her: I have given her
the realm and its governance; the possession is hers, and she is
in truth worthy of it. She is a rose newly opened, I am a flower
that is faded and blown: if her mind is decided, I can put up no
barrier. You would draw no murmur from me if you gave her
as a bride to a servitor. Who could wish to thwart you in any-
thing? Who, save a madman, could regard you with anger? —
For Avtandil, if he was not dear to me, why have I longed
for his return without ceasing? I declare before God that what
you ask for is granted."

When the king had made an end, Tariel touched the ground
with his forehead in a humble obeisance. The king too bowed
his head in a reverence; then he went up to Tariel. Each spoke
words of thanks to the other; great was the joy in their hearts
then.

Pridon mounted at once and galloped off with the good
news; greatly did he too rejoice at the outcome. He went back
to Avtandil and told him to come with him; the hero obeyed,
but he felt shame, his radiant splendor was darkened. The
king rose and came towards him; Avtandil got out of his saddle

on the approach of his lord, and hid his face in a kerchief that
he held in his hand. It was as when a cloud covers the sun and
the rose is frozen in darkness. . . . But what could ever have
concealed the bright rays of his beauty?

The king — his weeping[85] was done with now! — would have
kissed him, but Avtandil fell at his feet; the light of the hero's
countenance had the ground all illumined. "Rise and have done
with shame," Rostevan said; "you have given proof of your
quality. Why should you feel any guilt, when you have kept
always a loyal heart?" With that he embraced Avtandil and
kissed his cheek many times. "Those fires in my breast are now
quenched by your hand," he said. "Come, I will unite you, O my
lion, with her whose lashes are jet, who is as fair as the sun
itself." Once more he enfolded the lion, the hero; then he had
him sit at his side and talked to him, gazed upon him and kissed
him. Thus did the sun-fair lord receive his due then from
royalty: sweet indeed is joy when a man has made a passage
through sorrow.

"I wonder you are content to talk thus!" Avtandil said to
Rostevan presently. "Why are you not eager, impatient, to look
on her who is as fair as the sun? Let your heart be glad, go and
welcome her, bear her off to your palace; let the light of her
loveliness shine over all."

A word then to Tariel, and they mounted and rode over to
Nestan. The three heroes' cheeks were as bright as the sun;
their desire was achieved; they had found what they sought;
they had not girt on their swords to no purpose, but had made
right good use of them.

The king dismounted at a little distance and saluted the lady;
his eyes were quite blinded by her cheeks' flashing loveliness.
She had her litter moved forward; leaning out from it, she
kissed him in greeting. Filled with delight, he then spoke words
of eulogy: "Sun-fair lady, bringer of light," he said, "how can
I praise you? Those who run mad for your sake have cause
indeed to be crazed! You are like the sun, like the moon — what
star has your beauty! Roses and violets can hold no more de-
light for me!"

Her loveliness struck all who beheld her with wonder; she
dazzled their eyes like the rays of the sun. Wherever she went,

(1530-46)

the people ran, crowding; their hearts were on flame, and they gazed with delight on her.

The company mounted and set off for the palace. Only to the seven planets could Nestan the sun-fair be likened; her beauty lay beyond the apprehension of mortals. . . . Soon they arrived at the sovereign's gateway.

When they went in they saw Tinatin, her who made captive the hearts of beholders. On her head was her crown; in her hand was her scepter; very fair was she to look upon, robed all in purple. Her beauty shed its radiance upon those come before her. — When the Indian prince, that sun-fair hero, had entered, he and his bride made each a deep reverence: then they went forward and kissed her and spoke to her lovingly. The palace was filled now with the light of their beauty; their cheeks were crystal and ruby, their lashes were jet.

Tinatin would have had them take their seats on the high throne of the sovereign, but Tariel answered, "The place is yours; the Supreme Judge has willed it so. And today above all days it is right you should sit there; beside the fairest of sun-fair ladies I am going to set the most splendid of heroes."

They took her by either hand and led her up to the throne then: and by her side they placed Avtandil — Avtandil, who had been brought near to death by his longing. Never was there such a sight to behold, nor in time to come will there ever be; Vis and Ramin[86] themselves were not lovers such as these.

When they set Avtandil by her the maiden was startled and seized by confusion: her cheek's color changed, her heart began to beat faster. "What is this, my child? — Enough, come, what ails you?" the king said. 'In the end love will triumph'[87] is the saying of sages.

"Now, my children, may God grant you a thousand years of life, with splendor and joy and an end to all sorrow. May the heavens preserve your good fortune, may you know no more change than do they; may your hands cover me over with earth in time's fullness."

Then he ordered his warriors to make Avtandil obeisance: "Here is your king," he said, "king by the will of God. Today he has ascended my throne, for old age now afflicts me. Serve him as you have served me; let this command be obeyed by all."

The lords and the warriors bowed themselves down low: "We are," they said, "earth under the feet of him who rules over us: let him reward those who keep faith, let him root out the disloyal, let him overwhelm enemies and give our hearts valiance."

Tariel spoke then with words of joy and of praise. To the maiden he said, "I see you and your lover united; fires will consume you no longer. Your husband is my brother, and you I would have for a sister; I will destroy all who are traitors to you or rise in rebellion."

How the king of the Arabs held a marriage festival for Avtandil and Tinatin

That day Avtandil sat upon the throne as a sovereign: Tariel, his face illumined by joy, had a place at his hand. Nestan sat beside Tinatin; she enchanted all who beheld her. It was as though the sky had bent down to earth and two suns had found union.

The warriors sat down to a feast that was spread for them; cattle and sheep beyond number were slaughtered; gifts were bestowed then, gifts such as were fitting; the faces of all were like the sun in their radiance. The bowls were of jacinth; the goblets were fashioned from rubies; there were vessels marvellously chased, with most wonderful coloring. The bard who could sing of that festival would deserve to be praised by the sages: had you been there, you who read this, you would have counted yourself truly a happy man!

Singers came in on every hand; there was a sounding of cymbals; gold lay piled up in heaps with cut rubies; wine flowed from a hundred fountains for all men to drink of. They drank from dusk until dawn, until the coming of morning.

The halt and the lame were not left without gifts; pearls were brought forth and scattered everywhere lavishly; satins and gold ingots were to be had for the taking. And for three days the Indian prince played the part of a groomsman.

On the fourth day the king of the Arabs sat down to feast again joyously. "Fair indeed," he said to Tariel, "is your lady

(1547-63)

to look upon; she is your queen, and the king of all kings are you; the shoes of your horse ought to serve us for earrings. — O King, it is not for us to sit as your equals." He had the sovereign's throne set apart, with another. Below, he placed Avtandil and his bride, on a level. Gifts were brought then for Tariel, and they lay heaped in a mountain.

An unwearied host was the king of the Arabs, sometimes here, sometimes there, caring nothing for rank, state and dignity. His generous giving called praise forth from every man. . . . It was Pridon's due, as a monarch, to sit near Avtandil.

Great was the honor shown to the Indian princess and her bridegroom by Rostevan; he bestowed presents as fondly on them as he would have on a son and a daughter-in-law. Not even a tenth part of what he gave can be told of, but each received a scepter, a purple robe and a jewelled crown. Still he continued to shower gifts upon them, gifts that were splendid and fitting: a thousand jewels;[88] a thousand pearls as big as doves' eggs; a thousand magnificent steeds each the size of a mountain.[89] To Pridon he gave nine trays filled with pearls and nine fine horses with costly saddles upon them. — The Indian prince made obeisance: proud was his bearing and sober, not that of one in his cups. For all that he had been wining, he gave thanks like a man clear in mind.

To make an end, the diversions did not cease till a whole month had passed away; nor was there any break in all that time in the drinking. — Certain rare rubies were bestowed upon Tariel that threw light upon all like the rays of the sun.

At length, like flakes of snow upon a rose, tears began to fall upon Tariel's cheeks; and he sent Avtandil to Rostevan with a message to say that he must take his leave: "No greater happiness could I ask for than to stay here in your company, but the whole of my kingdom is being ravaged by enemies.[90] . . . Knowledge and skill will, however, yet bring destruction on ignorance. . . . Any injury suffered by me would, I know, cause you to grieve. I must be gone, for delay might bring sorrow; but God grant that I may see you once more, in the splendor of majesty."

This reply came from Rostevan: "Why, O King,[91] do you send to me words of such deference? Reflect well, consider closely, and then act as is best for you. Avtandil shall accompany you, with a great host of warriors; rend, cut in pieces, all traitors and enemies!"

"No more of this!" Tariel said, when these words had been conveyed by Avtandil. "Do not let me see those crystal-bright teeth any longer! How can the sun leave the moon when they have been so lately united?" Avtandil answered him, "You cannot bemuse me so easily. Do you want to leave me to go off to spread slander: 'He deserted me for love of his wife!' — talk of that kind? Are we to part, am I to bemoan then my cruel fate? . . . Woe to the man who turns his back on his comrade!"

Tariel smiled; his teeth shone like crystal between lips red as the rose. "A parting," he said, "would grieve me even more than you. Come with me then, since you are determined to have it so — I speak without flattery!"

Avtandil summoned warriors from all quarters to join him; soon he had the armies of Arabia mustered — eighty thousand men, all in harness for battle. Men and horses alike were in Khvarizmian armor.[92] . . . But sorely did the king of the Arabs grieve over this parting.

When they said their farewells the two ladies, sworn sisters, each with an understanding now of the heart of the other, embraced weeping; those who beheld them were stricken in soul.

When the moon rides by the morning star both shine bright in the heavens; but then they will part, and there is distance between them. It is not their own choice, but the celestial ordering: to see them the watcher must now climb up a mountain. — He who created them in the likeness of those two stars it was, not their own wish, that parted the ladies. Weeping, they pressed together their lips, those cleft roses: to those who had to part from them, life was no more than an emptiness.

"Better never to have known you," said Nestan-Darejan, "to have been spared, sun-fair one, the sorrow of parting. — You shall have news, and do you send word to me, write to me. Keep me close in your heart's core, as I will hold you."

Tinatin replied, "How, sun-fair lady, delight of beholders, can I endure to be severed, bear the grief of your going? No prayers will I say for length of days, I will hope for an early death. — May your years be as many as the tears of my shedding."

(1563-80)

They kissed once more, and then parted. She who was to remain could not tear her eyes away from her who was setting forth; many were the backward glances of Nestan-Darejan: fires burned in the breasts of both — I cannot put down here a tenth part of what I would!

The parting drove Rostevan more distraught than a madman; a thousand lamentations burst forth from him, sighs that were numberless. Tears streamed from his eyes, hot as though from a cauldron. Soft snow seemed to fall on the sadness of Tariel's cheek in his weeping.

The king embraced Tariel, the rose-fair, and kissed him. "The time of your sojourn here," he said, "seems like a dream to me. When you are gone I shall know, not one grief, but a hundred. You have been a bringer of life; death too will come from your hands."

Tariel mounted and took his leave of the king then; the tears shed by the warriors soaked all the ground round about. "The sun-fair one," they said, "would hasten to battle; you must carry her banner." "This parting," he replied, "will have me weep more tears than did Salaman."[93]

They set out on their journey, with the army and baggage-train. High resolve filled the breasts of Tariel, Avtandil and Pridon. At their backs they had eighty thousand well-mounted horsemen: and so they went on, the three, the best of good comrades. Never will their like be created by God again! For three months they traveled on; the people everywhere came forth to receive them with honor; no enemy was there so bold as to raise his head.

When morning was past they halted on the plain to take meat, and feasted in splendor. Wine was their drink then — yes, wine, and not buttermilk.

How Tariel learned of the death of the king of the Indians

A great caravan came into their view on a hill-top: the caravaneers, and the horses too, were all clad in black; the men had their hair coiled in plaits round their heads. "We will remain here for a while," said Tariel; "let them be brought here before me."

The merchants, with their chief, were led into his presence.

"Who are you," he asked them, "and why are you thus garbed in mourning?" They replied, "In the land that we come from it is the only apparel: we have made a long journey, from Egypt to India."

Well pleased were the heroes when they heard that the traders were come out of India; but they kept their joy from their faces, so as not to betray themselves. As they did not wish to reveal who they were, they did not speak in Indian: as though they had none, they spoke in another tongue, talked to the traders in Arabic.

"Merchants," they said, "what news can you give us of India?" "Heaven's wrath," replied the chief, "has in truth struck the land. Tears flow from the eyes of all, from the eyes of high and low alike; the minds of even the wisest there among them are darkened." And then he told his tale; told his tale with great eloquence:

"Parsadan, the king of the Indians, was blessed with good fortune. One daughter had he, who was fairer than the sun itself: her teeth were pearls, her cheeks rubies; her form was like the cypress, her hair resembled the raven's wing. She was loved by the amirbar, and his love was requited: he took off her bridegroom, and the business was not slow to come to the ears of the king. — The storm that was loosed then carried destruction through India! Her father's sister had had the care of the princess's childhood; a Kaj was she, and well versed in sorcery. A most dreadful thing did she do; she robbed the world of the sun-fair! Then, miserable wretch, she died; too evil was she to live any longer. But the princess had vanished; the cypress-beauty was lost to ken.

"As soon as the amirbar, the lion-hearted, had heard of this, he set out in quest of the sun-fair; but he, too, was seen no more. It was as though the sun and the moon had been darkened in India; both were gone, and small was the hope of their finding. 'O God,' said the king, 'why do you burn me in this grief, in this slow fire?' He could find a trace nowhere, he was driven distracted; throughout the land lamentation silenced the harp and the cymbal. . . . For a short space he endured in the furnace of sorrow, but then he died; he knew no more of this world and its agonies."

When the merchant had ended his story a loud shriek burst

(1580-96)

from Nestan; she tore off her veil in a transport of anguish. Tariel too gave a cry — and so their secret was out. From their narcissus-eyes tears broke, tears like the torrents that rush down through the melting snow.

The sun itself, by heaven, could not have matched the beauty of the lady whose head was uncovered now! She had the fragrance of the rose, she was as fair as the poppy; her teeth were like twin pearls in a casing of crystal. Even a sage, were he to seek to sing her praises, would sound like a braying ass!

Tearing her hair, she made piteous lamentation for her father with the voice of a nightingale. Tears ran down to cover her countenance; her cheek's rose turned to saffron, her lips' ruby to moss-green. A cloud covered the beauty that was like the orb of day's radiance; and the daylight was dimmed.

She rent her cheeks, tore them; she wept and she wailed aloud; blood and tears mingled to pour down from her eyes: "Oh, father, would I were dead, for I have been to you the worst of all children! In nought have I served you, in nought given joy! Father, light of my eyes, my fault has taken you forth into darkness! What word that might make your heart glad can you have of me? Sun, why do you keep your light, why do you shine yet upon the world? Earth, why do you not fall in ruins? Why do you still stand, you mountains?"

Tariel likewise lamented: "Oh, my dear lord, what bitter news is this that has come to me? Why does the sun still send forth light, why is it not closely shrouded in grief? You were like a sun to all creatures; now you are dead, and the world is no longer yours. Give me pardon, for God's sake, for the wrong that I did to you!"

Then he said, "Tell us the rest of your story." And the merchant continued: "In India a great war is being fought at this present time. The Cathayans' army has come and surrounded the capital; their king is one Ramaz,[94] and they all owe him allegiance. The queen is still alive — and yet she is more dead than the very dead. The Indian warriors fight on, but all hope has now gone from their hearts. All the outlying strengths have been taken, destruction is everywhere. Let the light of your countenance, sun-fair lord, shine forth; for lowering and dark is the sky now, in all truth!

"All the people there, and we too, put on mourning. — At

length we went before Ramaz and told him that we were Egyptians. He let us go unharmed; our king is a powerful monarch, and he desires to stay at peace with him."

Tariel pressed on in haste as soon as this tale had been told to him; in a single day's journey he traveled the distance of three. His banner floating above him, he marched forward openly. Behold him! How mighty of heart is the hero!

How Tariel arrived in India, and how the Cathayans made submission to him

Tariel came to a high mountain-ridge on the borders of India. Before him he perceived a huge army, and was amazed at its numbers. "Can I, my lords," he said, "trust to your valor now? With God and Fortune to aid me, I will soon have them turn and fly! Once before have those warriors made proof of my sword's edge; they attacked me, and I shattered their armor and made slaughter among them." "What need for such words?" said Avtandil in answer. "We will bring them to the dust, we will trample them underfoot."

Their hearts full of valiance, they made ready quickly for battle; then they mounted their best steeds and at once urged them forward. Swifter than the storm-wind they swept down the mountain; each of them strove to out-distance his comrades; loud in their praises were all who beheld them.

The Cathayan host's outposts were overwhelmed by the vanguard; put to flight and pursued and flung from their horses: then they were brought bound before Tariel, who at once asked them whose men they were.

"Grievously, lord, have we been abused," the Cathayans replied to him: "we are King Ramaz's soldiers, sent forward as sentinels." "Go, you wretched dolts," Tariel said, "and tell your master that warriors stout of heart are approaching. Say that Tariel, proud and mighty king, great monarch, destroyer of enemies, sends him this message: 'Your own guards can tell you of me: fear will not save you from death, grief will avail nothing! Who but one crazed would think that the mighty were thus to be overthrown? How, maddest of madmen, did you dare attack India? I come as a fire that will burn you to ashes, I will blunt my sword's sharpness with blows on your

(1596-1613)

carcass. I would not strike like a felon — make ready for battle and marshal your army; but first receive my defiance. Would you make it your boast, false of tongue, you will vanquish me? — I will cleave through your helmet as I would through a turban!' "

The guards made off pell-mell: holding back nothing, they told their story to Ramaz: "With a splendid army at his back, the king of the Indians is upon us now — none can hope to escape alive! Any one of those men could vanquish two of our warriors!"

Tariel raised aloft his banner, with its Indian blazon; beside it was carried the standard of the king of the Arabs. — Everyone knows that the lance is the Arabs' chief weapon.[95]. . . Pridon, the sun-fair, he who shed blood in rivers, was there in the company.

When they had gone on for a little they saw five hundred horsemen approaching. The Arab lords were eager to charge, but Tariel restrained them and quietened them. When the company drew near they were seen to be unarmed; they did not have even their daggers about them.

Ramaz came and clung to the legs of Tariel's charger; on bended knee he then made his entreaty: "Mercy, in the name of the God who created you! Do not leave life within me, but have me killed here and now; let there be no more than a corpse to be carried away! Fate has shattered this heart — this heart that owed you its fealty. Ten years since you departed, you vanished away: the birds were left without a king, the wings of the eagle were broken, and this hazard tempted me. But Fate has been quick to crush; I have diced, and lost all.

"Let me die alone, I beseech you, for no other is guilty. I have brought five hundred viziers here with me: cut off their heads if you will, let their blood flow in rivers — but spare the lives of my warriors, for no wrong has been done by them. From a heart full of wretchedness I beg this with tears."

Then they all fell on their knees before Tariel: "For the sake of the Lord who has had you in his heavenly keeping, let us live!" they implored him. Tariel remained silent, in thought; Ramaz fell on his face before him. — God pardons those who repent; how then can Man withhold his forgiveness?

The sinner may win mercy with tears, even as did the men of

Nineveh when they covered their heads with dust and with ashes:[96] thus may he escape from the anger of heaven. The working of Fate can always have a wrong turn put right again.

I came upon this, conning over the philosophers' writings: "To stay your hand and spare a vanquished foe is valor's loftiest pinnacle; remember these words, if you would be a hero."

Tariel's heart softened within him; he was filled with a righteousness that was like the divine. "I will have no killing," he said to Ramaz. "If terror enters the soul of the conquered, he will set straight once again what he had earlier twisted: now I have restored what was crooked to the shape that is right for it."

They made obeisance, and with one voice they called down blessings upon him; they made prayer to God that he should send the best fortune. They had escaped slaughter, their lives had been granted them; their flesh would not serve to gorge Tariel's ravening sword-blade.

Mushtar[97] appeared now, to gaze upon Tariel: the fires of the hero's wrath were put out by compassion. — They came thronging to look on him; close-pressed were the warriors in Ramaz's army, one man on another. Light came down from the sky in a column, to shine over India.

The joyful news was carried back to the Cathayans by messenger: "He is not going to kill you, you will all have his mercy!" And they then one and all raised their voices to bless him. The trumpet was sounded, the rejoicing was great indeed. "Here he comes," they said, "whose unaided hand has brought death to so many!"

The Indians went forth to meet Tariel; from a distance they gave salutation. They recognized their own banner among the flags that were flying there; but, still distrustful, they said, "This is treachery!" Tears bathed their cheeks, for they had had no hope of his coming.

Tariel rode forward: "It is I — your king!" he called out aloud. "And with me I have my star-fair lady, her whose face flashes loveliness: the Almighty has sent us his favor from heaven! Draw closer; I am eager to have you about me!"

They were sure who he was now; on all sides they came run-

(1613-29)

ning. Lights shone from the houses and the walls of the city. Great was the noise: "All our woes," they shouted, "have now fled away from us! God has put aside wrath, he has granted us mercy!"

They opened the gates and brought the keys of the city out: those who came forth to look were all clad in mourning. Tariel and Nestan both wept; the roses on their cheeks were bedewed then. They beat their heads, wailed aloud. . . . Their hair, black as the raven's wing, covered their faces' bright crystal.

Tariel grieved as it befits a man to grieve for his lord; tears fell from his eyes that burned hotter than fire. He struck his head, moaned aloud, wept — his heart full of affliction: his hand, a crystal rake, tore through locks like jet thickets. When he saw the lords and the viziers all apparelled in black, the cries that burst forth from him were even more piercing: from his eyes blood and tears poured out now in great torrents.

Like sons and like brothers they came up and embraced him; they clasped him to them, and they condoled too with him and his bride. Nestan swooned; she could weep for her father no longer; like a rose-bush whose fallen branches none can raise again was she. . . . Never a face there had the least light of laughter.

The queen came hastening out, and spoke in tones with reproof in them: "Why those tears? We must thank God for changing his wrath into mercy; in truth this is no time to make lamentation!" Shedding burning tears, she pressed Tariel to her. "The fierce fires within me," she said, "are raging no longer; gentler in its burning is the flame that consumes me now. Calm your spirit, be silent and give heed to the words I say: God, the comforter of the orphan, has filled my heart with joy, for he has given it to me once more to behold you!"

Nestan wept before her mother: "Oh, mother, what hope can there be for me! You were garbed in gay yellow and red when we parted; now I see you clad in weeds of mourning, in black! The royal throne, too, stands empty; my father sits there no longer!" The queen dried her tears, saying, "Do not weep — peace, unhappy one!" She kissed Nestan's cheek, and her lips, tender roses; she of the cypress-form was all but drowned in her tears. But then she said, "Why should we speak on this day of unhappy things? We must all rejoice — rejoice not once, but a thousand times!"

The lords came before them after a little, and made their obeisance. Tariel and Nestan, those sun-fair ones, went forward and fondly embraced them; each received a kiss, and his word, too, of greeting.

Avtandil and Pridon addressed the queen then with words of condolence. "These two," Tariel said, "O Queen, are unknown to you; but to them we owe everything. There is no time for the story now, but from the hands of those heroes we have both received life anew."

They rose, entered the city and repaired to the palace. The queen there addressed them; her words, though few, were each of the worth of ten: "God has brought destruction upon our enemies: no more harm can they do to us, and therefor my heart is now filled with great gladness."

And she gave her commands then: "Let there be an end to all mourning; let the drums and the cymbals sound; let our court now re-echo with joy and with revelry. Wear your richest apparel, put on golden girdles; let there be laughter and song, and an end to all tears."

How the marriage of Tariel and Nestan-Darejan was celebrated

Taking the bride and bridegroom by the hand, the queen placed them together upon the throne of the sovereign. She put away sorrow, her gentle heart found new strength; she changed grief into joy, she would let none weep thenceforward. Discarding her mourning weeds, she arrayed herself richly; she had gay clothing made ready for the lords to put on. All were furnished with raiment, the gifts bestowed then were countless. "Since joy has been granted to us," she said, "let all our woes be forgotten!"

There upon the throne Tariel sat with his lady; worthy indeed were they one of the other! A fit prize was Nestan for a hero so valiant. . . . Where is the master of words, who has the wit, that could tell of this? What child of Adam upon the earth is there like them?[98]

(1629-45)

Thus Tariel and his bride won all that their hearts desired; seven kingdoms,[99] and felicity beyond man's imagining. Bliss banished all sorrows endured now from memory: he who has not passed through grief can know nothing of happiness.

Behold the two now, seated there side by side! The sun itself, truly, is not more splendid to look upon. — Tariel was proclaimed king with trumpets, the drums sounded bravely. They brought the keys of the treasure-chambers and gave their allegiance: "All hail to our sovereign!" they cried out aloud.

Two thrones were set in place likewise for Avtandil and Pridon; they sat royally upon them and received praise in their majesty. — When did God create such as these among humankind? They told the tale of their sufferings; it was now known on all hands.

There was drinking and feasting; everywhere there was joyfulness; servants attended in hosts; such high festival was made as was fitting. The bride and the bridegroom received gifts in equal measure; great riches of alms were set apart for the poor.

"Bring the widows and orphans here; bestow treasures upon them; load them with gifts!" were the words of the queen. And with her own hand she gave away wealth such as the tongue cannot tell of. "Pray for length of days for them, ask this of God," was her bidding.

"O Queen," Tariel said, "I have a boon now to crave of you; grant pardon to Ramaz, I beseech you in God's name. The sight of him moved me to pity; great was the dread that he felt for our sword-blades. — God has mercy on the sinner when tears show his penitence."

"I will forgive him," responded the queen then in a gentle tone. King Ramaz was brought in, and he made obeisance to the royal throne. The voices of minstrels rose on all sides to blend in song; in the joy of that day all past sorrows found recompense.

In mountains of splendor gold, jewels and pearls lay piled everywhere, to tumble like torrents that water the plain: all men were free to carry off whatever they would then. . . . No care had the chamberlain for places or precedence.

Tariel, the great king, said to the warriors of Avtandil and Pridon, "You are my guests; do not scruple to take whatever may please you!" On each man he bestowed a mule charged with a load of pearls — but the sum of his gifts is beyond any reckoning.

Who could tell of the treasures showered on Avtandil and Pridon! The tongue cannot treat of them, but must needs fall silent. The queen did not withhold even her rarest possessions; smiling sweetly upon the two, she called them deliverers. The Indians felt beholden one and all to the heroes: "We are your debtors," they said, "for all the joy that has come to us!" They looked on them as masters, fulfilled their every desire, and were for ever coming to wait and attend on them.

Tariel bestowed gifts on King Ramaz, and said to him, "Send us the tribute that is proper and fitting." Ramaz made obeisance, touching the ground with his forehead, and called down blessings on Tariel; then he departed. Nothing was there now of the braggart about him!

To Asmat, sharer of his sorrows, the king of the Indians said, "More have you done than ever servant or lord did! Take a seventh of the Indian realm[100] as an appanage; give liegedom its due, and let there always be love and friendship between us. Have whom you will for a husband, rule over your lordship, serve us henceforward as a vassal in fealty." Asmat kissed his feet: "I am as nothing without you; what more could I ask than to have you for lord?" she said. Then further: "Do not be angered, but not for the whole world, O King, would I go from you. Enough to be near to you, near to the sun-fair one: nor can I depart from the lady to whom I have given my service."

"You have seen enough of sorrow," Tariel answered: "well do I remember your eyes swimming, wretched, with pity's tears. Listen to what I say, do not demur at what I intend for you; let bad be changed into good; warriors sharp of sword will be yours to command."

She acquiesced in his will: "Grief lasts but an hour," she said. Then they brought a certain lord forward, a man of valiance, sense and a keen understanding; and Asmat was given as a bride then and there to him. He took her by the hand. . . . And they gave him the dignity and title of king.

A few more days did the three sworn brothers spend together; they passed their time in diversion and received gifts of great

(1645-62)

splendor — pearls that were rare, and the finest of horses. . . . But the mark of longing showed soon on the brow of Avtandil. Tariel knew that he was pining for his bride, and he said to him, "Within your heart you are now thinking hardly of me; a crown, alas, has been given to your sorrows by memory. I know I must lose you; Fate grudges me happiness."

And then, in his turn, Pridon spoke of departure: "I must go home," he said; "but often in the years to come my foot will tread this soil and the floors of this palace. Summon me to your service as a lord does his vassal: as the deer thirsts for the spring shall I long to behold you."

Tariel gave him his leave to go likewise: "Take your way homeward," he said; "but do not forget me; return soon." Then he said to Avtandil, "What joy can life hold for me when once you have gone away? But what can I do, since you fret to be gone? — She who is as fair as the moon is awaiting her lion."

He gave him some fine cloaks to take as a present to Rostevan, also vessels encrusted with gems — no common spoons, nor yet ladles! "Take all these for him," he said; "now go, without argument!" "When I am no longer with you," replied Avtandil, "how is life to remain in me?"

Nestan sent a veil and cloak for Tinatin; such was their splendor, it would have befitted no other to don them! Also a jewel that no man would ever think was not worth the taking: it shone at night like the sun, and threw its light all around.

Avtandil mounted to set out, and then said farewell to Tariel; fiercely did the flames of grief burn within them on parting. All the Indians wept; the ground was soaked with their tears. "I have drunk this world's poison; now is my life near its end!" said Avtandil.

Pridon and Avtandil traveled for some days in company; each, when their roads parted, took his way onward in tears. Success had been granted to them, it had crowned their endeavors. . . . Avtandil reached Arabia with no untoward happening.

The whole realm was enriched by his return with a loveliness; all the Arabs came forth to give him their greeting; he saw his sun-fair one, and knew longing's pains no more. When

(1662-69)

he took his seat beside her upon the throne all who beheld them rejoiced; and the Almighty blessed his reign and sway.

Between those three monarchs there was love ever afterwards; many were the visits paid by one to another. Their desires found fulfilment; those who showed disaffection felt the weight of their swords. They enlarged their dominions, they reigned in glory and splendor. Their mercy descended upon all like the falling flakes of a snowstorm; the widow and the orphan received riches, the poor no longer had need to beg. There was no daring in evil-doers; no lamb would take the milk of another; the goat and the wolf fed together in peace.

Epilogue

Their tale is ended, like a dream of the night; they have passed away, fared forth, gone out beyond the world. Behold the treachery of Time! A man may think it long, but for him too it will last for no more than a moment.

This comes from the pen of me, Rustaveli, a poet of Meskhia.[101] For the diversion of David, lord of the Georgians[102] — David, who, excelling the risen sun in his splendor, strikes terror into the lands of East and West and brings destruction to traitors and joy to all loyal hearts — have I put this story into rhyme.

How could I sing of David's feats, of his valor? . . . But I have found and given to verse this wondrous tale, full of the praise of distant kings, of old-world manners and heroic deeds; thus have I sought to entertain.

Such a place is this world as no man should put trust in; the thing of an instant, past and gone with more speed than an eyelash's flicker. Why then should we struggle? From Fate comes only mockery. . . . Happy indeed is the man it is kind to through time to eternity.

Amiran, son of Darejan, was praised by Mosé Khoneli;[103] Abdul-Mesia by Shavteli[104] — much was his verse acclaimed: Dilarget was lauded by Sargis Tmogveli,[105] whose flow of words never faltered; Tariel by Rustaveli, who sheds for him tears without ceasing.

APPENDIX A

Personal beauty and planetary imagery

Rustaveli's endless insistence on the personal beauty of his heroes and heroines (in some measure, doubtless, a product of Neoplatonic notions; Neoplatonism had a home in medieval Georgia, and *The Lord of the Panther-skin* is permeated by it in language and feeling) is, particularly in its application to the young men, likely to appear tedious to the Western reader of today. The use of a single descriptive vocabulary for both sexes, furthermore, is somewhat disconcerting. To some extent these difficulties must be regarded as the mark of sympathies restricted in time as well as provincial in space; thirteenth-century Englishmen who knew how much in the romance of *King Horn* turned on the hero's fair outward seeming had no objection to hearing of beauty in the male; nor would they have been disturbed by interchange of image and epithet between man and woman.[1] Nevertheless it must be conceded that by comparison with the expressions customary in works written in the Persian mode the language of the Western poets when dealing with face and form is usually relatively sober; and, more particularly, that the splendor of the hero's person is described much less frequently, and with much less exuberance of hyperbole. It is interesting to set alongside any of Rustaveli's flights in this kind one of Chrétien de Troyes' comparatively rare attempts at descriptive bravura:

"I will try to describe Cligés' beauty in just a few words. . . . He was fairer and more charming than Narcissus. . . . His hair was like gold and his face was like a new rose. He had a well-shaped nose and a good mouth, and his build was of the best made by Nature. . . ."[2] Such effect as these banalities might produce is weakened, furthermore, by much digressive matter. It is all very half-hearted.

Most of the foregoing comment can also be applied to the
planetary imagery in which Rustaveli's cult of beauty finds its
principal mode of expression. The twentieth-century Westerner
will accept an occasional quiet suggestion of loveliness through
sun, moon or star, such as that in Sir Henry Wotton's poem on
Elizabeth of Bohemia; but, in general, conceits involving the
heavenly bodies do not have much appeal for him. His medieval
forebears, however, were ready enough to accept planetary
similes and metaphors very like those of the Persian tradition;
the passage in which Chrétien writes of the beauty of a pair of
lovers illuminating a palace like the morning sun[3] is only one of
many such in the literatures of the "Franks." But even when we
have achieved some adjustment of appreciation here, a diffi-
culty remains. The classical tradition has invested the sun with
specifically masculine, the moon with similarly feminine, asso-
ciations.[4] When Chrétien compares his hero with the sun and his
heroine with the moon,[5] or the Byzantine historian Anna
Comnena describes her father the emperor Alexius I as "the
shining light of the world" and his empress as "the moon that
brings light to all,"[6] the conceits may appear far-fetched or
florid, but the categories are at least familiar;[7] the male moons
and female suns that in figurative patterns of the Persian type
may occur almost as frequently as the opposite identifications
strike us, on the other hand, as bizarre.[8] Here again, however,
it is important to realize how limited in both time and place
is observance of the convention to which we have been schooled.
Historically, a regularly-maintained distinction of the Phoebus-
Artemis type has been very far from a general rule: not only
do such tropes as "the sunborn maid," "the sun-lovely girl,"
"the sun-child" (feminine) and (the girl) "more brightly flash-
ing than the sunny rays"[9] occur in the popular literature of a
Byzantine Asia Minor much exposed to Oriental influence; in
the Middle Ages Western Europe knew nothing of sex-discrimi-
nation in this field. Chrétien likens one of his heroes to both
"a moon among the stars and the sun above the moon";[10]
while in another of his works we find: ". . . in her there is more
beauty than there is radiance in the sun. . . ."[11] As late as the
sixteenth century, indeed, Spanish balladry could still tell of
a girl looking "so beautiful that people thought the sun was
rising."[12]

APPENDIX B

"Generous" weeping and the demonstrative gesture

Knights who weep as they make great dole are familiar figures; the spectacle of Chaucer's Troilus "in salte teres dreynte" causes no surprise; we know that no further back in time than the 1770s Henry Mackenzie's Man of Feeling could burst into tears as he left the room without incurring the slightest censure — but in spite of all this the tears in which Rustaveli's story is drenched may move us to echo the words of Chaucer's Pandare: "Lat be thy wepyng and thy drerynesse. . . ." Enough is surely enough.

But the point must be grasped that the tears of Troilus and those of Tariel are shed in two quite different worlds. Pandare's exhortation bears some relation to what in real life a man might say to a friend cursed with an over-charge of sensibility; with quite minor alterations in phrasing it could appear in a contemporary novel. Rustaveli, on the other hand, does not write as a novelist; he has many arresting things to say about the human situation, but the surfaces of life are of little concern to him.[1] The weeping in which his characters indulge so freely has in fact small connection with the world of the senses. Its true home is in literature of a heroic sort: tears of blood, for instance, are shed in the *Shah-nama* — not a work open to the reproach of facile emotionalism.

In the heroic world, archetypal figures are seen from a distance, in simplicity of outline: the valiant warrior, the crafty courtier, the lovely princess, the noble-hearted king. In the grandeur of elemental settings hyperbolic tears seem merely in scale; no sense of incongruity is aroused. Nor need it be when the tears are turned to the purpose of literary ornament in a more sophisticated context, where the atmosphere is one of pathos, as in *Layla and Majnun*, or of formalized amour, as in *Visramiani*. In a romance of chivalry, however, they may seem out of place. But the hyperbolic weeping in *The Lord of the Panther-skin* is not simply a conventional device for the signalling of emotion in traditional stereotypes; it is to be understood as a sign of the generous spirit, of a quality of response to the ebb and flow of life that is worthy of as high a regard as are courage, devotion, or constancy of purpose. The tears that Avtandil sheds over the tale of Tariel's sorrows are evidence of nobility of soul quite as compelling as his readiness to give a crew of pirates battle single-handed; Nestan's endless weeping in Gulansharo is not to be thought of as in any way out of character in the haughty princess whose imperious command had once sent her lover forth to war.[2]

Similar comments could be made on other elements in the behavior of Rustaveli's heroes; more particularly, it must be remembered how narrowly confined in time as well as space is the sway of our familiar ideas of well-bred reserve. The poet's Western contemporaries would have felt no surprise at the demonstrative gestures; a generation or two before his time Geoffrey of Monmouth had clearly regarded it as wholly natural that a man reunited with his brother after hazards should have "the solace of embracing him and kissing him to his heart's desire":[3] while in a period no more remote than the early years of the seventeenth century a Scottish writer of romance could have two young men meet in this fashion:

> Their soules by a diuine sympathy did first ioyne, preuenting the elementall masses of the bodyes: but ah, whilst they were clasped in others armes (like two graffes graffed in one stock) the high tide of ouerflowing affection restrayning their tongues with astonishment, as vnable to expresse an vnexpressable passion. . . .[4]

NOTES

The Lord of the Panther-skin

1. Cf. *Layla and Majnun* (p. 158): "It is he who . . . gives its span of life to every creature. . . . He has adorned the heavens with stars and filled the earth with people. . . . He has given them a soul. . . ."

2. Queen of Georgia, 1184-1212; the "hero" is the Ossetian prince David Soslan, who in 1189 became her second consort. His victories over Muslim armies played their part in the expansion of Georgian power and territory in the early years of the thirteenth century.

3. Cf. the invocation of Otarid (the planet Mercury), p. 115.

4. This seems like an echo of Firdausi's description of his precursor Rudaki as one who turned "scattered prose into ordered verse and strung those pearl-filled words in line" (*Epic*, p. 334). The image is however a favorite of the Persian poets; Nizami uses it several times in *Layla and Majnun*.

5. The name of several places in Georgia. Which gave the poet his appellation is uncertain, but the evidence of the Epilogue may be thought to give the village in the southwestern province of Meskhia a strong claim.

6. I.e., Tamar.

7. Arabic *maidān*, an open space used for sports, martial exercises etc. The word has been received in English through the Anglo-Indian vocabulary. The game in question here is polo.

8. I.e., "Tinatin."

9. See Introduction, p. xvii.

10. This is the opinion lying behind the assertion of the troubadour Bernard de Ventadour that fools cast reproach upon love through lack of understanding:

> Amor blasmen per no-saber,
> Fola gens. . . .

(Bernard de Ventadour, *Chansons d'Amour*, ed. Moshé Lazar [Paris: C. Klincksieck, 1966], p. 64.)

11. Cf. the sentiments expressed by Chaucer's turtle:

> "Nay, God forbede a lovere shulde chaunge!"
> The turtle seyde, and wex for shame al red,

"Though that his lady everemore be staunge,
Yit lat hym serve hire ever, till he be ded. . . ."

(*The Parlement of Foules*, lines 582-85). Also the troubadour Marcabru's assertion that false and faithless lovers debase love and promote crime:

Fals amic, amador tafur,
Baisson Amor e levo·l crim. . . .

(*Poésies complètes du Troubadour Marcabru*, ed. J.-M.-L. Dejeanne [Toulouse, 1909], p. 53).

12. With the suggestion in this passage that the code of love requires that the lover should at some time be denied the pleasures of his lady's society, cf. *Antar*, 1: 222: ". . . no lover is excusable but he who tastes the bitterness of absence after the sweetness of enjoyment. . . ."

13. Cf. *Visramiani*, p. 49: "This is sufficient grief for the lover, that he is always in sorrow, and must keep the longing for his beloved a continual secret in his heart, of no one can he receive consolation for his heart's woe." It cannot, however, be said that the obligation of secrecy, reminiscent of that contained in the Provençal code of courtly love, receives any very consistent observance in *The Lord of the Panther-skin*.

14. See Introduction, p. xvii. Cf. also Antar's lament for his lost lady (*Antar*, 2: 333): "I mourned thee in tears and blood — I wept for thee on the plains and the mountains. For thee my frame is exhausted and worn. I am become a tale and a proverb by my tears — I will traverse the rugged hills — I will follow the track of lovers over every desert." The same thought seems to lie behind another passage in the Arabian romance (Ibid., 2:245), in which a lover in a similar situation is described as wandering over deserts.

15. Cf. Bernard de Ventadour's declaration that he is so drawn to love that nothing else holds any interest for him (*Chansons d'Amour*, p. 60):

Si·m tira vas amor lo fres
que vas autra part no·m aten.

Also the dictum of the thirteenth-century writer on courtly love, Andreas Capellanus (*De Amore Libri Tres*, ed. E. Trojel, 2d ed. [Munich: Eidos Verlag, 1964], p. 312): "Verus amans assidua sine intermissione coamantis imaginatione detinetur."

16. This first quatrain of the story seems almost like a conflation of the openings of *Layla and Majnun* ("Once there lived among the Bedouin in Arabia a great lord. . . . Success and merit made him a

Sultan of the Arabs. . . . To strangers he was a generous host"), *Vis-ramiani* ("In the land of Khuarasan and Adrabadagan there was a great and mighty Sultan, Tughlurbeg, lord of many hosts, powerful, glorious, sovereign of all Persia") and *Amiran-Darejaniani* ("There was once in India a king Abesalom who was powerful, wise, and free from all sorrows"). More generally, we have here the archetypal picture of the monarch of a chivalrous society. Cf., save for the matter of age, that given by Gerbert de Montreuil:

> Il ot en Franche un roi jadis,
> Qui molt fu bials, preus et hardis,
> Jovenes hom fu et entendans,
> Hardis as armes et aidans;
> Molt hounora les chevaliers. . . .

(*Le Roman de la Violette*, ed. Douglas Labaree Buffum [Paris, 1928], pp. 5-6, lines 65-69.)

17. Etymologically, 'reflected light'.

18. Tamar was associated with her father, Giorgi III, in the exercise of royal authority in 1178.

19. *Avt'an* would be a proper Georgian equivalent for Arabic *au-ṭān*, plural of *waṭan* 'abode', 'native country'. The last syllable almost certainly represents Persian *dil* 'heart'. *Avṭāndil* might be conceived of as a composite signifying 'patriot': names such as Kohandil and Indil are to be found. Arabic *'awtan* 'continuing', on the other hand, might possibly be joined to *dil* to form a name to be interpreted as 'perseverance' — which would certainly be eminently appropriate to the bearer.

20. Though modern English does not take kindly to glass and crystal imagery as a means of suggesting personal beauty, it is familiar to Middle English literature: e.g., the thirteenth-century metrical romance *King Horn*, lines 13-14:

> Fairer nis non thane he was,
> He was bright so the glas. . . .

and Chaucer's "For as the cristal glorious ye shyne" (*To Rosemounde*, line 3). Nearer to the world of Rustaveli, we find the breast of the hero of *Digenes Akrites*, an eleventh-century ballad-epic of Byzantine Asia Minor, being likened to crystal (*Digenes*, p. 79, line 1179).

21. Cf. the description of the pains of love in *Eneas* (2: 61, line 7919; see Introduction, p. xxvii, note 10): "Pire est amors que fievre ague. . . ."

22. 'Socrates'.

23. Possibly an echo of Eccles. 1:7.

24. Cf. Homay's actions after assuming the Persian crown (*Epic*, p. 221): "She gave audience to her troops, opened the door of the trea-

sury and distributed money." Also those of Farayin in similar circumstances (ibid., p. 408): "He installed the army's muster-master in the royal treasury and summoned all his troops to the court. Whether in the dark night or in bright daylight he lavished money on them and presented many a robe of honor, so that within two weeks there remained of Shah Ardashir's treasure not as much as the price of a feather for an arrow." A Western analogy is provided by Geoffrey of Monmouth (*The History of the Kings of Britain*, transl. Lewis Thorpe [Harmondsworth: Penguin, 1966], [9.1] p. 212): "Once [Arthur] had been invested with the royal insignia, he observed the normal custom of giving gifts freely to everyone. Such a great crowd of soldiers flocked to him that he came to an end of what he had to distribute."

25. As a sign of humiliation.

26. Perhaps Persian *Sher* 'Lion', Arabic *Muḥyī 'd-Dīn* 'Reviver of Religion'. Cf. the Crusaders' turning of *Ṣalāh ad-Dīn* into 'Saladin'.

27. This nightingale-rose conceit is a commonplace of Persian poetry.

28. A whip is part of the regular equipment of a paladin in Georgian romance.

29. A note to Miss Wardrop's translation draws attention to the curious resemblance between this episode and that of the meeting of Arthur and Peredur in the *Mabinogion*. — "Know ye," asked Arthur, "who is the knight with the long spear who is standing in the valley above?" "Lord," said one, "I will go to discover who he is." Then the squire came to where Peredur was and asked him what he was doing there and who he was. And so fixed were Peredur's thoughts on the woman he loved best, he gave him no answer. He then struck at Peredur with a spear, but Peredur turned on the squire and hurled him over his horse's crupper to the ground. And one after another there came four-and-twenty knights, but he would make answer to one no more than to his fellow, save the same play with each one, to hurl him with one thrust over his horse to the ground (*The Mabinogion*, trans. Gwyn Jones and Thomas Jones [London: Dent; New York: Dutton, 1949], pp. 199-200).

30. The Georgian Pegasus.

31. The Georgian *devi* is derived from Persian *div* or *dev*, conventionally rendered by some such term as 'devil' or 'demon'. In this passage the reference is clearly to supernatural power, but in such works as *Amiran-Darejaniani* and *The Lord of the Panther-skin* Divs are usually conceived of as corporeal, mortal beings, with attributes approximating to the human: they tend, in fact, to appear in the character of a hostile people, of alien culture and religion.

32. Cf. the melancholy that afflicts the king of the Indians at the beginning of *Amiran-Darejaniani* (p. 3): after finding certain mysterious portraits while out hunting, he "would not eat or go out to hunt or have any feasting."

33. Cf. the advice given to the king of the Indians to send forth men in quest of information about the mysterious Amiran (*Amiran-Darejaniani*, p. 6).

34. Avtandil is likening himself to the moon, Tinatin to the sun.

35. For the significance of the lion-sun association in the zodiac, see p. 213, note 30. The common "lion" (hero) metaphor is probably also being brought into play here, likewise the various "sun" connotations (beauty, life, loved one).

36. See p. 11.

37. The period allowed for the quest was in fact three years; see pp. 18, 21.

38. The Pseudo-Dionysius, Neoplatonic writer of the 4th-5th century; his works were read throughout medieval Christendom.

39. Cf. *Visramiani* (pp. 137-38): "The king . . . had the earth for mattress and his own arm for a pillow."

40. The heroine and hero of *Visramiani*; see Introduction, pp. xv-xvii.

41. See p. 210, note 58.

42. See Introduction, p. xiv.

43. Mongol *Kitat*, Arabic *Khaṭāy*, Georgian *Khataet'i*; a name used first for the region on the northern border-land of China conquered in the tenth century by the Mongol Kitans, and subsequently for North China generally.

44. See p. 208, note 30.

45. Cf. *Antar*, 3: 268: ". . . tears, that flowing would moisten the saturated as well as the parched up soil."

46. The Arabic *'iṣmat* is used as a proper name in the Muslim world; the sense of 'chastity' may however have relevance to Rustaveli's selection of it.

47. The passage in *Antar* (3: 367-72) in which the hero mourns for King Zoheir and one of his sons is very reminiscent of Rustaveli's scenes of lamentation. A few brief excerpts will give a sufficient idea of its language:

"O my eyes, shed showers of tears for the anguish and calamities that have befallen me. Dry not on my cheeks, but flow in gushing torrents like the rain-charged clouds. . . . Oh! I will weep for them as long as the birds shall sing, or the drops of the pouring clouds shall fall" (pp. 367-68).

"Set is the full moon, though once it was in its zenith; hidden is its light, and all is dark. Eclipsed is the sun, and the morn no more returns in smiles. Fallen are the constellations; they have disappeared; the atmosphere is obscured; the dust of darkness is over it; all the seas are hollow, and are sunk deep; we have lost its dews and its clouds" (pp. 369-70).

When Antar had finished his verses, his tears gushed out in incessant streams, and he wept bitterly, till he could no more, and he fainted; but when he recovered from his swoon, he cast his eyes

towards King Zoheir's seat, and thus expressed himself:
"Weep abundantly, my eyes, in torrents of tears; aid me, relieve my woes with weeping!" (p. 370).

48. Both of these "partridge" similes occur in *Visramiani* (pp. 180, 240).

49. The fingers gesture has a significance of solemn entreaty; cf. *Visramiani*, p. 349.

50. Apparently an echo of Luke 17.4.

51. Tariel's numerous paroxysms may be something of a tax on our sympathy, but similar extravagances are not uncommon in the medieval literature of the Western world: e.g., Chaucer's description of the distraught Troilus (*Troilus and Criseyde* 4. 239-45):

> Right as the wylde bole bygynneth sprynge,
> Now her, now ther, idarted to the herte,
> And of his deth roreth in compleynynge,
> Right so gan he aboute the chaumbre sterte,
> Smytyng his brest ay with his fistes smerte;
> His hed to the wal, his body to the grounde
> Ful ofte he swapte, hymselven to confounde.

52. See p. 210, note 58.

53. The Academy edition has "Kurds"; "Turks" is however a common reading and more acceptable: the reference would be to the Turks of the region of "Cathay," where the brothers are lords of a city (p. 25). Elsewhere (p. 119) they are referred to as Cathayans.

54. Arabic *amīru 'l-bahr* 'commander of the fleet'.

55. Firdausi has Sohrab acquire the courage of a hero by his fifth year (*Epic*, p. 68).

56. Passages in which the poet breaks into a story told by one of his characters have been marked by square brackets.

57. In Persian literature lion-slaying is something of a conventional exploit for a youthful hero. A lion is killed "like a cat" more than once in *Amiran-Darejaniani*.

58. I.e., "the land of the Kajes". Kajes are properly demons, but Rustaveli's are merely sorcerers. See p. 150.

59. El-Jib, five miles northwest of Jerusalem; "the great waters that are in Gibeon" (Jer. 41. 12) may lie behind the allusion.

60. I.e., Asmat.

61. See p. 209, note 43.

62. I.e., the letter he had received from Nestan.

63. See p. 211, note 69.

64. The highest in the Ptolemaic cosmology.

65. This simile occurs in *Digenes* (p. 63, lines 944-45). In a variant of the figure an eagle swoops on partridges (ibid., p. 171, line 2606). The image of the pouncing eagle occurs a number of times in *Antar*.

66. I.e., himself.

67. "Treasure" for Rustaveli, as for other medieval Georgian writers, consists largely of costly raiment and fabrics.

68. The rending of cheeks in grief may appear characteristically Oriental, but it is in fact not uncommon in Western tales of chivalry; cf., e.g., the "cracchynge of chekes" in Chaucer's *Knight's Tale* (line 2834).

69. The Turkish Khvarizm-shah dynasts had the center of their power at Khiva: in a period of great expansion at the end of the twelfth and the beginning of the thirteenth century their empire absorbed the greater part of Western Persia. For Rustaveli the Khvarizm-shah is simply the ruler of the Persians.

70. This Christian reference is of course anomalous in a Muslim setting; cf. Avtandil's citing of the Apostles (p. 95).

71. See p. 210, note 58.

72. Arabic *Nūr ad-Dīn;* Persian *Farīdūn.*

73. Firdausi describes Rustam as a "tree" (*Epic,* p. 140).

74. Persian *marghzār shahr* 'city of the meadow'.

75. The highest heaven of the Jewish and Muslim cosmologies.

76. The thought seems to be that Parsadan, by his conduct towards Tariel, has forfeited his title to the throne, and that Tariel, as lawful heir, deserves recognition as king.

77. Presumably the two slaves who remained with him after the first period of voyaging; see p. 71.

78. The association of Divs with caves is traditional; Rustam's fight with the White Div in the *Shah-nama* takes place in one.

79. This recalls the vows made to Majnun by the Beduin prince Nawfal in a similar cave-setting: "I promise you, you shall have your Layla. Even if she became a bird, escaping into the sky, even if she were a spark, deep inside the rock, I would still find her. I shall neither rest nor relax until I have married you to your moon-like love." ". . . I shall make a pact with you. In the name of Allah the Almighty and his prophet Mohammed I swear that I shall fight for you and your cause. . . ." (*Layla and Majnun,* pp. 70, 72).

80. I.e., Tinatin.

81. An interesting irruption of the poet's love for the medium of his art.

82. One of the four heads of the river that flowed out of Eden (Gen. 2. 10-11).

83. The Academy edition puts the last statement into the mouth of the vizier.

84. I.e., Tariel.

85. The Oxus is very commonly put to figurative use of this kind in Persian poetry: references are frequent in *Visramiani.*

86. No relationship has been established between this "precept" and any passage in Plato's works.

87. This passage comes unexpectedly from the pen of the presum-

ably Muslim Avtandil.

88. Probably to be connected with the concept of the Nocturnal Evil, met with in *Antar* (1: 336-45, 350). Cf. also the references in the latter to nocturnal depredators (3: 296), and to night-wanderers and robbers (4: 37).

89. It may be doubted whether reference to any particular "Levi" is intended: the name helps with the rhyme.

90. Shermadin's story seems rather lacking in candor.

91. There are two similar figurative references to the Tigris in *Visramiani;* pp. 174, 269.

92. A curious image; cf. pp. 106, 162.

93. Instances of the characteristically Persian conceit of a river swollen by tears are to be found in the verse of Hafiz and Jami (*Persian Poems: an anthology of verse translations*, ed. A.J. Arberry [London: Dent; New York: Dutton, 1954], pp. 79, 82).

94. Cf. *Visramiani*, p. 134: "In China on a stone it is written. . . ."

95. I.e., Rostevan.

96. I.e., Tinatin and Tariel.

97. Beds of reeds seem to have a certain conventional association with the slaughter of wild beasts in some Near Eastern literatures; cf. p. 160. Such killings occur in several episodes in *Amiran-Darejaniani* (pp. 16, 168, 175, 176-77). In *Digenes* (p. 83, lines 1253-54) a lion is found dead in a reed-bed; another emerges from a withy-bed (p. 77, line 1142), to be slain.

98. This is strikingly at variance with the view of the place of tears in the heroic life that informs the poem generally. See Appendix B.

99. "Why do you behave as though incapacitated when you are in fact perfectly well, and why do you torture yourself with brooding on what is past?"

100. See p. 60.

101. Possibly an echo of Ecclus. 20. 30:

> Wisdom that is hid, and treasure that is out of sight,
> What profit is in them both?

1. Cf. p. 79.

2. Cf. p. 33.

3. The days about the time of the heliacal rising of the Dog-star, usually reckoned today as extending from 3 July to 11 August.

4. Through being torn.

5. I.e., Tinatin and Tariel.

6. Arabic *zuḥal*, Saturn, planet of disaster.

7. Arabic *mushtarī*, Jupiter, planet of justice. In *Layla and Majnun* Majnun, after surveying the moon, Mercury, Venus, Mars, Jupiter and Saturn in the night sky, addresses first Venus and then Jupiter, "the star of just rulers and judges" (pp. 145-46).

8. Arabic *mirrīkh*, Mars, planet of vengeance. The thirteenth-

century Persian historian Juvaini describes Saturn and Mars as "the two malefic planets" (*The History of the World-Conqueror*, trans. John Andrew Boyle [Manchester: Manchester University Press, 1958], 1:109).

9. (Hesperus) Venus, planet of healing.

10. Arabic '*oṭārid*, Mercury, planet of intelligence.

11. This simile occurs twice in *Visramiani* (pp. 264, 278).

12. The seven planets of the Ptolemaic system.

13. In the Oriental sense of Western Europeans in general. The quatrain is one of those whose authenticity is commonly held to be doubtful.

14. It would probably be a mistake to attempt to furnish these "Turks" with a location, even in Rustaveli's geography.

15. A note to Gustavo de la Torre's Spanish translation of the poem suggests that the feathers would be used for arrows (*El Caballero de la Piel de Tigre*, Santiago de Chile, 1964, p. 176).

16. A king of the Seas figures in one of the stories in *Amiran-Darejaniani*.

17. The situation recalls that of the caravan immobilized by fear of brigands in *Amiran-Darejaniani* (pp. 95-96).

18. Possibly a perversion of 1 John 4. 18.

19. Persian *gulān shahr* 'city of roses'.

20. Arabic *malik* 'king'; Persian *Surkhāv* (*Suhrāb*).

21. Turkish *khātūn* 'lady', 'dame,' etc.

22. Rustam plays the part of a merchant in the city of Khotan in somewhat similar fashion (*Epic*, pp. 168-69).

23. The heroine and hero of *Visramiani*; see Introduction, pp. xv-xvii.

24. This seems rather like an echo of a misogynic tirade in *Layla and Majnun*, (pp. 115-16): "For a while she looks upon you as a hero, and then, all at once, you are nobody. . . . Never trust a woman!" In its unexpectedness the outburst resembles Antar's ". . . what misfortune can drive man to his destruction, but a woman who is the root and branch of it!" (*Antar*, 1: 222).

25. The crow-nightingale contrast is proverbial; other instances will be found on p. 151.

26. Thereby giving his threat the quality of an oath.

27. The Persian New Year's Day; falling on the vernal equinox, it initiated a week of festivities.

28. It is not clear how Fatima knows these men, "black of face and of body," to be "Indians."

29. The eclipse-dragon appears with the sun or moon several times in the imagery of the poem, as it does in that of *Layla and Majnun* and *Visramiani*.

30. The zodiacal Leo: when the sun is in this sign its power is at its greatest.

31. A color of mourning; cf. the blue and green worn in Arabia

for Avtandil's sake (p. 180). Blue has a similar significance in the *Shah-nama* (*Epic*, pp. 174, 402), *Layla and Majnun* (pp. 156, 160) and *Visramiani* (pp. 11, 164).

32. I.e., the Cup-Bearer.

33. Possibly an echo of Ecclus. 37. 1-2; but it might be a mistake to look for a specific source for the expression of a sentiment so widespread.

34. See p. 150.

35. The first element may represent Persian *dil-āwar* 'brave'; the second is Persian *dukht* 'virgin': sovereigns bearing the names of Azarmidukht and Purandukht figure in the *Shah-nama*.

36. Probably Persian *rosh* 'wicked' and *ak* 'vice'.

37. For her sister's death; see p. 147.

38. Dulardukht evidently regards her nephew as an adopted son.

39. It is interesting to compare Avtandil's conduct with that of Chrétien de Troyes' Lancelot; Lancelot's devotion to Guinevere requires him to reject the advances of a chance hostess (*Le Chevalier de la Charrette*, ed. Mario Roques [Paris, H. Champion, 1958], pp. 37-39, lines 1192-1265). There is no place in the French romancer's world for a hero of Avtandil's pragmatic cast of mind — or for the spirit of comedy.

40. The poet's use, in consecutive lines, of derivatives of the Greek *aedōn* and the Persian *bulbul* for 'nightingale' might serve as a summary of the major external influences on the culture of medieval Georgia.

41. The reference is to Avtandil's second departure from Arabia.

42. An odd statement. Avtandil has indeed searched for Tariel over the whole earth (see p. 23), but his quest for news of Nestan has taken him only to Mulghazanzar and thence to Gulansharo.

43. Presumably one of the two slaves Fatima has already sent on a mission to Kajeti (p. 149).

44. There is an association in the poem of dark skins with magic and the supernatural; cf. Nestan's description of her captors ("black" on p. 76 and pp. 135-36) as sorcerers (pp. 154, 156).

45. See p. 136.

46. See p. 61.

47. See pp. 61, 153.

48. Cf. p. 170. The revolving heavens are referred to several times in the *Shah-nama*, as also in *Layla and Majnun*.

49. Though the poem contains a number of references to sorcery and sorcerers, actual magic is found only in the flights of Fatima's slaves to Kajeti and, perhaps, in the qualities of the arms in the Divs' treasure-hoard (p. 164).

50. See p. 112.

51. A rather curious passage: we have heard nothing of any special services rendered by the slaves, and Avtandil makes over all the

plunder from the pirates' ship to the merchants of the caravan (p. 127).

52. I.e., Tariel.

53. The sun enters this sign on 21 June.

54. This passage reads like an expression of the pathetic fallacy, but it may be just one more instance of the imagery of weeping.

55. In *Visramiani* (pp. 300-01) Ramin swoons on receiving a letter from Vis and recognizing her token.

56. I.e., Qays-Majnun, the hero of *Layla and Majnun*.

57. The hero of the story of Salaman and Absal, best known in modern times in the version of the fifteenth-century Persian poet Jami.

58. A stock metaphor is here used in word-play.

59. The moon represents Tariel, the sun Avtandil.

60. Literally, 'the king of the Indians'. From this point on Tariel is frequently accorded this title: no doubt he is seen as the legitimate heir of Parsadan, who, although still alive when Nestan wrote to Tariel, or at any rate believed by her to be so (p. 157), is perhaps now to be thought of as dead (p. 190). 'The Indian prince' is used in the translation, until near the close, for the sake of clarity.

61. See p. 79.

62. The connection of Divs with treasures locked away in caverns is, like the general association with caves, traditional: see e.g. *Amiran-Darejaniani*, pp. 35-36. According to Italo Pizzi (*Storia della poesia persiana* [Turin, 1894], 2: 7, 9) it reflects the mining activities of aboriginals who were regarded as evil spirits.

63. A sword of Basra (a city near the head of the Persian Gulf) is the equivalent of a Toledo blade.

64. From this point onwards Pridon the minor ruler and Avtandil the feudatory tend to treat Tariel with something of the distinction due to a great monarch.

65. See p. 149.

66. The council of war here entered upon is very reminiscent of that held by Amiran outside the city of Balkh (*Amiran-Darejaniani*, pp. 218-19).

67. This argument seems rather out of harmony with the advice Pridon himself has given against bringing a large army on the expedition (p. 166).

68. Pridon's prowess as an acrobat is one of the marvels of the poem. The handling of a lariat is however one of the regular skills of a warrior in the *Shah-nama*, and there are instances therein of the use of rope and noose to make an ascent: the tyrant Zahhak climbs to the roof of a palace by this means (*Epic*, p. 24).

69. Avtandil's plan recalls the surprise attack which Rustam launches on the king of Turan under the cover of a merchant's disguise (*Epic*, pp. 167-72).

70. See p. 78.

71. On p. 115 and again just below, the disaster-planet appears un-

der its Arabic name. Like the "nightingale" instance (p. 214, note 40), this variation affords a good example of the freely eclectic manner in which the poet uses terms of Greek and Oriental origin.

72. For Mushtar and Zual, see p. 212, notes 7 and 6. Astrologically, this conjunction is indicative of great happiness.

73. Cf. p. 164.

74. It is seldom that courtly romance remembers battle casualties in this way. Cf. p. 175.

75. Tariel now definitely assumes the leadership of the company.

76. A province of northern Afghanistan, famed for its rubies.

77. So in the original.

78. Golden-girdled attendants are part of the décor of such works in the tradition of Persian story-telling as the *Shah-nama*, *Amiran-Darejaniani* and Nizami's *Iskandar-nama*.

79. A twelvemonth passes between Avtandil's departure from Tariel's cave and his return from Gulansharo (pp. 112, 159-60): we must suppose a period considerably longer than a year to have elapsed since the "wrong" done Rostevan.

80. See p. 209, note 38.

81. The sun represents Nestan; the moons stand for the three heroes.

82. See p. 165.

83. The sun represents Tinatin.

84. A symbolic halter of submission.

85. I.e., his weeping for Avtandil.

86. The heroine and hero of *Visramiani*; see Introduction, pp. xv-xvii.

87. Possibly an echo of 1 Cor. 13. 8.

88. The text appears to say, "a thousand jewels laid by a Roman hen": an enigmatic passage, carrying perhaps a reminiscence of the episode in the *Shah-nama* in which the emperor of Rum agrees to pay the Persian monarch an annual tribute of a hundred thousand golden eggs containing jewels (*Epic*, p. 229).

89. Persian hyperbole makes free use of mountain-comparisons of this kind.

90. Cf. Nestan's reference to her father's plight in her letter to Tariel, p. 157.

91. It seems appropriate to render Tariel's royal title literally from this point forward.

92. Cf. p. 49.

93. See p. 215, note 57.

94. See pp. 49-57.

95. In the *Shah-nama* the lance is a weapon closely associated with the Arabs.

96. Jonah 3. 5-10.

97. See p. 202, note 7.

98. The fifty-eight quatrains that lie between the heading "How

Tariel learned of the death of the king of the Indians" (p. 189), and this point are omitted in many editions; much of their language is very obscure.

99. For India's seven realms, see p. 38.

100. Presumably one of the seven kingdoms that had been ruled over by Parsadan; see p. 38.

101. See p. 205, note 5.

102. See p. 205, note 2.

103. See Introduction, p. xv.

104. "Abdul-Mesia" (Arabic *'Abdu'l-Masīḥ* 'the servant of Christ') is the eponymous hero of a sequence of encomiastic odes, dating probably from the early years of the thirteenth century, by Ioané Shavteli; he has been identified with both Tamar's husband and her ancestor David the Builder (1089-1125), Georgia's greatest king.

105. Dilarget was the hero of a romance *Dilariani*, now lost; for Sargis Tmogveli, see Introduction, p. xv.

Appendix A

1. "It is notable in *Ipomedon* [an Anglo-French romance of c. 1185] how very closely the hero and the heroine approximate to each other" (Gervase Mathew, *The Court of Richard II* [London: Murray; New York: Norton, 1969], p. 130).

2. Translated from *Cligés*, ed. Alexandre Micha (Paris: H. Champion, 1957), pp. 83-84, lines 2721-40.

3. Ibid., p. 83, lines 2714-20. Such generalized statements are commoner in Chrétien's works than detailed descriptions of the beauties of hair, cheek, nose and mouth.

4. When Romeo says (*Romeo and Juliet*, act 2, sc. 2, lines 2-3):

> . . . what light through yonder window breaks?
> It is the east, and Juliet is the sun!

— the situation requires something stronger than moonlight to "break": the image is not a piece of conventional ornamentation but a bold effect.

5. *Le Chevalier au Lion* (see p. xxvii, note 10), pp. 73-74, lines 2395-2413.

6. *The Alexiad of Anna Comnena*, trans. E.R.A. Sewter (Harmondsworth: Penguin, 1969), p. 514.

7. The argument is not affected by the circumstance that these writers are concerned with character or position rather than appearance.

8. In the West female sovereigns may of course be invested with monarchy's familiar solar associations; cf. Spenser's apostrophe

(*The Faerie Queene*, bk. 6, canto 10, stanza 28):

> Sunne of the world, great glory of the sky,
> That all the earth doest lighten with thy rayes,
> Great *Gloriana*. . . .

9. *Digenes*, p. 95, line 1429; p. 171, line 2595; p. 103, line 1558; p. 113, line 1714; p. 123, line 1886; p. 183, line 2790. Other instances of "light" figures in the ballad-epic are: "The youth . . . flashing like the sun" (p. 81, line 1229); ". . . there she lay, and seemed to shine with light" (p. 21, line 313); "my light" (p. 121, line 1844; p. 123, line 1884). The imagery in *Digenes* deserves the attention of every student of Rustaveli.

10. *Le Chevalier au Lion*, p. 99, lines 3244-45.

11. *Erec et Enide*, ed. Mario Roques (Paris: H. Champion, 1971), p. 55, lines 1781-82.

12. Quoted in Margaret Wilson, *Spanish Drama of the Golden Age* (Oxford and New York: Pergamon Press, 1969), p. 65.

Appendix B

1. His poem does admittedly contain one or two expostulations rather similar in tenor to Pandare's; but the phrasing is different.

2. The reflections of John Barbour (1375) on weeping in his *Bruce* (bk. 3, lines 515-34) are sufficiently typical of the mind of the medieval West. There is no traffic in heroic hyperbole, and no particular virtue attaches to tears; they are simply accepted as part of life, having a natural connection with anger and sorrow and associations with joy and pity:

> For I trow traistly, that gretyng
> Cummys to men for mysliking;
> And that nane may but anger gret,
> Bot it be wemen, that can wet
> Thair chekys, quhen thaim list, with teris,
> The quethir weill oft thaim na thing deris.
> Bot I wate weill, but lesyng,
> Quhat euir men say off sic greting,
> That mekill ioy, or yeit pete,
> May ger men sua amowyt be,
> That watir fra the hart will ryss,
> And weyt the eyne on sic a wyss,
> That it is lik to be greting,
> Thocht it be nocht sua in all thing.
> For quhen men gretis enkrely,

The hart is sorowfull or angry.
Bot for pite, I trow, gretyng
Be na thing bot ane opynnyng
Off hart, that schawis the tendirnys
Off rewth that in it closyt is.

It will be noticed that the tears of women are regarded as facile: from this view there evolves a tendency to devalue all weeping by association; tears in the male become womanish or woman-provoked. An illustration may be drawn from *Henry IV, Part 1* (act 3, sc. 1, lines 95-96): Glendower evokes a scene — the parting of two noblemen from their ladies on the eve of a perilous adventure — that might come straight from the quatrains of *The Lord of the Panther-skin*. So too might the image he employs:

> . . . there will be a world of water shed
> Upon the parting of your wives and you.

The import of the passage is, however, most conspicuously un-Rustavelian. Rustaveli would certainly have conceived of Hotspur and Mortimer as shedding quite as many tears as their wives, and the flood would have afforded proof of the quality of soul of all four: for Glendower — no longer prepared to accept such phenomena in the workaday spirit of the fourteenth-century Scottish poet — tears are simply a consequence of the presence of the womenfolk at a difficult moment, and one which it is worth taking pains to avoid. For this scene is not in fact to take place: Glendower has just told the husbands that they are to steal away without leave-taking.

3. Geoffrey of Monmouth, *The History of the Kings of Britain*, trans. Lewis Thorpe (Harmondsworth: Penguin, 1966), [9.1] p. 214.

4. Sir William Alexander, supplement to Sir Philip Sidney's *Arcadia* (Dublin, 1621), 3: 331-32.

THE LORD OF THE PANTHER-SKIN
A GEORGIAN PERSPECTIVE

A.G. Baramidze
Member of the Academy of Sciences
of the Georgian S.S.R.

Georgia, the homeland of Rustaveli, is a country with an ancient culture. The origins of Georgian literature lie in remote antiquity, before the development of the feudal system and the spread of Christianity throughout the country (fourth century A.D.), but no examples of pre-Christian literature have survived. The earliest known example of Georgian literature is *The Life and Martyrdom of St. Shushanik*, by Jacob Tsurtaveli (fifth century A.D.).

The social and political conditions of Georgia in the early feudal period led to the development of exclusively ecclesiastical and religious literature until the end of the eleventh century. Of particular importance are the achievements of Georgian hagiography, hymns and theology. Though designed essentially for the doctrinal and missionary purposes of the church, this native hagiographic literature contains considerable elements of belles-lettres and historiography, and much material throwing light on the history and life of the Georgian people and their struggle against foreign invaders and conquerors. A number of works of Byzantine and Eastern Christian hagiography were translated into Georgian and several literary monuments of the highest rank, the originals of which have been lost, have been preserved in their Georgian translations. Georgian hymns often used meters borrowed from the oral folk poetry. In the tenth century, there appeared a collection of hymn-books in Georgian, complete with musical notations. In their works, Georgian hymn-writers gave sincere expression to both religious and patriotic feelings.

A certain monk of the Monastery of St. Saba in Jerusalem composed a *Song in Praise and Honor of the Georgian Language.* Inspired, as he himself puts it, by the profundity and grace of his native tongue, but aware of its minor position in relation to the dominating world languages of the time, the author of the *Praise* predicted a brilliant "triumph" for it in the future. There is even a hagiographic poem written in Georgian on a romantic theme *(The Chronicle of the Monastery of Saint Saba).* In the realm of philosophical thought, "the Georgians of the eleventh and twelfth centuries were interested in the same problems as were then exercising the leading thinkers of the Christian world, in both West and East — but they differed from others, particularly from the Europeans, in that they reacted earlier to the latest philosophical trends and carried out what must be considered, for that period, a model of direct textual criticism of Greek originals."[1] The scope and significance of ancient Georgian ecclesiastical and religious literature as a whole may be judged indirectly from the opinion of the eminent German scholar, A. von Harnack, in connection with the publication of N. Ya. Marr's *Preliminary Account of the Research done at Sinai and Jerusalem during the 1902 Expedition:* "The fact that the Georgians belonged in ancient times to the great Graeco-Christian family of nations is made abundantly clear by Marr's account. Will young scholars be found in Germany to study the language, literature and history of this people — related as it is to us through its ancient culture — and to familiarize us with its treasures? Here, surely, is a new task for our universities."[2]

Politically, economically, socially, and culturally, medieval Georgia reached the peak of its development in the twelfth century, in the reigns of David the Builder (1089-1125). Giorgi III (1156-1184) and especially the celebrated Queen Tamar (1184-1213). The Georgia of that period was a strong feudal state, playing an important part in the history of the peoples of the Near East. This period in the life of the Georgian people was marked by a great material and spiritual upsurge. We are amazed by the grandeur and beauty of the surviving monumental works of architecture of the time, and by the delicacy and grace of the painting, jewellery, chasing, and embroidery.[3]

The end of the eleventh century saw the rise of ancient Georgian secular literature which — especially poetry — flourished luxuriantly in the following century; at the same time, ecclesiastical and religious literature lost its earlier dominating position and acquired a doctrinal, bookish and scholastic tone.

The twelfth century was the classical period in the history of Georgian ecclesiastical culture. The secular literature of the time was highly original, even though it developed in close contact with the literatures of neighboring countries, above all Persia, Azerbaijan and Armenia. The works of ancient Greek writers were translated into Georgian, as were also the finest works of Persian and Azerbaijani writers (Firdausi's *Shahnama*, the poems of Nizami, Unsuri, Gurgani, etc.). On the other hand, the high standard of Georgian culture was also reflected in the works of great poets, such as Khaqani and Nizami.

A very large and valuable part of the Georgian classical literary heritage was lost as a result of the catastrophic events in the subsequent centuries (the Mongol invasions); even so, those works that have survived enable us, to some extent, to form an idea of the general state of literary life in the country.

Ancient Georgian secular literature is represented by a variety of genres, epic poetry being particularly developed. One of the early works of secular literature is the heroic tale *Amiran-Darejaniani*.[4] A story of a deeply human and passionate love is told in *Visramiani*, the Georgian version of the Persian poem.[5] A high degree of national consciousness marks such remarkable examples of Georgian panegyric poetry of the twelfth century as Ioané Shavteli's *Abdulmesia* and Chakhrukhadze's *Tamariani*, as well as works by Georgian historians, particularly the *History and Eulogy of Monarchs*. Very curious is the fate of a widely-traveled Georgian poet of the twelfth century, who visited many Eastern and Western countries and won renown by reciting his own poems, apparently in Persian and Arabic (his story is told in *Tamariani*). His name, however, is unknown. But the crowning achievement and unsurpassed masterpiece of Georgian classical poetry is Shota Rustaveli's *The Lord of the Panther-skin*.

There are very few well-established facts about Rustaveli

himself. The principal source of historical and literary facts concerning *The Lord of the Panther-skin* and its author is the Prologue to the poem itself. Following a literary tradition, Rustaveli dedicates his poem to Queen Tamar, respectfully singing her praise in the opening stanzas (3-4). This dedication provides a clue to the date of the poem: it could not have been written before the 80s of the twelfth century, or later than the first decade of the thirteenth. In the Prologue there are two references (7-8) to the author of the poem, Rustaveli (or more correctly, Rustveli), which means literally 'owner of the Rustavi estate (or castle)' or 'coming from Rustavi.' The poet's Christian name, Shota, is confirmed in literary documents relating to the sixteenth and seventeeth centuries. Apparently Shota Rustaveli owned the estate (or castle) of Rustavi, belonged to the military class of Georgian feudal society, and was close to court circles.

Several localities in Georgia bear the name Rustavi. Shota Rustaveli is usually considered to have come from the South-Georgian' Rustavi, in the province of Meskhia. Numerous folk stories, mostly of Meskhian origin, add further material to the poet's biography; but many of these tales and legends are scarcely more than fiction. According to both literary and oral tradition, toward the end of his life Rustaveli became a monk in the Georgian monastery at Jerusalem and died there. There is a portrait of Shota Rustaveli, dressed as a courtier, in the Monastery of the Holy Cross.

The story of *The Lord of the Panther-skin* has great appeal. Rostevan, the aged and renowned king of Arabia, having no male heir, destines his throne to his only daughter, the beautiful and intelligent Tinatin, who is in love with the valiant Avtandil, both army commander and courtier. One day, during a hunt, Rostevan and Avtandil meet by the side of a stream a mysterious, mournful knight clad in a panther-skin. All attempts to speak with him are vain. The disappointed king falls into depression. It is then that Tinatin charges her beloved to find the mysterious stranger at all costs. Avtandil is eager to serve his lady. After long and arduous wanderings, he finds the mysterious knight, whose name is Tariel. Tariel tells Avtandil his sad story: he is the scion of a royal family and an *amirbar* (military commander and admiral) of the Indian king Parsadan, and he is passionately in love with the radiant princess Nestan-Darejan, daughter of the king. But fate has been unkind to the lovers. King Parsadan has decided to marry Nestan-Darejan to a Khvarizmian prince and proclaim him heir to the throne, even though Tariel is the lawful heir. Nestan-Darejan persuades her lover to kill his rival and seize power. The princess is accused of sinful love for the rebel and severely punished: after a cruel beating, she is secretly taken away beyond the borders of India. Tariel undertakes a vain search for his beloved, and, having lost all hope of finding her, he turns his back on his country. Avtandil becomes Tariel's sworn brother, consoles him, gives him fresh hope and sets out himself in search of Nestan-Darejan. He finally discovers that she is held captive in the impregnable fortress of Kajeti. With the help of Pridon, another sworn brother, Tariel and Avtandil take the fortress and free Nestan. The joyful heroes then return home. Tariel marries Nestan-Darejan and Avtandil marries Tinatin. Peacefully and humanely they rule their countries and their happy peoples.

Rustaveli unfolds the plot of his poem with all the masterly skill of a great poet. To this day, *The Lord of the Panther-skin* keeps the reader enthralled. The poet successfully avoids the repetitions and tedious passages which are a feature of most epic-narrative works. Rustaveli's poem is highly dynamic; its action develops rapidly and with increasing intensity in a natural and logical sequence. It abounds in tense, dramatic situations. The reader is moved by its lofty pathos, which is especially intense at the crucial points of the story.

The Lord of the Panther-skin is a poem which is to a large extent free of the fantastic and fairytale elements encountered in works of that epoch. Even Rustaveli's *Kajes* (evil spirits) are humanized and endowed with the physical features of men. In reply to Avtandil's puzzled question (1245): ". . . the *Kajes* are spirits — how then have they taken flesh and blood to themselves?" Fatima replies (1246): "These are not true *Kajes*, but mortal men who live secure among steep rocks."

Despite the extreme complexity of its subject, *The Lord of the Panther-skin* is an integral, complete poetic composition, skillfully combining two basic story cycles (Indian and Arabian), besides other important narrative episodes (the story of King Pridon, the merchant land of Gulansharo, etc.). In unfolding his narrative, Rustaveli brilliantly reveals the characters of his heroes, disclosing their rich and complex inner world, while at the same time concisely expounding his own lofty conceptions with artistic conviction. The profound psychological analysis of his heroes and the penetrating treatment of the inner essence of events are striking features of the innovations that Rustaveli — an unsurpassed master of style and verse — brought to Georgian literature.

Rustaveli succeeded in creating a whole gallery of living, complete and artistically convincing characters, both men and women, who, selflessly and fearlessly, wage their battle for the triumph of justice on earth. The principal heroine of the poem, the chaste, virtuous and gentle princess Nestan-Darejan, is seized by the fury of the panther, the spirit of rebellious protest, when she hears that she is to be married against her will. Stoically and courageously she endures her imprisonment in the fortress of Kajeti, that symbol of tyranny, darkness and fanaticism. The titanic efforts of the three noble brothers in arms, their unshakable faith in the ultimate triumph of justice, and the selfless struggle they wage in its name are crowned with complete victory. Kajeti is destroyed, Nestan-Darejan is delivered from "the jaws of the dragon," and justice triumphs. "Good has overcome evil, for its essence is lasting" (1361). This optimistic and positive idea of the victory of justice over arbitrary power, of good over evil, is the underlying theme of *The Lord of the Panther-skin*: man must go on seeking, for he can achieve complete happiness in this world.

Although the geographical scene of the story as it unfolds is vast and the characters belong to different nations (some of them fictitious), Rustaveli is a wholly original national poet.

In the ninth stanza of the Prologue he says: "I came upon this Persian tale and turned it into Georgian; a thing until now like a rare pearl passed from hand to hand has been put into verse." The first learned publisher of the poem and its erudite commentator, Vakhtang VI (1675-1737), wrote, as early as 1712: "There is no such Persian story. . . . Rustaveli invented the story and told it in verse himself." All attempts to discover indications that the plot of *The Lord of the Panther-skin* was borrowed from Persian literature have proved vain: neither in Persian nor in any other literature is a similar story to be found. It seems certain to us that Rustaveli resorted to a "camouflage" familiar in the works of medieval literature.[6] Apparently Rustaveli deliberately resorted to this "camouflage" device in order to veil the obvious allusions contained in his poem to the acute political conflicts of his time; and perhaps also in order to avoid too much criticism of his own political, social and philosophical ideas. Be that as it may, Rustaveli gave an artistically truthful picture of the great variety and complexity of Georgian life in the twelfth century. His religious and philosophical, as well as his social and political views, are expressed with clarity and precision.

The Lord of the Panther-skin is a moving poem of love and the worship of woman. In 1910, N. Ya. Marr noted that "the cult of woman, the idealized love and worship of woman, originated in the refined and enlightened Georgian society of Tamar's time."[7]

In the Prologue to his poem Rustaveli clearly defines the essence of love and sets forth its complicated code. The poet distinguishes three fundamental kinds of love. First, there is celestial love, "whose nature is heavenly" (20). He admits that this is the most important, most valuable form of love, but "far is it beyond the understanding of even the wisest men." Obviously leaving aside this kind of love, Rustaveli champions the second kind, elevated earthly love — adding that he himself had sung only of an earthly, human, "carnal" feeling, "which has yet some likeness to the mystic when there is nothing wanton in it" (21) — so the poet tells the reader. At the same time, he absolutely rejects the third kind of love — base, crudely sensual love, which is akin to debauchery (24-25). The love he preaches is not an abstract and objectless spiritual passion, but a deep human feeling. Such love can be experienced only by a hero of high moral qualities, great valor, spiritual strength, and lofty intellect (23):

> A lover should be even as fair as the sun itself,
> deep of mind, possessed of riches, generous of heart,
> in the flower of youth, and with time at command.

He should have eloquence of tongue, a good under-
standing, endurance, and the strength that brings
victory over mighty antagonists. He who falls short
of this is not to be reckoned a lover.

The theory of love propounded in the Prologue is subsequently
demonstrated in the poem itself, where the poet deals with a
love which is earthly but at the same time chivalrous, a morally
elevating and ennobling passion.

His treatment of the various aspects of love has much in com-
mon with that of the medieval poems of Western Europe,
but in these, love "is not a complete system of life,"[8] as it is to
Rustaveli. According to *The Lord of the Panther-skin*, love
brings out all that is best in human nature, and stimulates heroic
deeds and self-sacrifice in man. Rustaveli feels that love is a
hard ordeal for both men and women: only by heroism and
valor can man win the heart of his chosen one; only by chival-
rous self-denial and the perfect fulfilment of his duty to society,
and by selfless devotion to his homeland can he deserve the
full confidence of his beloved. Thus Nestan exhorts Tariel (377):
"Vapors, swoonings, expirings — is this how you would play
the lover? Deeds of prowess were a far better offering to make
to your lady!" Tariel fulfils his difficult task honorably, and
Nestan writes to her beloved after his triumphant return from
Cathay (494): "Never shall I be another's; that do I swear."
Avtandil likewise wins Tinatin by performing heroic deeds.
And in the end, Nestan and Tinatin, the heroines of the poem,
are worthily rewarded for their bitter sufferings.

Rustaveli's understanding of love is closely related to his
theory of poetry, which also is expounded in the Prologue.
While regarding poetry as "a branch of philosophy" and paying
tribute to its divine character, Rustaveli simultaneously stresses
is earthly, worldly, instructive and even utilitarian purpose (12):
". . . divine, fit for heaven," he says, "it delights those who
hear it. Even here below it gives pleasure to noble souls. . . ."

It is noteworthy that Rustaveli considers love to be the basis
of the family and marriage. The poet proclaims the freedom of
personal feelings and severely condemns any coercion or con-
straint in the choice of a spouse. The tragedy of Nestan-Darejan

arises from King Parsadan's decision to marry her to a stranger she does not love. Parsadan, of course, guesses at the mutual attraction between Nestan and Tariel, but, in his conservative way, he holds that it is a father's right to decide his daughter's fate; her personal happiness must, if necessary, be sacrificed to consolidate his own political power. As he explains his motives to Tariel (508-9):

> . . . we do not grieve over the lack of a son, since we have a daughter of a dazzling loveliness. Now we wish to find a husband for her — but where are we to find one whom we can have sit on our throne, whom we can mold in our own image and make the realm's defender and ruler, that we may not suffer destruction, that our enemies may not sharpen their swords for us?

King Parsadan's actions are quite understandable. Friedrich Engels pointed out in his *Origin of the Family, Private Property and the State* that it was unheard of that in the ruling classes mutual attraction between the parties should take precedence, as a basis for marriage, over other considerations. In the same work Engels stressed that, in medieval society, for a knight or a baron, or for the prince himself, marriage was a political act, an occasion for increasing power with the help of new alliances; the decisive role had to be played by the interests of the house, not by personal sympathies. And he asked how, under such conditions, the last word in the question of marriage could belong to love.

The contempt shown for their innermost feelings produces a violent and passionate protest on the part of Nestan and Tariel and compels them to stand up bravely in defence of their human rights and their love. Bloody events ensue, and Nestan becomes their tragic victim. Rustaveli shows how unwise and unjust are the acts of Parsadan and how severely he himself is punished. Rostevan, the king of the Arabs, acts differently and, having learned of the mutual love of Tinatin and Avtandil, he helps them and blesses their union. Thus the great Georgian poet of the twelfth century glorified an ideal "unheard of" in the Middle Ages.

Rustaveli's poem is imbued with the specifically Georgian worship of woman. The social and political conditions of Georgia favored the development of that idea and the secluded "harem" way of life for women was thoroughly alien to its people. In the *Life and Martyrdom of St. Shushanik* (fifth century) and the *Life of St. Nino* (eighth to ninth century) it had already been affirmed that man and woman were one, and equal in the eyes of the Most High. The greatest Georgian writer of the tenth century, Giorgi Merchuli, created a number of admirable female characters. Women often played an important role in the political and cultural life of the country.

According to national church traditions, Georgia was regarded as the appanage of the Mother of God, and the conversion of the Georgians to Christianity was attributed to a woman, St. Nino of Cappadocia. Nicoloz Gulaberisdze, an ecclesiastical writer of the twelfth century, and a contemporary of Rustaveli, composed a special treatise in defense and in praise of woman's honor and dignity. Finally, it is noteworthy that Rustaveli himself witnessed the power of Georgia and its splendid flowering as a state in the reign of a woman, Queen Tamar. The age of Rustaveli was thus fully prepared ideologically for the acceptance and promotion of the "cult of woman." This was reflected in the general ideological trend of the Georgian poet's work, in his rapturous hymn to woman's honor, to the freedom of a woman's love, and in the undying character of Nestan-Darejan which he created (her prototype was Queen Tamar herself). In Rustaveli's general poetic scheme Tinatin is not meant to play a leading part; but her moral qualities, her intellectual capacities and her appearance are in complete harmony with the poet's general conception of the ideal woman. Not only do Nestan-Darejan and Tinatin embody the purity of woman's love: they are fully rounded human characters, endowed with high intellectual and moral qualities. Weak in body but strong in spirit, Nestan even under unusually arduous conditions does not lose her self-control, her courage or her clear-mindedness, but utters words of profound wisdom (1191): "What man in his right mind will yield himself up to death before needs must? It is when we are in straits that wit can provide its best service!"

Nestan-Darejan does not brood over her personal hardships. She does not yield to despair, even when she sees no solution; she appraises the situation soberly. She does not value her life above all else. She does not think of herself. What depresses her is the thought of her country's fate, of her beloved India, of her disconsolate parents. Shedding tears, she writes to Tariel (1296-97):

> I had believed, upon my faith, that you were with the dead; life, I thought, had gone from me, with nothing remaining. This news has made me praise the Creator, humble myself before the throne of God; the sorrow that was mine is now changed into joy. You are alive — that is enough; my heart has something to hope for, my heart that is afire and covered over with wounds. Think of me, remember me, as one who is lost to you. . . .

And the letter ends with this appeal (1307): "Set out, ride to India and bring aid to my father; he is beset by his enemies and has no one to help him."

The letter of Nestan-Darejan is the brilliant poetic expression of the greatness of a woman's love, of the triumph of reason over passion; it is the inspired confession of a woman capable of any exploit and any sacrifice for the sake of lofty ideals, for the defense of her country against its enemies.

In the words of the well-known Russian poet Balmont, the author of the first Russian translation of *The Lord of the Panther-skin*, "this is the best love poem ever composed in Europe."[9]

It is not surprising that the creator of the character of Nestan-Darejan should give a poetic justification for the equality of men and women, at least in a certain society, by saying that, like lion cubs, whether male or female, they are equals (39).

Certain scholars (e.g., Academician N. Ya. Marr and I.A. Javakhishvili) consider that in Rustaveli's poem the *motif* of friendship prevails over that of love. While not sharing this view, we agree that in *The Lord of the Panther-skin* friendship indeed plays an exceptionally important part and may even at times seem to be the most important thing of all. As the poet says (854): "His own enemy he who will not seek for a friend." In Rustaveli's poem the closest bonds of friendship unite, not two (which is usually the case in medieval poetry), but three paladins (a pattern common in Georgian folklore). The friendship of Rustaveli's heroes takes the specific Georgian form of sworn brotherhood. Tariel and Avtandil become sworn brothers and take an oath of eternal friendship. To help a friend in dire need, Avtandil leaves his homeland and his beloved, suffers great hardships, but fulfils the duty of a paladin and a brother (703): "For the sake of a friend a man should shrink from no sorrow, but give heart for heart, love as a road and a bridge." The manly decision to renounce personal happiness for a brother-friend's sake is also approved without hesitation by Avtandil's sovereign lady, Tinatin. Even though exposing her beloved to grave dangers, and so losing her own peace of mind, she is as capable as her champion of any sacrifice for the love of a friend.

In Rustaveli's poem brotherhood is not in any sense opposed to love; on the contrary, they are indissolubly linked. Brotherhood may be said to be an organic part and a result of the sentiment of love. Rustaveli's heroes become brothers on the basis of the universal power of love, for the sake of rescuing Nestan-Darejan, the bearer and embodiment of this love.

The brotherhood of the three heroes of *The Lord of the Panther-skin* symbolizes the friendship of different nations. Avtandil the Arab, Tariel the Indian, and Pridon the Mulghazanzarian not only become friends, but also forge bonds of friendship between their peoples. Although Rustaveli's heroes are of different nationalities, they are filled with the same noble aspirations. They are united by the same will and the same aim. It is as a result of their united efforts that they win their victory over evil, injustice and violence. Returning with honor to their countries, the sworn brothers grow still more united; they continue to help one another and so safeguard the peace of their countries and the progress and prosperity of those over whom they rule. Rustaveli sings the praises of this inspiring, manly, and selfless friendship among sworn brothers and of friendship among their peoples.

Also radiant and touching is the friendship between a man and a woman (Tariel and Asmat), as related in Rustaveli's poem. Further, the whole poem is imbued with a noble idea of patriotism. Tariel's glorious military campaigns for the restoration of Indian sovereignty against Ramaz, the perfidious king of the Cathayans, are described with great poetic fervor. The Indians are filled with ardent patriotism during the anxious days of conflict between King Parsadan and the amirbar Tariel. Nestan and Tariel discuss thoroughly and at length their plan of action in case the Khvarizmian prince arrives as a bridegroom and heir to the throne. They place the welfare of their country and the state above their own private interests. They rebel against any recognition of a foreigner's claims to power over their native land: ". . . never must it be said that the Persians lord it here at our court!"[10] they say (540). Nestan advises Tariel to appeal to King Parsadan (544): ". . . speak to your lord, my father, saying, 'I cannot let the Persians devour all of India; my inheritance it is, and not one jot will I yield of it!'" It should be remembered that Tariel belongs to the royal family, and has been brought up by Parsadan as heir to the throne of India. Tariel boldly reminds Parsadan that he has broken his royal word and disregarded the interests of the state. To defend the violated rights and dignity of his country, Tariel places himself at the head of a rebellion and turns to the Indian people for help. This is how he subsequently relates the story to Avtandil (560): he "sent out messengers with this call to the warriors: 'Rally to me now, all those who are for me!'" We have already spoken of Nestan-Darejan's ardent, patriotic appeal from the fortress of Kajeti.

Rustaveli's political ideal is a united, powerful, independent monarchy, ruled by a brave, enlightened and humane king. The poet condemns feuds and the separatist ambitions of vassal princelings and stands for the complete centralization of power, limited to some extent by a council of wise statesmen. He holds absolute monarchs in high esteem and inculcates respect for their dignity and unconditional submission to their authority. But, at the same time, he expects justice and wisdom from the rulers themselves. Through the mouth of Tariel, Rustaveli sharply condemns Parsadan's political shortsightedness (563): ". . . a king should always deal justly."

Rustaveli denounces all despotism and tyranny. He idealizes a relationship between suzerain and vassal which was humane enough for the time. Rustaveli's principal heroes, Tariel and Avtandil, are ambitious, courteous, and valiant men of arms, always true to their feelings of love and loyal to their homeland and to their king. Their characters have much in common, the spiritual and physical qualities of the chivalrous ideal, courage, valor and nobility; and, at the same time, they are richly endowed with specific individual qualities of their own.

Tariel is clever and rational but good-natured and sensitive almost to the point of sentimentality. He is a predominantly emotional personality. Avtandil has a more balanced nature — he is reasonable, resourceful, adroit and optimistic. To some extent Tariel reminds us of Achilles, and Avtandil of Ulysses.

The Lord of the Panther-skin is a poem that glorifies life itself. Rustaveli's heroes love the spiritually rich, reasonable, and beautiful life worthy of the most advanced men of their time. But their love of life is inseparably linked with their struggle for human rights. In this struggle they do not fear death. Rustaveli puts these words into Avtandil's mouth (800): ". . . better a glorious death than a life without honor!" In the poet's view, life is ennobled by this striving for the good, by the desire for a good name (799): "Better to win glory than all else beside." Life is an arena where a man can show his true worth, his physical and spiritual strength. Only by courageously overcoming the obstacles on the hard and dangerous road he must follow can man create a life worthy of himself. Only one who can endure ordeals and triumph over them will enjoy life, and he alone has the right to taste of the sweet fruits of victory (1637): ". . . he who has not passed through grief can know nothing of happiness," or (1533) ". . . sweet indeed is joy when a man has made a passage through sorrow."

Rustaveli opposes nobility, honesty and valor to perfidy and treachery (162): "For treacherous falsehood a lance-thrust is fitting." The poet abhors traitors who conceal their evil and wicked intentions behind a mask of kindness and friendship (1211): "The false friend is the worst of all foes. . . ."

Rustaveli sternly denounces those who break their oath, who betray their country and their friends, and who try to hide their inertia and insignificance behind a noisy display of bravado and boasting. The poet puts these words into the testament of Avtandil to express his contempt for cowardice (799): "Miserable indeed is the wretch who, face contorted with terror, fearful of death, will shrink back in battle! In what way is a coward of more worth than a weaving-woman?" Every warrior, every paladin, every man valuing his own dignity must be brave, valiant and bold (875): ". . . a man should bear himself like a man, and weep as seldom as may be. In grief we should strive to show the strength of a wall of stone. . . ."

Rustaveli's hero, brave and self-sacrificing, albeit merciless to his enemies, is, at the same time, a model of kindness and generosity. He is the patron and defender of the weak and helpless, the poor and the oppressed.

Rustaveli's favorite personages are models of perfection. The poet, of course, exaggerates their worth and idealizes the heroes and their ladies. But in drawing his material from contemporary life, Rustaveli generously endows his characters with the finest features of the military and chivalrous society of Georgia which, for the twelfth century, was highly advanced. Exaggeration and hyperbole in *The Lord of the Panther-skin* are, of course, only natural, as in any medieval romantic epic.

In his poem Rustaveli deals, in the main, with the life of two social spheres of Georgian feudal society: warriors and heroes on one hand, merchants and traders on the other. Rustaveli is obviously hostile to the merchant class. In the land of Gulansharo, dominated by merchants, the leading role is played by a merchant named Husain, the closest friend and counsellor of the king. In commercial affairs Husain is enterprising and cunning, but he is morally contemptible, and his ugliness is a reflection of his base inner motives. Rustaveli describes him in these contemptuous words (1165): "Behold the merchant in his cups now, false, faithless and thoughtless!" Husain's wife, Fatima, is destined to play a very important part in the land of Gulansharo. Rustaveli is generously condescending to her, but there is, nevertheless, an unmistakable touch of irony in his description of her (1077): "This Fatima Khatun was a woman who had her attractions, and she was none the less lively because her first youth had now passed away. She had a good figure and dark coloring, and her face was well-rounded. She was a great one for singers and minstrels, and was fond of her glass of wine: many were the fine gowns and head-dresses possessed by her." Fatima is a frivolous and amorous woman, caring nothing for her family's honor, and abusing her husband for his physical shortcomings (1205): "I have no use for my husband; he is ugly, all skin and bone." The character of Fatima is artistically true to life and, despite her defects, she is still capable of deep feelings and a human warmth characteristic of women. She does much to save Nestan-Darejan. It is significant that, having learned of the real aim of Avtandil's journey, Fatima makes no attempt to detain her lover for even a short time.

And yet, in this mercantile society, love is very much like that base and lustful sensuality which Rustaveli speaks about in the Prologue to his poem (25-26): "Love-making with no heart to it I find utterly hateful. This one today, that other tomorrow; parting without a pang — this is not worthy of the name of love! It resembles nothing so much as the idle games boys play together: the true lover is he who can endure the woes that Fate sends him."

People of the merchant class put their mercenary interests above all else; they are miserly and grasping and always strive for easy gain. Among them, selfishness and other base instincts take the place of chivalrous magnanimity.

Rustaveli was among the first in the whole of world literature to paint a realistic and colorful picture of merchant life, which he sets against his idealized picture of chivalrous society.

Prominent medievalists who have studied *The Lord of the Panther-skin* all agree that Rustaveli is much more of a freethinker in religion than his European fellow-poets (e.g., Wolfram von Eschenbach or Chrétien de Troyes). To quote the academician V.F. Shishmarev: "Unlike the most famous medieval poets of Western Europe, Shota is quite unconcerned with any religious or ecclesiastical doctrine"[11] — even though the poet is, obviously, well-read, and familiar with biblical texts. The same view is suggested by Bowra[12] and others.

At the center of Rustaveli's attention is his love of man,

with all his spontaneous feelings, experiences, passions and strivings. In opposition to medieval mental withdrawal and ecclesiastical morality, Rustaveli proclaims the freedom of the human personality, freedom of thought and of all spiritual life. He sings the praises of the intellectually exalted and morally pure man, and his beautiful earthly, material ideals. *The Lord of the Panther-skin* extols a full and purposeful life, and a human personality unhampered in its actions by either a blind Fate or a Divine Providence. Rustaveli is a great humanist in the fullest sense of the word. His humanism is reflected in his advocacy of the freedom of love, in his idea of the brotherhood of men and peoples, in his selfless love of his homeland and his burning hatred of all its enemies. In his free-thinking attitude Rustaveli is well in advance of his contemporaries, anticipating the humanistic ideas of the early Renaissance.

The poet rendered his profound feelings and thoughts in graceful, supple and sonorous lines known as *shairi*. He is the law-giver and unsurpassed master of this meter in Georgian versification. The *shairi* is a sixteen-syllable line. Rustaveli uses two types of this line — the high type (4-4-4-4) and the low type (5-3-5-3). The high type is used chiefly to give dynamic vigor to the narrative, while low *shairi* are used in the more static (e.g., descriptive) passages. This variety of meter helps Rustaveli to escape the monotony common to so many works of medieval literature. The different *shairi* are combined with a definite order in the system of rhymes. The low *shairi* have three-syllable rhymes, while the high *shairi* have two-syllable rhymes. The *shairi* stanzas are quatrains always following the rhyme pattern *aaaa*. As a rule, Rustaveli's rhymes are rich in variety, sonorous and original, and the poem itself is exceptionally melodious, with an unsurpassed harmony of sounds. Rustaveli is a master in the use of alliteration and assonance. Unfortunately the verse of this great poet loses much of its inimitable expressiveness in translation.

Rustaveli's poetic speech is particularly rich in metaphors and aphorisms. His poem is, indeed, full of complex and detailed metaphors. His profound, terse and beautifully expressed aphorisms have passed long since into the spoken language, and continue to thrive as maxims of popular wisdom. But they are very far removed from moralizing epigrams or ordinary "rules of conduct."

His aphorisms, lyrical preludes, epistles and brief but pointed descriptions do not interfere with the dynamic development of the narrative but, on the contrary, add a colorful framework to the story and greatly enliven it. Rustaveli did not accept the archaic and bookish style of ancient Georgian ecclesiastical literature; his language is relatively simple and, at the same time, elegant and expressive. Rustaveli is deservedly regarded as the father of a new literary language, which still flourishes in Georgia. The vocabulary of *The Lord of the Panther-skin* is unusually rich and varied, and admirably reflects the wealth and suppleness of the Georgian language.

Rustaveli absorbed all the riches of ancient Georgian literature and at the same time followed the best traditions of the folklore of his native land, thus developing Georgian poetry and raising it to a level never before attained. The ideas propounded in Rustaveli's poem are original and peculiar to the Georgian people. He sang of their finest ideals and aspirations, and yet any form of national exclusiveness or isolationism is wholly alien to him. The world of Rustaveli's ideas belongs to the whole of humanity.

Even though the lofty ideas of love, patriotism, friendship and heroism in Rustaveli's poem are essentially Georgian, such ideas also belong to other nations, both great and small. It is remarkable that the Georgian poet should have succeeded in expressing these advanced ideas in admirable poetic form as early as the twelfth century — that is to say, in the Middle Ages, when society was still dominated by religious and mystical ideology. Rustaveli's ideas are today as fresh, beautiful and original as his verses are delightful and unequalled. Rustaveli's humanistic outlook and the exceptional popularity of his poem aroused the animosity of the clergy in Georgia. Some of the poem's enemies deliberately corrupted its text, while others did all they could to abuse and discredit its author; others again tried to destroy both manuscript and printed copies of the poem. But the clerics failed to destroy *The Lord of the Panther-skin* or to weaken its inspiring influence on the development of Georgian poetry down to the present time. Rustaveli's genius rose high above the society of his age. His vision penetrated far into future centuries, giving him a natural kinship with the forward-looking elements of every new epoch, and of every people.

Rustaveli is close to the peoples of our time, and his advanced ideas are in harmony with the world of today.

NOTES

1. N. Ya. Marr, *Ioann Petritskiy, gruzinskiy neoplatonik XI-XII vekov* [Ioané Petritsi, a Georgian neoplatonist of the eleventh-twelfth centuries] (St. Petersburg, 1910), p. 130.

2. Adolf von Harnack, *Forschungen aus dem Gebiete der alten grusinischen und armenischen Litteratur*, Sitzungsberichte der preussischen Akademie der Wissenschaften, vol. 39 (Berlin, 1903), p. 840.

3. G.N. Chubinashvili, *Peshchernye monastyri David Garedzh* [The Cave Monasteries of David Gareja] (Tbilisi, 1948); also his *Gruzinskoe chekannoe iskusstvo s VIII po XVIII vek* [The Georgian art of clashing from the eighth to the eighteenth century] (Tbilisi: 1957); Sh. Ya. Amiranashvili, *Istoriya gruzinskoy monumental'noy zhivopisi* [History of Georgian Monumental Painting] (Tbilisi, 1957) and his *Beka Opizari* (Tbilisi: 1956).

4. There is an English translation by R.H. Stevenson (Oxford: 1958).

5. Translated into English by Sir Oliver Wardrop (London, 1914). An abridged German translation of the same work by R. Neukomm and K. Tschenkeli was published in Zurich in 1957.

6. This device has also been frequently resorted to in more recent times. Thus the French writer Montesquieu (1689-1755) claims no more than the honor of having translated from the Persian, and polished, his well-known *Lettres persanes*. In reality, the book has nothing whatever to do with either Persia or Persian literature. Similarly, the Russian writer Lermontov (1814-1841) claims that his famous novel *A Hero of our Time* was written by its principal character, Pechorin. Lermontov wrote: "Recently I learned that Pechorin had died on his way back from Persia. This news pleased me very much, for it gave me the right to publish his notebooks, and I took advantage of the opportunity to sign my name to another man's

work. God forbid that the reader should penalize me for such an innocent deception" (Trans. Martin Parker [Moscow: Progress Publishers, 1965]). This "camouflage" device was also well known in Georgia.

7. N. Ya. Marr, *Vstupitel'nye i zaklyuchitel'nye strofy 'Vityazya v barsovoy kozhe' Shoty iz Rustava* [Introductory and closing stanzas of 'The Lord of the Panther-skin' by Shota of Rustavi] (St. Petersburg, 1910), p. xxxviii.

8. Sir Cecil Maurice Bowra, *Inspiration and Poetry* (London: Macmillan, 1955), p. 53.

9. Shota Rustaveli, *Nosyashchiy barsovu kozhu* [*The Lord of the Panther-skin*] trans. K.D. Balmont (Paris, 1933), p. viii.

10. In Rustaveli's poem 'Khvarizmian' is synonymous with 'Persian'.

11. *Bulletin de l'Institut des Langues, d'Histoire et de Culture matérielle*, vol. 3 (Tbilisi, 1938), p. 266.

12. *Inspiration and Poetry*, pp. 58-59.